W9-AEZ-942

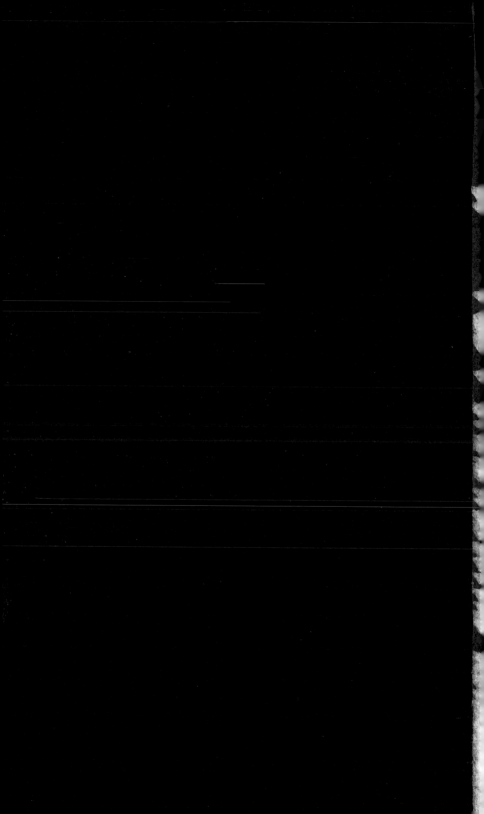

THE
DEADLY BET

Montante Family Library
D'Youville College

THE
DEADLY BET
LBJ, VIETNAM, AND THE 1968 ELECTION
WALTER LaFEBER

ROWMAN & LITTLEFIELD PUBLISHERS, INC.

Lanham • Boulder • New York • Toronto • Oxford

ROWMAN & LITTLEFIELD PUBLISHERS, INC.

Published in the United States of America
by Rowman & Littlefield Publishers, Inc.
A wholly owned subsidary of The Rowman & Littlefield Publishing Group, Inc.
4501 Forbes Boulevard, Suite 200, Lanham, Maryland 20706
www.rowmanlittlefield.com

PO Box 317
Oxford
OX2 9RU, UK

Copyright © 2005 by Rowman & Littlefield Publishers, Inc.

All rights reserved. No part of this publication may be reproduced,
stored in a retrieval system, or transmitted in any form or by any
means, electronic, mechanical, photocopying, recording, or otherwise,
without the prior permission of the publisher.

British Library Cataloguing in Publication Information Available

Library of Congress Cataloging-in-Publication Data

LaFeber, Walter.
  LBJ, Vietnam, and the 1968 election / Walter LaFeber.
    p. cm. — (Vietnam. America in the war years)
  Includes bibliographical references and index.
  ISBN 0-7425-4391-9 (cloth : alk. paper) — ISBN 0-7425-4392-7 (pbk. : alk.
paper)
  1. Presidents—United States—Election—1968.   2. Johnson, Lyndon B.
(Lyndon Baines), 1908–1973.   3. Vietnamese Conflict, 1961–1975—United
States.   4. United States—Politics and government—1963–1969.
I. Title.   II. Series.
  E851.L33 2005
  324.973'0923—dc22   2004020834

Printed in the United States of America

∞™ The paper used in this publication meets the minimum requirements of
American National Standard for Information Sciences—Permanence of Paper
for Printed Library Materials, ANSI/NISO Z39.48-1992.

E851
.L33
2005

This book is for
David and Martha Maisel,
class of 1968

NOV 1 0 2006

Mrs. Alving: Ghosts! . . . But I almost think we are all of us ghosts, Pastor Manders. It is not only what we have inherited from our father and mother that "walks" in us. It is all sorts of dead ideas and lifeless old beliefs, and so forth. They have no vitality but they cling to us all the same, and we cannot shake them off. Whenever I take up a newspaper, I seem to see ghosts gliding between the lines. There must be ghosts all the country over, as thick as the sands of the sea. And then we are, one and all, so pitifully afraid of the light.

Manders: Aha—here we have the fruits of your reading. And pretty fruits they are, upon my word! Oh, those horrible, revolutionary, freethinking books!

Mrs. Alving: You are mistaken, my dear Pastor. It was you yourself who set me thinking; and I thank you for it with all my heart.

Manders: I!

Mrs. Alving: Yes—when you forced me under the yoke of what you called duty and obligation. . . . It was then that I began to look into the seams of your doctrines. I wanted only to pick at a single knot; but when I had got that undone, the whole thing ravelled out. And then I understood that it was all machine-sewn.

—Henrik Ibsen, *Ghosts: A Family Drama in Three Acts*
(London: 1888, 1900)

CONTENTS

ACKNOWLEDGMENTS

David Anderson suggested that this book might be useful in classroom discussions on the Vietnam War, and I am most indebted to him—for his suggestion and his unbelievable patience, editorial prowess, and many years of friendship. Lloyd Gardner and Tom McCormick have not only written important analyses of the politics of the 1960s war, but they have also carried on a nearly five-decade-long discussion with me about that topic and many others—and our friendship somehow nevertheless continues to grow. Frank Costigliola, who has also discussed parts of this book and many other subjects, Anne Foster, Joel Silbey, Ted Lowi, Dick Polenberg, Michael Kammen, Andy Rotter, Glenn Altschuler, Mel Small, George Herring, David Langbart, Jim Siekmeier, Evan Stewart, Ambassador Eric Edelman, Jim Moore, Frank Annunziata, Jeremi Suri, Art Kaminsky, and Milton Leitenberg have provided, both in writing and in conversation, important analyses and ideas relating to the decade's politics and culture from which I have happily stolen, usually without explicit acknowledgment.

Ruth Bower Anderson and the staff of the Minnesota Historical Society were exceptionally helpful and efficient in making available the Hubert H. Humphrey papers. The staff of Cornell's Olin Library has set the highest standard for helping research scholars, and once again

I am especially grateful for that staff's expert, always available assistance. Hunter Rawlings (former president of the university and now, happily, a member of its faculty), Andrew Tisch, and James Tisch provided help, both tangible and intangible, that made the completion of this book possible; I'm grateful for their friendship and their commitment to Cornell. Over the past several decades, Steve Weiss has been one of the university's most important friends; over the past decade, and especially the past year, he has been an important and valued personal friend. Wayne Isom's contribution was crucial and timely, his conversations, especially given the circumstances, memorable. Rebecca Meyer and Julia Russo have been exemplary research assistants with their saving sense of humor and irony, as well as their imaginative discovery of sources. I am particularly indebted to Laura Roberts Gottlieb, Andrew Boney, and Terry Fischer at Rowman & Littlefield for their good advice, unfailing professionalism, and awesome patience. As always, Sandy LaFeber, Scott LaFeber, Suzanne, Tom, Matt, and Trevor Kahl have made it worthwhile as well as always interesting. This book is dedicated to David and Martha Maisel, with profound thanks for a thirty-five-year friendship and their invaluable help on many levels to Cornell's Department of History.

Walter LaFeber
February 2004

INTRODUCTION

War and Democracy: The Life-or-Death Bet

Looking back more than three decades later, a witness to the 1960s wrote that 1968 "was a year of fearful portents and strange exhilaration. Everything—on every scale, from the global to the personal—seemed to be coming unmoored. The sweep of events was like a hurricane."[1]

A hurricane indeed struck the United States, as well as many other countries, in 1968. Resembling other such storms, this hurricane had causes that can be analyzed and continue to be instructive in the twenty-first century: during the 1960s U.S. presidents made a life-or-death bet that Americans could fight a long war against a determined foe, and, at the same time, maintain order and protect constitutional rights in their own society. If the presidents were wrong, their own society could be torn apart, and two hundred years of U.S. democracy endangered, by the war they believed they had to fight. The presidents, especially Lyndon B. Johnson, lost their bet. The result was a hurricane that struck American society with greater fury than any destructive force since the Civil War.

In the late 1940s, the United States had begun a long struggle against an enemy it knew little about. Americans set out on this mission because they believed their presidents, who after World War II consistently warned them that the enemy—communism—threatened not only their own way of life but also the safety of the global community in which they lived and earned their living. For nearly one hundred fifty years, Americans assumed that the Atlantic and Pacific Oceans formed huge barriers to overseas attack. The Japanese strikes, first on Pearl Harbor in 1941 and then by primitive balloons that actually took lives on the West Coast, destroyed much of that illusion. The rush of post–World War II technologies, including intercontinental missiles, nuclear weapons, and jet planes, ripped away any remaining hope for intelligent Americans that foreign relations could be comfortably ignored. After 1941, these citizens had no place to hide from worldwide cataclysms, although, as U.S. history repeatedly demonstrated, many Americans tried to deny—or caricature—the rest of the world with the same passion they devoted to creating the globe's greatest consumer society.

Many Americans went into the post-1941 world confident that they were fighting for their self-defense and doing God's will. They knew that they possessed the most powerful military and economic machine in history. Such power sometimes made them believe they could ignore global realities. By the 1960s, the United States enjoyed a clear superiority in nuclear weapons, had military bases in twenty countries, was locked in security commitments with forty-two allies, stationed a million soldiers abroad, and deployed history's mightiest air force with the most advanced technology.[2] U.S. military might was nearly matched by the power of American culture. Jazz, Hollywood, and fast food ("Coca-Colonization") were popular in many societies. As Secretary of State Dean Rusk boasted in early 1968, "When we sneeze, the rest of the world catches the flu."[3]

Among the many corners of the globe these overly confident (and, as it turned out, ignorant) Americans moved into was Vietnam during 1950–1954. They voluntarily replaced the French colonial power that was being defeated by Vietnamese commanded by the national communist leader, Ho Chi Minh. In the 1954 Geneva Accords, the nation was divided between North (communist) and South Vietnam (soon tied to the United States). This division was supposedly to last only until a national election was held in 1956. The American control of the South became more blatant between 1954 and 1964, but communist power nevertheless grew. President Lyndon Johnson ratcheted up his bet by dispatching 550,000 U.S. troops to fight Ho's forces between 1965 and 1968. The planned election to reunify the nation was never held.

Confident U.S. officials believed they knew what Vietnamese society required to develop and find contentment. President Johnson, from Texas, and his vice president, Hubert Humphrey from Minnesota, had become national political leaders during the 1930s, 1940s, and 1950s, when Franklin D. Roosevelt's New Deal modernized the United States with electrical grids, dams, government-subsidized industry, and massive welfare programs aimed at alleviating poverty and easing old age. As he swept his historic Great Society legislation through Congress in 1964–1966, Johnson swore to carry on Roosevelt's work by reforming education, ensuring voting rights and civil rights protection for minorities (especially African Americans), and providing Medicare so U.S. health programs could finally begin to move into the mid-twentieth-century. Similar development and welfare programs, Johnson and many other Americans believed, could be exported— especially to such developing nations as Vietnam—to create a better, happier world. Who could resist the American success story?

But these programs could work only after communist power was either destroyed or forced to surrender. The development plans were meant to work in capitalist societies. After all, they were designed in the United States, and it was the U.S. model that others were to follow. This requirement meant, in turn, that the world could be safe for Americans and their capitalism only after communism in such places as Vietnam was eradicated. In August 1967, Vice President Humphrey declared that Americans had made "a pledge to ourselves and to posterity to defeat aggression, to defeat social misery, to build viable, free political institutions and achieve peace in Vietnam." This was a large order, but he believed the world's leading power could do it. "I think there is a tremendous new opening here for realizing the dream of a great society of Asia," Humphrey concluded, "not just here at home."[4] Americans could go about doing good while also doing well by increasing their own power, influence, and opportunities.

If anyone could work such wonders, it was Lyndon Baines Johnson. He had risen out of the Texas back country and, after a thirty-year career in Washington, became the political master of the city—indeed, of the nation. After winning national elective office in a special election to the House of Representatives in 1937, LBJ ascended to the U.S. Senate in 1948. By the mid-1950s he had become the most powerful majority leader in the 160-year history of that august body. The tall Texan combined an unsurpassed memory for the political weaknesses and needs of his Senate colleagues, with the "Johnson treatment"—in which the six-foot-four LBJ glared down inches from the face of an awed politician and, accompanied by a pull on the victim's coat lapels or an arm around the shoulder, talked incessantly until the captive surrendered to Johnson's wishes. (Once the "treatment" included Johnson kicking the shins of Vice President Humphrey.) Desiring the presidency in 1960, LBJ reluctantly agreed to run as the vice presidential nominee with John F. Kennedy of Massachusetts. Johnson served Kennedy's purpose: he helped deliver the South to the Democratic ticket. It would be the next-to-last time that the historically Democratic region remained united. Kennedy's assassination on November 22, 1963, in Johnson's home state suddenly catapulted LBJ to the White House.

In 1964, he captured the presidency over Republican Barry Goldwater of Arizona in one of the great landslide victories in American political history. The country then began to pass through the storms that climaxed with the hurricane in 1968. Johnson whipped more than sixty reform measures through Congress in 1965 alone. At one point, the president paraded his raw power by forcing the House of Representatives to remain in session nearly fourteen hours and into early morning, until it voted through a highway beautification measure desired by his wife, Lady Bird Johnson.

His control of foreign policy, however, eventually proved to be less sure. In August 1964, he passed by overwhelming votes in both the Senate and House the Gulf of Tonkin Resolution that, in his view, gave him a blank check to respond to North Vietnam's attacks on the South. By mid-1965, however, the South Vietnamese government—largely put and kept in place by the United States—was tottering. After months of agonizing, Johnson began a major build up by sending 50,000 troops to help South Vietnam. The escalation continued until in 1966 more Americans than Vietnamese were dying in action. Yet communist strength continued to grow.

As he prepared for the 1968 presidential election, Johnson was losing his life-or-death bet. The war seemed stalemated while American cities were exploding with racial and antiwar demonstrations. He nevertheless believed he had no choice but to continue raising the stakes in Vietnam even as he accelerated his drive at home to pass his beloved Great Society legislation. He was determined not to become the first American president to lose a war. Johnson believed, moreover, that he had to make good on the commitments of the three previous presidents (Harry Truman, Dwight D. Eisenhower, and Kennedy), who had set out to save South Vietnam from communism.

But the heart of Johnson's bet was on the American people and their political system. He assumed they had the patience, foresight, and willingness to sacrifice—and the necessary money and power to fight a vague, undeclared, unending war abroad while carrying through his reforms at home. LBJ vividly remembered how Truman had made such a bet—and won. In 1947, in his Truman Doctrine, the president from Missouri defined the world as divided between the democratic and the totalitarian (i.e., communist) nations. Truman bluntly asked Americans which side they were on. The country responded by fighting the Cold War with billions of dollars and few reservations. Throughout the 1950s and early 1960s, U.S. officials came to believe (too easily, as it turned out), that Americans would remain united and committed to fight communism, regardless of the enemy, regardless of the costs.

The top-secret U.S. policy document of 1950, NSC-68 (National Security Council paper no. 58) set out principles Washington officials followed in waging the Cold War over the next forty years. A pivotal section of NSC-68 discussed why the document's authors (Truman's top advisers) believed the American people would agree to sacrifice at home over a long period of time in order to fight the enemy abroad:

> The vast majority of Americans are confident that the system of values which animates our society—the principles of freedom, tolerance, the importance of the individual and the supremacy of reason over will—are valid and more vital than the ideology which is the fuel of Soviet dogmatism. Translated into terms relevant to the lives of other peoples, our system of values can become perhaps a powerful appeal to millions who now seek or find in authoritarianism a refuge from anxieties, bafflement, and insecurity.

So far, so good, although it was by no means clear in the 1950s that American "values" were winning over the hearts and minds of Vietnamese who had been giving their lives for over a thousand years to prevent foreign "values" from taking over their country. Then came NSC-68's bet on the American people: "Essentially, our democracy also possesses a unique degree of unity. Our society is fundamentally more cohesive than the Soviet system. . . . This means that expressions of national concensus in our society are soundly and solidly based."[5]

Johnson believed this American "consensus" was "solidly based." He had closely watched Roosevelt keep the nation together through World War II, witnessed firsthand Truman's success in creating an anticommunist consensus with the Truman Doctrine, and as Senate leader personally supported Eisenhower, a Republican, in nearly every foreign policy initiative during the 1950s. Once in the White House, LBJ believed that between his intimate knowledge of Washington politics and his vigorous use of the "Johnson treatment," especially on reluctant members of Congress, he could keep the anticommunist consensus—and American society—pieced together as he escalated the war in Vietnam.

Committing a democracy to war is a highly risky business, especially if the bloodshed lasts over a long period of time and results in boatloads of treasure going out and the body bags of dead soldiers coming back. Committing a democracy to both war and, as Johnson demanded, deep reforms at home in order to help minorities, the poor, the young, and the elderly—that combination was especially risky, perhaps politically explosive. War demanded both vast expenditures and a single-minded focus on the fighting. But Johnson's reforms also were expensive and required a single-minded focus on their implementation if they were to work. Trying to carry out both war and reforms, however, seemed to be a contradiction in terms. War demanded the complete allegiance of the American people (an allegiance they had willingly given in the War of 1898, World War I, and World War II). The demands of such conflicts left little time for a highly diverse population to give complex social reforms. In World Wars I and II, Americans largely gave up their reform programs to fight the wars effectively. As President Roosevelt said bluntly during World War II, "Dr. Win-the-War" would have to replace "Dr. New Deal" (his pre-1941 reform program) in giving helpful prescriptions to the American people. Johnson, however, did not want to replace his Great Society program with "Dr. Win-the-War-in-Vietnam." He was determined to do both. It turned out, however, that not even the unbelievable wealth of the American people allowed U.S. officials to do both.

Such huge demands threatened to bear down on Americans until, like an overloaded electrical circuit, their society began to explode in the mid-1960s. Those who knew their history, especially American history, should not have been surprised at this possible contradiction between fighting wars and maintaining democracy. One hundred and thirty years earlier, Alexis de Tocqueville, perhaps the most observant foreign visitor ever to analyze the United States, had issued a warning to future generations of Americans in his classic two-volume work, *Democracy in America*. A "protracted war," the French aristocrat wrote, would endanger American democracy not because a victorious general would take over in "the manner of Sulla and Caesar" but because war centralizes power. Tocqueville implied that Americans would allow such slow centralization in return for the state giving them the comfort of security from outside threats. War "is the surest and the shortest means," he summarized, for those who want to destroy democratic liberties.[6]

Americans know about Tocqueville's warning in their bones even if they have never read his work. At least since 1776, when they broke away from the British monarchy, they have mistrusted government, and many have even mistrusted government during wartime, when the demand for governmental protection is necessarily at its peak. During the Civil War, for example, thousands, especially in New York City, violently protested in the streets against being drafted for the war when the wealthy could buy their way out of the military. The protesters were put down in bloody riots. During World War I, those who opposed U.S. participation in the conflict were sentenced to jail terms that cooler heads overturned only after the war. In World War II, U.S. citizens of Japanese American ancestry were stripped of their constitutional rights and locked away in concentration camps because they were unjustly charged with threatening the American effort.

These constitutional crises occurred during wars in which the enemy was both obvious and seen as a clear danger to U.S. interests. The enemy in Vietnam, however, was much less obvious. Indeed, a major debate erupted over whether the Vietnamese communists posed any danger at all to U.S. interests—were they, for example, more nationalist than communist and thus fighting only for their independence from foreign control (and not for the advancement of Russian or Chinese communism)? By 1965–1967, as Johnson escalated the number of U.S. troops fighting in the conflict, many Americans were coming to believe that Ho Chi Minh's forces in Vietnam posed no danger to the United States and, as a consequence, the war was not worth the loss of tens of thousands of their young men and women.

But by the mid-1960s, the opposition to the war had become more complex and diverse. It moved well beyond that particular calculation. Led by the Reverend Martin Luther King, Senator Robert F. Kennedy (Democrat of New York), and considerably more radical civil rights leaders, many Americans were reaching the conclusion that correcting several centuries of injustice and improving the lives of minorities, especially African Americans, was more important than killing Asian people 10,000 miles away. They believed the mighty economic and political resources of the United States had to be devoted to righting wrongs at home, not fighting this particular kind of communism. President Johnson, on the other hand, was convinced that the war for equal rights at home had to be waged simultaneously with the war against communism abroad. This fundamental disagreement between increasing numbers of Americans and their president triggered massive political problems for both sides in 1966–1967. As popular demands for civil rights and Johnson's demands for fighting the war intensified, they finally climaxed in the hurricane of 1968, as many Americans frantically sought to return to some order, some sense of tranquility and law, by voting for the presidential candidate who most effectively sold his law-and-order message: Richard Nixon.

The causes of this hurricane in the civil rights movement went back at least to the institution of slavery in American society during the seventeenth, eighteenth, and early nineteenth centuries. The movement took on new momentum after the Civil War, when all slaves were finally emancipated. Organizations of African Americans and whites were formed to ensure that the former slaves and their descendents would enjoy equal rights with whites. The movement accelerated during World War II, when Americans condemned Nazi theories of "Aryan" superiority. Led by the National Association for the Advancement of Colored People, NAACP, (founded in 1908), African American and white leaders convinced President Franklin Roosevelt to create federal agencies to ensure nondiscrimination in employment. They also pushed President Truman to desegregate the U.S. armed forces in the late 1940s. The historic 1954 Supreme Court decision, *Brown v. Board of Education*, provided legal and constitutional support for ending segregation. Then, in 1955, a calm, courageous forty-two-year-old NAACP activist, Rosa Parks, electrified the civil rights movement by defying a Montgomery, Alabama, law that required African Americans to sit in the back of public buses. When she was arrested, a boycott of Montgomery buses followed that focused world attention on one of the city's church leaders, Reverend Martin Luther King, a Baptist minister who was piecing together a civil rights movement based on nonviolent principles.

In 1957, Senator Lyndon Johnson responded to these and many other demands for racial equality by pushing through the first national civil rights bill. President Eisenhower meanwhile ordered federal troops to force the desegregation of Little Rock Central High School after Arkansas authorities refused to recognize the national government's right to make schooling equal for blacks and whites. Johnson's legislation, however, was weak, and the U.S. government did little as the civil rights movement stalled. New groups, with no commitment to King's nonviolence principles, appeared in the early 1960s. The Student Non-Violent Coordinating Committee (SNCC) began to confront white officials in the South and North to demand immediate equality. In 1963, Medgar Evers, a black Mississippi NAACP leader, was gunned down by whites. Governor George Wallace of Alabama defied federal laws requiring desegregation of Alabama schools.

The most horrible events occurred in Birmingham, Alabama. Under the command of "Bull" Connor, police used dogs and high-pressure fire hoses (capable of tearing bark off a tree) to attack civil rights demonstrators. The confrontation was viewed on television by millions of Americans, including a sickened President Kennedy. Next, bombs set in a Birmingham church by white racists murdered four African American children. President Johnson and Congress responded by passing meaningful legislation, including a 1964 act guaranteeing civil rights and a 1965 bill guaranteeing voting rights. It proved to be too little, too late.

Many African Americans, frustrated by decades of unfulfilled promises and a rising economy that continually passed them by, turned to movements of black racial pride (that excluded even sympathetic whites), black nationalism, and violence. Mere days after Johnson passed the 1965 act, the largely African American section of Watts, a district of Los Angeles, erupted in fires, looting, and violence that killed thirty-four people while destroying millions of dollars in property. Watts exemplified the poorer, inner-city ghettoes where a majority of African Americans lived. The hot summers of 1966 and 1967 turned red, not from communism but from reflections in the sky of cities burning. Twenty-six died in Newark and forty-three in Detroit, where more than $85 million of property was destroyed. Over one hundred racial clashes occurred in 1967 alone. For the first time, Johnson sent U.S. troops into the inner cities to try to restore order. Black leader Stokely Carmichael demanded that African Americans use guerrilla war to achieve "total revolution."[7] As had happened before in American history, the war being fought overseas had come home.

The president's popularity began to sink as white voters concluded that his Great Society was threatening to destroy, not reform, their society. Anger also grew as African Americans noted their children were being sent to fight in Vietnam and die in jungle battles in numbers far higher in proportion to their population than were whites. But many whites, especially those who had less education and made low wages, believed Johnson's administration was unfairly trying to help African Americans, often at the expense of whites. British politicians visiting the United States told Vice President Humphrey that "they found an undercurrent of resentment concerning civil order and gains made by the Negro population."[8] Johnson was not surprised. He knew his civil rights legislation was a historical necessity, but he also knew he and his Democratic Party would pay for it politically. When a young assistant congratulated him in 1965 for passing the legislation, the president was quiet for a moment, then said, "I think we just delivered the South to the Republican Party for a long time to come."[9] He had accurately seen the future.

Quite contrary to NSC-68's assumptions (and Johnson's bet), the American consensus was cracking wide open. Protests against the president's Vietnam policies erupted alongside protests in the inner cities. As the war dragged on in 1966 and U.S. casualties mounted, Republicans took advantage of Johnson's terrible dilemma by positioning themselves for the 1966 congressional and 1968 presidential elections. Everett Dirksen of Illinois and Gerald Ford of Michigan led the minority Republicans in the Senate and House, respectively. During press conferences that became known as the "Ev and Jerry Show," Ford generally lambasted Great Society programs as giveaways, while Dirksen more carefully questioned White House foreign policy. The Illinois senator wondered aloud whether Johnson was being sufficiently open with Americans about the war. Dirksen's friendship with the president had spanned decades, and he believed it unpatriotic (and also bad politics) to condemn publicly a president during a war. When one Senate Republican did so, Dirksen sharply, and revealingly, corrected him: "It don't sound good and it don't look good. Have you heard the British demean their king or queen? You don't demean the ruler—the president is not our ruler—but you don't demean him in the eyes of the people abroad, because when you do you demean the prestige of this republic, and I don't mean to do it."[10]

While Dirksen acted as the moderate, loyal opposition, Richard Nixon emerged as the immoderate Republican opposition. Nixon had played this role on the national political stage before. Between 1949 and 1952, he rushed to the forefront of those attacking President Truman and the Democrats for not ferreting out communists who supposedly infested the U.S. government. As vice president under Eisenhower between 1953 and 1961, Nixon had been the Republicans' political nose gunner, spraying Democrats with political buckshot while the president usually remained above the battle. After Kennedy defeated him in 1960 for the presidency, and he then lost a 1962 race for the California governorship, Nixon withdrew from the arena to make money by practicing law while maintaining his extensive political ties.

The growing political struggle over Vietnam in 1965–1967 was a godsend to a foreign policy addict like Nixon. And the eruption of violence in the inner cities also helped his political popularity. He had

long campaigned as an outspoken law-and-order candidate, whether
he was opposing communists or those setting fires in American cities.
By 1966, he had gone much farther than Dirksen to join the growing
protests against the war. But Nixon did so from the hard-line, "hawkish" right wing. In an August 1966 speech before the annual American
Legion convention, he warned that "if Vietnam falls, the Pacific will be
transformed into a red ocean and the road will be open to a third world
war." He was careful in his criticism of the president, but not of Johnson's party: "Republicans have stood behind the president in his efforts
to deny reward to aggression. . . . It has been the President's party that
has harbored those who have counseled appeasement of Communist
aggression in Vietnam." A number of Democratic senators and House
members, Nixon continued, "whose cries for peace at any price have
given heart to Hanoi," the capital of communist North Vietnam, have
"thus been directly responsible for encouraging the enemy, prolonging
the war," and greatly raising "the risk of American casualties."[11]

The Vietnam War had become a bloody mess, Nixon was arguing,
because the Democratic Party, which had strongly supported Johnson's sending a half million men and women and tens of billions of
dollars to fight communism in Vietnam, was soft on communism.
When a democratic society begins to believe such arguments, it is
in considerable trouble. And Nixon was emerging as the clear front-
runner for the Republican presidential nomination in 1968.

Johnson and the Democrats who supported him were trapped by
1966. On one side were African American groups, many college students, influential faculty members, and various politicians who believed
the war to be an endless, bloody quagmire, and the Great Society to
be insufficient. On the other side were many Republicans and white
middle-class voters, especially those in and around the burning cities,
who wanted massive force employed both to win once and for all in
Vietnam and restore order at home. With good reason, Johnson had always feared the right wing of American politics—that "great lurking
monster," as he called it—more than his liberal or leftist critics.[12]

The "monster" dramatically appeared in one of the most stunning
polls taken in early 1968. The results were best characterized by those
conducting the poll as "appalling from a civil libertarian point of view."
When asked whether they approved or disapproved of those people

"taking part in protest meetings or marches that are permitted by the local authorities," fewer than 20 percent of all respondents were willing to approve. But more than half disapproved of the protesters, even though such protests were entirely legal.[13] Public opinion polls consistently showed that Americans agreed with Nixon: they wanted a quick win in Vietnam, not a retreat, and they also wanted a quick end to the lawlessness—as the poll indicated, even an end to lawful protests—in the streets. Tocqueville would not have been surprised.

But the demand to win the war, and win it quickly, revealed another terrible trap for Johnson. If he escalated the war to win total victory, he and his advisers knew they would have to attack North Vietnam massively. Such an attack would kill Chinese troops and advisers who were helping the communists in northern ports and other strategic areas, and would take the war to China's borders. Johnson, Secretary of State Dean Rusk, and others who had been in Washington during November 1950, knew the grave dangers of such an expanded war. In late 1950, Truman, advised in part by Rusk (then an assistant secretary of state), had allowed U.S. troops to try to win all-out victory in the Korean War by driving across communist North Korea to the Yalu River separating Korea from China. Suddenly faced with the possibility of powerful U.S. forces positioned on their border, the Chinese responded with human wave attacks that killed thousands of U.S. troops. China's stunning, unexpected counterattack turned the war into a near disaster and then stalemate, triggered years of hatred and possible further conflict between Americans and Chinese, and—especially remembered by Johnson—ruined Truman politically and led him to withdraw from the 1952 presidential race. LBJ, therefore, had no intention of provoking China. Or, as he told one of his assistants, "I'm not gonna spit in China's face."[14]

No end to the war appeared in sight, however, unless he attacked North Vietnam. It was the source of endless communist soldiers and supplies who filtered into the South to fight and kill Americans, as well as a control point for the National Liberation Front, the communist organization that waged the war in the South. Johnson grew increasingly frustrated over the possibility of losing his life-or-death bet. Meanwhile cities went up in flames. Antiwar and civil rights organizations became more radicalized. The president warned about a "white backlash issue" that was splitting the nation "at a very critical time," but his remark had no calming effect.[15]

In the 1966 elections, Republicans scored a stunning victory by gaining forty-seven seats in the House and three in the Senate. Republicans remained in the minority, but Johnson's triumph of 1964 was going into reverse. In California, a one-time movie actor, Ronald Reagan, who had gained national attention campaigning for Goldwater in 1964, ran for the governorship on a law-and-order platform and handily defeated the incumbent. Divided in 1964 by the conservative Goldwater's candidacy, the Republicans—taking advantage of an increasingly unpopular war overseas and growing riots and discontent at home—were reuniting under a more moderate Ford, Dirksen, and (when compared with Goldwater) Nixon.

It was Nixon, proud of his knowledge of American history, who drew a devastating parallel between Johnson in 1966–1968 and President Woodrow Wilson in 1918–1920. Wilson had appealed for national support in 1918 as he set off to Paris to make peace after the unparalleled bloodletting of World War I had finally ended. But Americans seemed to repudiate him by voting a Republican Congress into power in the 1918 elections. Wilson was undercut, then further weakened by deep divisions within his own party, Nixon pointed out. He implied that the same kind of repudiation was now being suffered by Johnson.[16]

Nixon could have added that another parallel between Wilson and Johnson was developing. Wilson's hope in 1918–1919 for an American-led peace was fatally undermined at home by racial upheavals, postwar witch-hunts for communists in the United States, and a growing economic recession. Some of the worst race riots in the nation's history occurred in St. Louis and Chicago immediately after World War I. Short-tempered Americans tried to find the causes for these eruptions and other postwar frustrations by attacking supposed communists—new immigrants whose "Americanism" might be suspect. As Tocqueville would have understood, in the aftermath of the bloodiest war in history, and as Russia's communist revolution threatened to spread across Europe, Americans wanted order and security at home above all else—even above a world brought together in Wilson's League of Nations. In 1920 they swept a conservative Republican ticket into power. Wartime President Wilson—who, like Lyndon

Johnson, had also pushed through a reform program that frightened and angered many conservative Americans—stood repudiated. Actually, Wilson had prophesied this failure. As he took the nation into war in March 1917, a deeply troubled president privately uttered words that echoed Tocqueville's of ninety years earlier, and that, fifty years later, Johnson would have thought profound: "a nation couldn't put its strength into a war and keep its head level; it had never been done."[17]

In 1967, the president and his advisers feared less that the nation was keeping "its head level" than that it was losing its head completely. Inner-city riots, antiwar protests, and the business community's growing concern about war draining the domestic economy and triggering a destructive inflation—all accelerated as the U.S. effort in Vietnam seemed to be stumbling. Throughout the year, the two sides on the battlefields agreed to five truces. Americans hoped the truces would allow peace talks to begin, but both the U.S. and North Vietnamese governments exploited them to send more troops and supplies into battle zones. Secretary of Defense Robert McNamara declared that 165,000 enemy soldiers had been killed in 1967, but, somehow, communist troop strength actually increased. Not even U.S. firepower could kill young Vietnamese as fast as they reached draft age. The communists controlled in varying degrees about 5 million of South Vietnam's 17 million people. The U.S.-supported southern government controlled about the same number. The other 7 million switched back and forth, usually anticommunist by day and procommunist by night. The U.S. commander in Vietnam, General William Westmoreland, had proclaimed 1967 the Year of the Offensive, but as the calendar pages flipped by, even the general admitted it might be another two years before South Vietnamese troops could take on more of the fighting.[18] By that time, thousands more Americans died in jungle battlefields. Nearly 10,000 were killed-in-action during 1967, double the number of 1966.

In September 1967, Johnson tried to explain to increasingly angry Americans that the war, compared with earlier conflicts the nation had fought, was incredibly complicated: "doubt and debate are enlarged because the problems of Vietnam are quite complex. They are a mixture of political turmoil, of poverty, of religious and factional strife of ancient servitude and modern longing for freedom."[19] The problems, he seemed to be saying, had to be political and cultural. It certainly could not be a problem of inadequate U.S. military power. The United States had the greatest military force in the world. These forces had set out to resolve the "complex" problems simply by bombing Vietnam until parts of the country resembled pockmarked surfaces on the moon. U.S. planes dropped more bombs on this small country in two years than they had exploded on all of Nazi-dominated Europe between 1941 and 1945. "We seem to be proceeding on the assumption," a top presidential adviser remarked in 1967, "that the way to eradicate the Viet Cong [the South Vietnamese communists] is to destroy all the village structures, defoliate all the jungles, then cover the entire surface of South Viet Nam with asphalt."[20]

Until mid-1967, Johnson used the selective service system and draft to obtain the troops he needed. Because college and graduate school students could obtain deferments, the brunt of the fighting and dying fell on poorer African Americans and white blue-collar workers who could not afford to attend, or were not interested in, college. During 1967, Congress, at the president's request, tried to devise a fairer system by ending graduate school deferments and eventually setting up a lottery to decide who would be drafted. As one of his White House advisers recalled, "All hell broke loose. . . . The fact that every economic and social class stood at equal risk . . . ignited furious opposition to the war across a broad spectrum of Americans who believed that the national interest in Vietnam was not sufficient to risk their sons' lives."[21]

Thousands of those potential soldiers fled to Canada, Australia, the Scandinavian countries, and elsewhere to defy the new draft. Some 75,000 others paraded in Washington in October 1967 to stage a massive protest. Many of the protesters marched on the Pentagon, where antiwar leaders were arrested for defying police orders to disperse. Worldwide television pictures showed the marchers carrying pictures of North Vietnamese leaders and flags. One group of counterculture hippies claimed their chants would "levitate the Pentagon"—that is, raise the massive structure four feet off the ground so the "evil spirits" could escape. Johnson secretly ordered U.S. troops stationed in government buildings to protect his administration from its own people. At the Pentagon itself, 8,500 soldiers from the elite 82nd Airborne Division kept most of the protesters away from the building. U.S. troops were again confronting U.S. citizens.

Antiwar movements had now spread throughout much of the world. As Americans marched on the Pentagon, Europeans cooperated by demonstrating against U.S. military bases in Germany and holding anti-American rallies in a half dozen other countries. Many protests turned increasingly radical as they demanded basic changes in their nations' capitalistic systems and relationships with the Johnson administration.[22] The Vietnam conflict seemed to be igniting a mass challenge to the governments of much of the Western world.

American political leaders, even conservatives, argued that the United States was enduring not merely a war but a profound crisis that marked the mid-1960s as a turning point in its history—a point equal in importance to 1776 and 1861. Senator J. William Fulbright, Democrat of Arkansas, was the powerful chairman of the Foreign Relations Committee, a former intimate friend of Johnson who had bitterly broken with him over the war, and a southern conservative on racial issues, In a mid-1967 article entitled "The Great Society is a Sick Society," Fulbright declared that American "souls" were being seized "by the false and dangerous dream of an imperial destiny." Such a destiny would soon make the "empire" a "moral if not [as in Vietnam already] a physical wasteland." Then the empire itself would collapse. Fulbright thought the great hope was "this generation of young men and women who reject the inhumanity of war in a poor and distant land, who reject the poverty and sham in their own country," and who were telling "their elders what their elders ought to have known—that the price of empire is America's soul and that the price is too high."[23]

Despite Tocqueville's warning, Johnson had made his bet. By late 1967, American protesters and potential voters alike were proving Tocqueville right, Johnson wrong. The president decided to throw the dice again. He ordered his commander in Vietnam, General William Westmoreland, to return home so he could tell the nation, and especially such political dissenters as Fulbright, that the war was actually being won. This action created such a full-blown crisis that, for only the second time in nearly two hundred years of American history, a sitting president was forced to conclude he could not successfully run for reelection.

General William Westmoreland meeting with President Lyndon B. Johnson in the Oval Office, November 16, 1967
Photo by Yoichi R. Okamoto, Courtesy of the LBJ Library and Museum

❶

GENERAL WILLIAM WESTMORELAND: THE TET OFFENSIVE

In late summer 1967, a survey by an influential periodical, *U.S. News & World Report,* announced that President Lyndon Johnson would have to deal with at least one of three large problems if he and his Democratic Party hoped to avoid "something approaching disaster at the polls" in November 1968. The problems were "war in Vietnam, which is increasingly unpopular with the voters"; "riots and crime in the cities that alarm people all over the country"; and "the high cost of living, which—with taxes—is to move steadily higher." Johnson knew he had no chance of finding quick fixes for "riots and crime in the cities" or even "the high cost of living," but he believed the war was going better—despite the thousands of U.S. lives (and tens of thousands of Vietnamese lives) being lost every year. On September 19, 1967, the president proudly announced "forward movement" in the conflict and asserted that "the Vietnamese with our help" were making "progress."[1]

Johnson no doubt assumed, and with good reason, that if he could deal with the war, the effects would be felt on the other two problems. By somehow scaling down the war, he could more easily find resources to deal with crime, turmoil in the inner cities, and the growing economic dilemma. He decided to launch a major strike on American public opinion—seize the initiative from his critics by launching a major propaganda offensive to convince the nation the war was going to be won. The centerpiece of the campaign was to be the photogenic, strong-chinned U.S. commander in Vietnam, General William Westmoreland. Johnson ordered "Westy" home for a series of speeches in late 1967.

Born in Spartanburg, South Carolina, the fifty-three-year-old general had a soft southern accent and confident manner that had charmed his superiors—and a war record that impressed everyone. From the first, he had benefited from his and his family's political connections. Westmoreland was nominated to the West Point Military Academy by none other than Senator James F. Byrnes, Democrat of South Carolina. Byrnes was a legendary (and highly racist) political "fixer" who later became U.S. secretary of state and a South Carolina governor. After graduating in 1936 from West Point, where he had been top dog (commander of the Corps of Cadets), Westmoreland fought in North Africa against the famous German general Erwin Rommel and then served under the equally famous U.S. tank commander, General George Patton. He later went into the Korean War as the commander of an airborne division.

"Westy" witnessed firsthand the horrible casualties inflicted on U.S. troops by the surprise Chinese attacks and the bitter Korean winter in November 1950. He drew the appropriate conclusion: Americans should never again get trapped in a limited, conventional war on the Asian mainland. He studied those lessons and burnished his already outstanding record when Eisenhower appointed him superintendent of West Point in 1960. In late 1963, Johnson made him second in command of U.S. forces in Vietnam. He became commander in June 1964. As the president escalated the war in 1965, he depended on Westmoreland to direct the effort.[2]

The general, remembering the horrors of Korea, understood the danger of fighting another limited war in Asia, especially in the dense jungles of Southeast Asia. But as a career military officer near the top of his profession, Westmoreland had become an expert in American politics, especially the labyrinths of Washington. He knew that Johnson had to fight a limited war precisely because the president had no intention of "spitting" in China's eye and finding himself in a much larger conflict against 800 million Chinese. LBJ's number one priority from 1964 to 1966, after all, was his Great Society program—not killing Vietnamese, let alone Chinese.

"Westy" therefore devised a plan for a war of attrition in which he hoped to slaughter as many communist troops as necessary to force Ho Chi Minh's government into retreat and agree to leave South Vietnam alone. To do this, he accelerated American bombing to historic proportions by 1967. The bombing aimed to kill enemy soldiers and tear up their transportation systems. Of course bombing roads and bridges from 30,000 feet could also kill large numbers of civilians, as antiwar protesters in the United States constantly pointed out. Civilian casualties approached an estimated 300,000 each year by 1968. Westmoreland thought this result of the bombing unfortunate, "but it does deprive the enemy of the population, doesn't it?"[3]

Such views did not endear him to antiwar protesters. In 1967, they burned effigies of Westmoreland in New York City as he looked on. ("It was sobering to see a representation of oneself to go up in flames," he later wrote.) At the same time, he caused headlines by declaring that he and the soldiers fighting in Vietnam were "dismayed . . . by recent unpatriotic acts here at home." Editorial writers and politicians who were cooling toward the war condemned his statement for criticizing Americans who were exercising their constitutional rights in opposing the conflict.[4]

Such remarks, and the general's growing frustration in being unable to kill Vietnamese rapidly enough, led him in 1967 to demand, secretly, 200,000 more soldiers so his forces would total some 670,000. Given this background, Westmoreland, for all his political success in rising through army ranks, was not the best person to make Johnson's case to the American people. By late 1967, the president's back was to the wall. His own political future was darkening along with the charred ashes of burned American and Vietnamese cities. Westmoreland was the good soldier who did as his commander in chief ordered.

But the general discovered the cost was rising higher than even he had thought. During an overnight visit to the White House, Johnson asked how the U.S. troops in Vietnam would react if their president "failed to run for reelection in 1968? Would they consider that their commander in chief had let them down?" LBJ added that his health was bad. He was tired. His family wanted him to step down. Johnson said he was afraid of becoming an invalid in the White House, much as a paralyzed Woodrow Wilson had been in 1919–1920. Westmoreland replied the troops would understand if they knew the president's reasons. Johnson swore him to secrecy about the conversation.[5]

Given his knowledge of what was going on behind the scenes and his secret request for more troops, the general was surprisingly upbeat in his public appearances of November 1967. "We have reached an important point when the end begins to come into view," he announced. The enemy had not won a major battle in a year "in his desperate effort to take the world's headlines . . . by a military victory." The "enemy's guerrilla force is declining at a steady rate." When pressed, "Westy" thought that "it is conceivable to me that within two years or less it will be possible for us to phase down our level of commitment" and let his Vietnamese allies fight more of the war.[6]

Westmoreland's happy talk occurred just as South Vietnamese elections in 1967 officially put Nguyen Van Thieu and Nguyen Cao Ky at the top of the Saigon government. Neither man (unlike communist leaders) had fought for Vietnamese independence against French colonialism between 1945 and 1954. Vice President Ky, moreover, was on record as admiring Nazi Germany. But the White House and State Department loudly praised this supposed democratic election. Critics noted that Ky and Thieu used their control of the army and treasury to fix the voting and then, just to be doubly sure, jailed some of their leading political opponents.

After a quick visit to South Vietnam, Johnson returned home to report at the end of 1967 that "victory" was indeed being "won" on the battlefield and also "in the cities and the villages all over Asia." The "distinguished Vice President Ky" had told him so, while emphasizing "the progress that they were making."[7] In private, however, Johnson had leveled with Westmoreland. The president was tired and feared that the war was unwinnable. When Johnson gave his State of the Union message on January 17, 1968, the British ambassador to the United States, Sir Patrick Dean, secretly reported back to London that many commentators had remarked on the speech's "pedestrian and uninspiring tone." But one part, Dean underlined, received the loudest applause of the evening: the president's demand that "crime

and lawlessness" be stopped. The British ambassador then propheti-
cally outlined how the 1968 presidential race would develop:

> Many people believe that this [the issue of law and order], no less than
> Vietnam and perhaps even more so, will be the real issue of the election
> campaign. It is perhaps even more relevant than Vietnam to his [John-
> son's] question about why there should be restlessness in the United
> States. As James Reston [*New York Times* columnist] commented, "We
> come to see that prosperity is not after all the goal in the pursuit of hap-
> piness and that after all the boasts of 83 months of economic boom
> something is still wrong, even with the economy."[8]

That economy, after nearly seven years of unparalleled prosperity,
was now suffering under growing war expenses and the unpre-
dictability of which U.S. city would explode next. Johnson had delayed
asking Congress for necessary new taxes to fight in Vietnam (and fund
his Great Society program) until after the 1966 elections were safely
past. When he finally urged more taxes, the president ran into massive
opposition. Opponents seized on the opportunity to open another major debate on the entire war effort. No wonder, as he told Westmoreland, that he was tired. But at least the general could assure him the
war was going better and, indeed, that "there was light at the end of
the tunnel," to use the phrase that became Westmoreland's most famous remark.

On January 31, 1968, even this hope evaporated for Johnson and his
loyal vice president, Hubert Humphrey. Westmoreland's "light at the
end of the tunnel," antiwar critics declared, turned out to be an accelerating train that crashed head-on with Johnson, Humphrey, the
entire U.S. war effort, and the Democrats' hope for election triumphs
in 1968. On that last day of January, communist Viet Minh troops, dis-
guised as civilians, infiltrated many South Vietnamese towns and cities
to launch the Tet (New Year's) offensive. U.S. military commanders
and their Vietnamese allies, most of whom were celebrating the New
Year, were largely taken by surprise. The Americans felt further embarrassed because for weeks the communists had fooled Westmoreland, Johnson, and their military experts into believing the showdown
battle was occurring in the far north, at Khe Sanh. Johnson had sternly
ordered Khe Sanh to be held at all costs. Westmoreland shifted troops

and planes to the north. Then the communists suddenly struck in the south.

They even took over parts of Saigon. For a few hours, communist forces penetrated the supposedly impenetrable grounds of the U.S. embassy in Saigon. The communists had built complex underground tunnels to furrow into the capital city. The tunnels had been discovered when American B-52 bombers pounded them, then huge earth-moving machines covered up the passageways with mountains of dirt. The Viet Minh patiently rebuilt the tunnels so they could were usable in late January.

The communists bet everything on their Tet offensive. Having suffered from U.S. firepower in 1967, they now hoped their surprise offensive would trigger a general uprising against the Thieu-Ky regime and its American sponsors. The communists hit thirty-six of forty-four provincial capitals, five of the six largest cities, fifty hamlets, and, most notably, the U.S. embassy, presidential palace, and South Vietnamese Army headquarters.[9]

But no general uprising against the Thieu-Ky regime and its U.S. sponsors occurred. Although it took several weeks of terrible hand-to-hand fighting, the Viet Minh were driven back from nearly all their Tet conquests. The losses were staggering. As many as 40,000 communists were killed in a matter of weeks. It took months to rebuild their troop strength. In many ways, the Tet offensive was a bitter disappointment to North Vietnamese leaders.

Tet, however, marked the turning point of both the war and the U.S. presidential campaign of 1968. Johnson's credibility, Westmoreland's military plans, and the optimism that both had paraded in late 1967 were in shambles. Contrary to the general's assertions, after two years of heavy bombing and a half million U.S. troops (along with 800,000 South Vietnamese soldiers) on the ground, the United States could not prevent the Viet Minh from carrying on the war—even into areas where the communists had never before penetrated. Some 1,100 U.S. (and over 2,000 South Vietnamese) soldiers were killed in the first two weeks of the offensive. Thousands of civilians perished, and, most ominously for U.S. plans, perhaps a million new refugees appeared as fighting drove them out of their homes. They joined 4 million other refugees who already strained U.S. aid agencies to the breaking point, while also providing a mass of people among whom communist agents could hide. It was now clear that Westmoreland's hope for Vietnamization (the replacement of U.S. troops in battle by efficient South Vietnamese soldiers) had rested on sand. As one besieged American observed in Saigon, "If the [South] Vietnamese won't defend their capital, what will they defend?"[10]

Johnson and his advisers moved quickly to put the best face on what was clearly a political, if not military, catastrophe. Secretary of Defense Robert McNamara declared, "Our forces have won every major battle in which they have been engaged since their commitment to Vietnam." But it was dawning on more and more Americans that they might win every battle and still lose the war. The Viet Minh could take huge losses yet launch surprise attacks anywhere. (American humorist Art Buchwald compared McNamara's and Westmoreland's optimism after Tet with General George Custer's supposed upbeat words just before he and his troops were massacred by the Indians at Little Big Horn: "We have the Sioux on the run," Buchwald had Custer say. "Of course we still have some cleaning up to do.")[11] McNamara publicly admitted that despite the heaviest U.S. bombing in history, the communists were sending about the same number of troops south at the end of 1967 as they had at the start of the year. He furnished statistics indicating the communists actually had the capability of tripling their troop numbers if they deemed it necessary.[12]

Privately, Johnson and his advisers turned deeply pessimistic. The Tet offensive was repulsed, but there was no end in sight to the war. McNamara, once a highly confident—indeed arrogant—prime architect of the U.S. effort, was now unable to sleep, unable to understand how victory could be won, unable to comfort his wife (who suffered from the intensifying public condemnation of her husband) or his children (who, along with the sons and daughters of other U.S. officials, joined antiwar protests). Seeing no way out, McNamara had wanted to resign for some months. He finally left the government in February 1968. The top U.S. military official, General Earle Wheeler, chairman of the Joint Chiefs of Staff, privately told Johnson that the Tet offensive had been a "very near thing." The bravery of U.S. forces had barely averted a military nightmare. At the annual presidential prayer breakfast in Washington, Johnson publicly blurted out, "The nights are very long. The winds are very chill. Our spirits grow weary and restive as the springtime of man seems farther and farther away."[13]

Just how serious the crisis had become was revealed when the *New York Times* headlined its discovery that Westmoreland and Wheeler had asked Johnson for 205,000 more troops. The president earlier had declared no more were needed above the "objective" of 525,000. Tet seemed to turn the war into a bottomless pit for American bodies. Newspaper stories circulated indicating that an unexplainable war was becoming irrational as well. When a U.S. officer was asked why his troops had to fight suspected Viet Minh by burning a village to the ground, he replied, "We had to destroy it in order to save it." Another widely published photo showed a public street in Saigon as the South Vietnamese police chief fired a pistol and blew out the brains of a suspected Viet Minh. Fed up with such reports from Vietnam and growing choruses of criticism at home, Secretary of State Dean Rusk, Johnson's leading prowar adviser, finally shouted at journalists to demand they tell him which side they were on.[14]

As the first presidential primaries approached in New Hampshire, Johnson turned over the Westmoreland-Wheeler request for 205,000 more troops to Clark Clifford, who had replaced McNamara on March 1. Clifford was the Washington insider's insider. Tall, white haired, impeccably dressed, courtly, with a carefully cultivated soft southern accent from his home state of Missouri, Clifford had been one of the most influential Americans for more than twenty years. As a young assistant to President Truman, he helped mastermind the president's upset 1948 election victory over the Republican, Governor Thomas Dewey of New York. It was perhaps the most surprising win in U.S. presidential election history. Clifford had next become a powerful lawyer, with offices close to the White House. But his number one client became Lyndon Johnson. The president greatly admired Clifford, not least for his winning advice to Truman in 1948 (which LBJ hoped could be repeated in 1968), and his hard-nosed, hawkish views on the need to win in Vietnam.

Clifford began his evaluation of the troop increase with the understanding that both the U.S. war effort and the Johnson presidency were at stake. The president had indicated there would be no further increases, and the Tet offensive had shredded LBJ's and Westmoreland's happy optimism of late 1967. But on January 23, a week before Tet, the communist North Korean government had captured the *Pueblo,* a U.S. intelligence ship, off the Korean coast. Despite Johnson's demands that the crew (and the body of one U.S. sailor killed in the capture) be released, the North Koreans defied him. They claimed the ship had been spying on them within their twelve-mile territorial waters and, thus, was fair game. The world's most powerful country was being put down by a Third World country, which was mistreating the crew as well. The crisis and Johnson's and Humphrey's failure to be able to resolve it only worsened their credibility, already badly damaged by Tet.[15] (The crew was finally released in December, a month after the 1968 election, when U.S. officials admitted the ship had been spying.)

Clifford's post-Tet evaluation thus involved not only Vietnam but also a larger question: whether the United States could send more troops to the war and, at the same time, have sufficient forces left to deal with crises elsewhere—such as the *Pueblo.* Many were also worried in early 1968 about whether the United States had the military force necessary to maintain order in the face of the crises of race, poverty, and antiwar rallies that were burning U.S. cities and causing chaos on college campuses. As a Defense Department memorandum bluntly phrased it, Americans had to know they "still had the resources left for the ghetto fight."[16]

Vietnam was the first war covered, and shaped, by television. The Korean conflict of 1950–1953 produced pictures shown on a few television sets, but the films were often bland and, since they had to be shipped by plane back to the United States, usually days old. Vietnam's pictures were graphic, largely because the Johnson administration feared trying to restrict U.S. reporters or censor what they filmed. Television sets now blanketed the nation and film footage, whether of police dogs attacking civil rights marchers in the South or the Tet offensive in Saigon, was transmitted rapidly. Viewers had only three networks (ABC, CBS, and NBC) and, therefore, resembled an audience locked in a theater with little choice about what they saw. Bitterly divided, fighting each other in the streets, Americans of the 1960s had nevertheless become much alike in their dependence on a small number of similar television news programs.

Johnson employed all his considerable persuasive powers on the three networks so he could dominate those news programs. But American politicians, resembling politicians elsewhere, are known for their love of the limelight and good publicity. Nothing provided better exposure than talking before tens of millions of viewers at suppertime. Until the Tet offensive, moreover, the three networks offered little criticism of the war and usually accepted whatever the Johnson administration said. Television seemed to be much less critical, for example, than such leading newspapers as the *Washington Post* and *New York Times*. Several reasons accounted for the difference. The newspapers appealed to a more literate, sophisticated, and cosmopolitan audience that followed politics and expected different perspectives and stories in some depth. A less educated, informed, and interested audience depended on television for its news (or at least this audience was uninterested in foreign relations until it was too late, and their sons and daughters went off to face death thousands of miles away). The television audience tended to be less questioning and more patriotic, while seeing complicated issues in moralistic, black/white terms. For these reasons, the mass of Americans received news about Vietnam and U.S. policies from a medium that reinforced their belief in both the American mission and Johnson's and Westmoreland's explanations.[17]

In other words, uncritical television coverage of the war, at least until early 1968, reinforced Johnson's popularity. In early January 1968, just three weeks before the Tet offensive, a Gallup public opinion poll reported that Americans who were asked approved the way the president "is handling his job as President" by 48 percent to 39 percent. (Those with only a grade school education gave 51 percent approval; those with a college degree 44 percent.)[18] In light of the disappointing course of the war and three years of major riots in American cities, these approval ratings were more favorable than LBJ might have expected. They no doubt were in part a reaction to Westmoreland's and Johnson's optimistic statements in late 1967.

Surveys taken during the first week of February—immediately after Tet—changed the findings of January. Now 41 percent disapproved of Johnson's "handling [of] his job," while 41 percent approved. More interestingly, in early December 1967, 39 percent of those asked had approved of how "Johnson is handling the situation in Vietnam," while 49 percent disapproved. In early February, after Tet, approval only sank to 35 percent and disapproval rose only a single point to 50 percent. But a most fascinating, and telling, response came when Gallup asked how respondents would classify themselves—as "hawks" (wanting to escalate the U.S. military effort) or "doves" (wanting to reduce that effort). Sixty-one percent identified themselves as hawks, only 23 percent as doves.[19] Antiwar protests on college campuses were by no means representative of American opinion as a whole.

Several conclusions may be drawn from these figures. First, the effect of television's relatively uncritical handling of the war and the impact of the Westmoreland–Johnson reassurance campaign in late 1967 lasted beyond Tet for the mass of Americans. Most did not like the president's handling of the war, but then they had not liked it for some time. Second, in addition to being pressured by antiwar protests that made colorful headlines, Johnson and Humphrey were being whip-sawed between those voices and the already large number (even a rousing majority of 61 percent) who wanted to escalate U.S. military involvement. On the one hand, LBJ feared that if he followed the antiwar protesters, his and his nation's international credibility would be ruined (he would be the first American president to lose a war). On the other hand, the president equally feared that escalating the military effort, as the hawks demanded, could lead to war with China or at least tremendous bloodshed. Johnson consequently tried instead to walk down the middle of the road—usually the most dangerous place to walk.

Being trapped by hawks and doves was not Johnson and Humphrey's only problem, according to early 1968 polls, if they hoped to be reelected in November. In early January 1968, Gallup asked, "What do you think is the most important problem facing the country today?" Only a bare majority, 53 percent, replied that it was Vietnam. "Crime and lawlessness" and "civil rights" ranked just behind Vietnam. In February, Gallup asked, "What is the most important problem facing this community today?" The number one response, "crime and lawlessness," was mentioned nearly twice as often as any other local problem.[20] Americans were concerned about Vietnam, but they were also worried over a possible breakdown in their own communities.

Besieged by both hawks and doves, discovering that his Great Society program seemed to be doing too little, too slowly in dealing with major social problems, Johnson began to resemble a tired boxer who could no longer trust his original fight plan. Then two more blows hit him. On February 20, the Senate Foreign Relations Committee, under the leadership of J. William Fulbright (Dem-AR), began holding public hearings on the war. These led to a series of statements by Fulbright and other antiwar voices condemning the president's policies. The attacks were well covered by the media.

On February 17, the man many believed to be the most trusted person in the country—Walter Cronkite of CBS television—returned from a trip to Vietnam and reported his findings on his widely watched evening news program. "We are mired in a stalemate," Cronkite concluded. In a jab at Westmoreland and the president, Cronkite told his tens of millions of viewers: "To say that we are closer to victory today is to believe, in the face of evidence, the optimists who have been wrong in the past." Johnson privately remarked that if Cronkite had turned against him, it would be impossible to keep drumming up public support for the war.[21] Tet marked a dividing point for many issues, less so for others, but after the communist offensive seemed to undermine Westmoreland and Johnson's credibility (and even raise questions about their knowledge of what was actually occurring in Vietnam), television coverage turned more critical.[22]

In early March 1968, Sir Patrick Dean nicely summarized for the Foreign Office in London some of the Tet offensive's results. The crisis had produced "the widest spectrum of opinions from say Walt Rostow [Johnson's national security adviser and an ardent hawk] who holds that the effects of the Viet Cong insurgency will be largely a bonus to the Allies' cause, to Senator Fulbright who takes them as conclusive proof that the Americans are fighting the wrong war in the wrong place and heading now even more rapidly for disaster," Dean wrote, "with the bulk of the Press taking the Senator's side."[23]

Dean's view was supported by Ellsworth Bunker, U.S. ambassador to South Vietnam. Returning to the United States in April 1968, Bunker was stunned by what he saw on television. "As an example of the effect of the reporting and TV coverage from here [Vietnam], the Tet offensive had a far greater impact in the United States than in

Viet-Nam," Bunker privately wrote a friend in New York. "No one got panicky here and nothing fell apart, but when I returned to Washington . . . in April, I was shocked to see the effect it had in the United States. This, of course, is Hanoi's main objective." The ambassador emphasized that Americans' perspectives tended to become blurred because "this is the first war in history which has been fought on television and it is the sensational aspect of it which comes into everyone's home." Meanwhile, he lamented, "the very definite improvements in the military situation . . . are largely passed over."[24]

Such beliefs as those expressed by Bunker and Cronkite later led some observers to argue that it was television and the press that weakened the will of the American people to the point that they were no longer willing to send their sons and daughters to die in Vietnam. The media, not the battles in Vietnam, these observers claimed, decided the outcome. Such a claim, however, ignored the points that Americans, along with some U.S. officials in Washington, were beginning to appreciate. Tet, for example, was indeed a communist military defeat, but it also demonstrated that Westmoreland and Johnson's optimism of late 1967 was unwarranted. The communists had further demonstrated that the United States could not kill enough of them fast enough to destroy their will to continue the war. This led to another point: U.S. media, including television, had originally been quite sympathetic to Johnson's war policies, but after Tet the media began to question the entire American war effort. In other words, reporting from Vietnam became more, not less, balanced and accurate.

Finally, Americans were coming to realize that the war was an integral part of a larger crisis they faced: inner-city rioting and death, growing racial conflict, economic downturn, and the seeming breakdown of civil society. One surprising presidential candidate began emphasizing those points. He did it so effectively, moreover, that he managed to pull off the unthinkable in American politics. He led the way in forcing a president who had won four years earlier in a landslide to drop out of the race for reelection.

Senator Eugene McCarthy during presidential primary campaign in Connecticut, April 3, 1968
Courtesy of the Minnesota Historical Society

SENATOR EUGENE McCARTHY:
THE COLLEGE STUDENT CRUSADE

The Tet offensive symbolized much of 1968. It was the first unexpected event in a year to be filled with the unexpected. It profoundly upset the hopes of Lyndon Johnson and, indeed, of most Americans. The communist campaign produced results that, like ripples in a stream, kept on multiplying and transforming the landscape. One of those ripples turned into a giant wave: the rise of a politics largely generated by college students that produced the explosive presidential candidacy of Senator Eugene McCarthy, Democrat of Minnesota. The wave washed over and helped change the course of the 1968 presidential election.

McCarthy's stunning showing in the March 12, 1968, New Hampshire Democratic Party primary was a major reason why Lyndon Johnson dramatically announced at the end of the month that he would not run for reelection. There was considerable irony here. McCarthy's campaign had been energized by college students who were determined to bring Johnson down and end the Vietnam War. Yet only four years earlier, the college-age generation had been so quiet that the president, running to be elected in his own right, thought it necessary in 1964 to lecture it:

> Our country very much needs the influence of this generation. I have read the tags often applied to your age group, the "quiet generation,"

the "apathetic generation," the "cool cookies" . . . interested only in sports cars, a split-level, and an annuity. But I am not really impressed by those statements because I just don't believe in labels. As a matter of fact, I believe it would be appropriate to say that yours is the "volunteer generation." You seem ready and eager to take on the tasks which call for a real personal sacrifice. This country needs those virtues. We need your boundless energy.[1]

Four years later Johnson was a victim of the generation's "boundless energy." He had become highly doubtful about its "virtues," especially when it turned out to be a "volunteer generation" that volunteered to help another candidate defeat him.

The baby boomers (the generation born between 1946 and 1964) began to enter their college years in the mid-1960s. The sudden population increase strained higher education's classrooms and dormitories. This was a young generation used to the prosperity and open choices of the late 1950s (an era that produced Elvis Presley, James Dean, and civil disobedience to protest racial segregation), and early 1960s (marked by the idealism of John Kennedy's New Frontier presidency, the Beatles, and Martin Luther King's "I have a dream" speech exalting racial equality in 1963). By 1964, college students involved with the civil rights protests in the South had lost their lives to the brutality of white racists. By 1965–1966, colleges had begun a massive teach-in movement against the Vietnam War.

In January 1966, Johnson made one of his most significant political errors: his administration announced it would draft college students who ranked in the lower grade levels of their classes. The war had suddenly come home for many baby boomers and their parents. Almost as galling to them, the colleges were cooperating with the government in ranking and exposing the young men to the draft to fight in a war that seemed to many both useless and endless.[2]

The teach-in movement and the antiwar rallies picked up in numbers and intensity. By 1966–1967, the American antiwar movement and, to a somewhat lesser extent, the civil rights movement were joined by supporters in Europe and Asia. Such protests easily translated into anti-U.S. and anticapitalism rallies around the globe.

For most Americans, especially those over age thirty who disliked
having their government condemned—and, at times, their own
daily activities upended—by such protests, their personal world
seemed to be disintegrating before their eyes. In early 1966, antiwar marchers from West Germany, Austria, France, Sweden, Nor-
way, Italy, and the Netherlands declared support for their American
counterparts. When 75,000 marched on the Pentagon in October
1967, coordinated anti-U.S. demonstrations erupted in West Germany, England, France, Italy, Japan, and the Scandinavian countries. In Paris, leftists attacked the American Express Company
building. Mass antiwar rallies occurred several times in London.
Latin American students swore to create new Vietnam-type wars
throughout the Southern Hemisphere that would throw out U.S.
influence.[3]

These movements profoundly affected politics in various countries,
especially France, Italy, and Latin American nations. But they also
began to transform U.S. policies. In mid-1967, at the convention of
the National Student Association (NSA), the country's largest student
organization, two leaders, Allard Lowenstein and Curtis Gans, triggered a movement to drive Lyndon Johnson out of the presidency.
Notably, the Lowenstein-Gans group had come to dominate the NSA
the year before when, after a bitter fight, it drove out a faction that believed regular political action would no longer work, but that only civil
disobedience—perhaps violent clashes—could effectively change a
system that produced bloody devastation in Vietnam and racial injustice at home.

Lowenstein was a young lawyer (he taught at New York University
Law School) and able politician (gaining election in 1968 to Congress) who still believed in working through the political system to
bring about change. Despite the usual factionalism and vicious back-
stabbing in such organizations, Lowenstein began his "Dump Johnson" campaign by looking for a suitable candidate to run for the presidency. He hoped that Senator Robert Kennedy (D-NY) would lead
the effort. Kennedy was distancing himself from Johnson and the war
but did not yet want to go the last step and divide the Democratic
Party. Others also rejected Lowenstein's offer.[4]

Then he talked with Senator Eugene McCarthy. After considerable soul-searching, in late 1967 McCarthy finally accepted Lowenstein's offer to head the anti-Johnson movement. The gray-haired, fifty-one-year-old Minnesotan was by no means the most likely person to lead a messy, fractious, free-for-all crusade. He resembled a monk from a secluded seminary more than a bare-knuckled fighter in the public lion pit of American politics. And with good reason: After growing up in a small town, McCarthy had studied at St. John's University in Minnesota, where his grade point average was the highest in the school's history. McCarthy taught high school and then returned to St. John's to teach and became for a time a novice in the Benedictine Order. He gave up a seminarian's life, however, when he worked in military intelligence during World War II and then married in 1945. Three years later he won a race for the House of Representatives. Over the next decade, McCarthy retained the seat with ever larger majorities. In 1958, he stunned political observers to win a Senate race by defeating a two-term Republican incumbent. He was reelected in 1964 by the largest popular majority of any Democratic candidate in Minnesota's history. Since Vice President Hubert Humphrey had several times run for the Senate from the state as a highly popular Democrat but had been elected by smaller majorities, it was clear that McCarthy had remarkable political talents.

At the same time, however, McCarthy seemed an unlikely politician. An accomplished author, he published four books on American politics between 1960 and 1967. He was also an original poet, and his poems, like their author, were sometimes otherworldly and quite detached from their immediate surroundings. A successful politician, he refused to be a backslapper and had a caustic sense of humor that could alienate those who were trying to like him. Its inhabitants called the U.S. Senate the "world's most exclusive club," or "the greatest debating society in the world." McCarthy, however, labeled it "the last primitive society left on earth." He came from a long-time progressive state and rode the political coattails of Franklin D. Roosevelt's sweeping New Deal reforms, but privately he preferred small, isolated communities that recalled attempts in the early nineteenth century to create gentle American utopian towns. His wife, Abigail, recalled that "Gene was caught up in the vision of the Catholic rural life movement whose ideal was the land as a source of freedom and security and as a base of community."[5]

A nineteenth-century utopian and poet who liked the monastery was, understandably, not Lowenstein's first choice to lead a movement to depose a sitting president. But those traits actually helped McCarthy in 1968. Given his age, restrained voice, sophistication, and yearning for a quieter life, he seemed the polar opposite of the students and their publicity-seeking leaders who marched on the Pentagon or clogged city streets with antiwar protests. The senator had publicly turned against the war in early 1967. He declared he saw no end to the killing and feared that Johnson would try unsuccessfully to escape his trap by killing yet more Americans and Vietnamese.

McCarthy had never been a fan of Johnson's and since 1964 had deeply mistrusted him. Before the 1964 Democratic Convention, LBJ hinted that McCarthy might be his vice presidential candidate. The senator was willing, but as Johnson delayed in order to arouse media curiosity, and as McCarthy's fellow Minnesota senator, Hubert Humphrey, seemed the front-runner, McCarthy declared he was no longer interested—and thus barely missed being humiliated by Johnson who indeed had long planned on asking Humphrey.[6] The senator again become angry in 1967, when a top State Department official, Nicholas Katzenbach, told the Senate Foreign Relations Committee, of which McCarthy was a member, that Johnson had the constitutional power to do anything he wanted in Vietnam. "This is the wildest testimony I have ever heard," a furious McCarthy told waiting reporters. "There is no limit to what he says the President can do. There is only one thing to do—take it to the country."[7]

He was ready to accept Lowenstein's offer for another reason. McCarthy feared the antiwar movement was moving sharply to the left and being increasingly shaped by Marxist thought. The Roman Catholic communitarian wanted to do everything he could to halt that trend. The longtime politician and thoughtful critic of overweening presidential power planned on doing all he could to stop another baby boomer trend: dealing with the complexities of Vietnam and domestic crises by getting high on drugs and music while dropping out of the political arena. As a devout admirer of Sir Thomas More (1478–1535), who was beheaded because he chose his Roman Catholic belief over loyalty to the British king, McCarthy believed Vietnam was shaping up to be the ultimate test for people of conscience. He wanted to stop the war and save both the baby boomer generation and the American political system.[8]

This sense of obligation came through clearly in his November 30, 1967, announcement opposing Johnson for the party's nomination:

> I am hopeful that a challenge may alleviate the sense of political hope-lessness and restore to many people belief in the processes of American politics and American government . . . [and also hope] it may counter the growing sense of alienation from politics which is currently reflected in a tendency to withdraw in either frustration or cynicism, to talk of non-participation and to make threats of support for a third party or fourth party or other irregular political movements.[9]

It is striking that McCarthy, who would increasingly be seen by many as a kind of radical, was so conservative that he refused to consider running other than on the Democratic Party ticket. He thought even a third party to be "irregular" and dangerous. (The Republicans themselves had been a third party in the 1850s, and McCarthy himself had started his political career as a member of a kind of third party, the Farmer-Labor Party in Minnesota.)

This conservatism was what was most important about McCarthy. It explained why he was able to change American politics in 1968 and why his run for the presidency revealed so much about how American democracy can react to the growing dangers of a long war. Like Toc-queville a century before, McCarthy had come to the conclusion that a long conflict undermined the nation's democratic principles—and, in McCarthy's view, thus American freedom itself—by creating an all-powerful presidency. It had become an endless war that would allow that president to have even more power, while student movements took out their frustration by turning either dangerously to the left or opting out through a drug-infested counterculture. (A decade later, McCarthy published a book discussing Tocqueville and his famous visit to the United States during the presidency of Andrew Jackson.)[10]

His overriding concern was Tocqueville's: finding a way to avert having American democracy corrupted by a long war. His emphasis was on saving democracy, not winning the war. McCarthy's views on the conflict in late 1967–early 1968 were hardly radical. Staunchly committed to fighting the Cold War against a godless communism, he believed Vietnam had become a needless distraction in that all-out struggle. McCarthy did not want to withdraw immediately from Vietnam but create enclaves in South Vietnam that could be defended. From these improved positions of strength, he hoped negotiations could begin to work out a settlement with North Vietnam. The senator opposed further escalation, thus breaking from Johnson, who had concluded he could not save South Vietnam unless he went much farther than simply hunkering down in an enclave strategy.[11]

The Minnesota senator seemed so wedded to the idea of staying in Vietnam until some settlement was worked out that observers wondered whether he would not merely serve as a figurehead for the antiwar movement until a more prominent, tougher, leader, such as Robert Kennedy, decided to run for the presidency. The speculation caused McCarthy to bristle. He had never cared for the Kennedys, who, although Roman Catholic, had certainly never considered living the simple, celibate life with the Benedictines. "I am not a stalking-horse for anybody," McCarthy pointedly proclaimed when he announced his candidacy.

The challenge McCarthy issued on November 30, 1967, was the second blow Johnson suffered in forty-eight hours. A day before, the worn-out, increasingly pessimistic secretary of defense, Robert McNamara, had resigned from the cabinet. Johnson responded to these two blows with a slashing attack on his opponents, including McCarthy, without ever mentioning the senator's name, in a December speech before the convention of the largest U.S. labor union, the AFL-CIO. "I am not going to be influenced by a bunch of political, selfish men who want to advance their own interests," the president told the cheering thousands. "I am going to continue . . . doing my duty as I see it for the best of all my country, regardless of my polls or regardless of the election."[12]

Such words fit well with the Johnson–Westmoreland propaganda offensive of late 1967. McCarthy clearly had not merely an uphill, but an up-mountain road to climb, according to polls, if he hoped to challenge the president. Nearly 60 percent of Americans asked had never even heard of the Minnesota senator. In a preference poll taken among Democratic voters, he trailed Johnson 63 to 17 percent. Not surprisingly, given his frequent condescension toward fellow senators, few of them or other Democratic Party leaders indicated any interest in his campaign. Nor at times did he seem personally to have much interest. He did not enter the first primary in New Hampshire until January, then campaigned so lazily that he drove away supporters.[13]

The Tet offensive of late January 1968 transformed McCarthy's prospects, if not his laziness and disinterest in campaigning. February polls showed that for the first time in the war, Americans believed, 49 percent to 41 percent, that committing troops to Vietnam had been a mistake. This by no means meant they wanted to retreat, but questions were now being raised by many who had long supported Johnson. The Americans for Democratic Action (ADA), an influential Democratic group that was anticommunist and pro–New Deal, suddenly endorsed McCarthy—although, notably, several labor union presidents who were pro-war and pro-Johnson resigned from the ADA so they could campaign for the president.[14]

Of more significance, Lowenstein and other supporters mobilized some five thousand college students to campaign door-to-door in New Hampshire for McCarthy. "We do not want hippies or flower children," organizers announced. When McCarthy supporters heard housewives commenting that some of the senator's female workers wore miniskirts and smoked, a set of rules—"Clean for Gene"—was issued. For men, "No beards. Wear a coat and tie, . . . NO BLUE JEANS OR WORK SHIRTS." For women: "Absolutely no slacks, no miniskirts. . . . Extreme dress of any kind—exotic jewelry, make-up, etc.—should be AVOIDED . . . NEAT hairdo. Long flying tresses should be restrained in a barrette." Anyone not obeying these rules would be sent away on the spot. The payoff was immediate. An estimated 60,000 doorbells were rung by the Clean for Gene campaigners. One New Hampshire Democrat declared, "These college kids are fabulous. . . . [They] knock at the door and come in politely, and actually want to talk to grown ups, and people are delighted." This "Children's Crusade," as it was soon tagged, attracted free media attention that would otherwise have cost the nearly bankrupt McCarthy campaign tens of thousands of dollars. And if the media tired of the students, Hollywood was available. As *Time* magazine noted, "Actors Robert Ryan and Tony Randall took to the stump" for McCarthy, "but Paul Newman's appearances had to be circumscribed for fear of a riot among Hampshire women."[15]

Lowenstein and McCarthy seemed to be reaching their objective. They had aimed to create a grassroots student movement that was both involved politically (and not lost somewhere in the drug-laden counterculture) and vigorously anti-Johnson. It became clear, however, that most of the newly involved came from elite colleges. Students at most of the 2,000 American colleges were apathetic, unwilling, or unable to question the president publicly, or too busy putting themselves through school to have time for door-to-door campaigning. Lewis Hershey, who headed the military draft program, believed that draft dodging did not plague American colleges—except among the student bodies at the top fifty universities, the most prominent and prestigious colleges in the country—and Johnson badly wanted their support. When the presidents of MIT, Duke, Cornell, Yale, and Princeton met to issue a tepid statement questioning the war, Cornell President James Perkins tipped off the White House. The Johnson administration unleashed its considerable powers of persuasion to convince these leaders of American higher education to back down. Many of their students, however, were out in the field for "Gene."[16]

In February, McCarthy finally aroused himself to campaign more vigorously in New Hampshire. He broadened his message beyond his moderate opposition to the war because of his deep belief that problems threatening the country went far beyond it. Johnson's refusal to increase taxes had created a skyrocketing government debt, the threat of dangerous inflation in prices, and—in order to pay growing U.S. debts abroad—an outflow of the gold that had been underpinning the dollar. On January 18, 1968, McCarthy broadly attacked the president's economic policies and tied them directly to the costs of the war. He had long blasted the Central Intelligence Agency and the

Department of Defense for acting as arrogant, secretive agencies that threatened the independence of American democratic institutions: "By establishing the criteria by which certain kinds of students are drafted and certain others are deferred, the military even influences the subjects that our young people are studying and really, therefore, is affecting our whole culture."[17]

McCarthy underlined his main message: the Vietnam War was not only wrong in itself. It corrupted American democracy. "The presidential election should be in part a referendum on the military—industrial complex [that increasingly controlled both domestic budgets and foreign policy], on the militarization of our foreign policy, and, increasingly of our domestic life," he told New Hampshire voters.[18] In a book published in May 1968 that summarized his campaign themes, McCarthy portrayed the state of the country in bleak terms and in judgments that went well beyond the war:

> For the first time since the Depression [of the 1930s], Americans are asking whether our republic, as we know it, can survive its present course. We are not threatened with imminent attack, economic collapse, or sectional dismemberment. There is no single danger that can be precisely pinpointed. Yet all around us are signs that something is gravely wrong.

He then outlined the dangers: "alienation" and a growing military that somehow made the nation "more isolated and more suspect than at any time in our history." He also cited the "violence and lawlessness in our cities; and an accelerating polarization of our society into hostile black ghettoes surrounded by hostile white suburbs." The senator related these broad threats to Vietnam: "What is new, and what is very much a product of the Administration's single-minded preoccupation with the war . . . is the feeling that these problems are not being solved *and are not about to be solved.* It is the disappearance of *hope* . . . that is the most unsettling fact about America." Then McCarthy told Americans to get their priorities straight:

> The most important struggle for the future welfare of America is not in the jungles of Vietnam; it is in the streets and schools and tenements of

our cities. Yet the commitment of resources and moral energy to the
problems of our cities has been but a fraction of the amount committed
to the Saigon regime.[19]

Throughout many of his speeches, McCarthy demanded, as he
once phrased it, "maintaining public order." He stressed the need "to
forestall and contain rioting and to insure that forces of order—
whether they be local police, National Guardsmen, or federal
troops—serve to reduce, and not augment, the level of violence."[20]

The problem as McCarthy defined it was as follows. Americans, as
they had for several centuries, faced growing problems of race, ur-
banization, class, and economic fairness. Since the 1950s, however,
many groups, led by civil rights advocates, had mobilized and demanded change. They were tired of waiting for solutions to these
problems, especially after Johnson's Great Society legislation had
overpromised and underdelivered in its attempt to solve them. The
continuing Vietnam War worsened an already unfair and increasingly
tense situation by diverting money and attention to killing foreigners
10,000 miles away instead of taking care of Americans at home. The
war further militarized the nation's life, heightened the already im-
mense military-industrial complex's power over U.S. budgets, and
raised to a most dangerous level the role of crime and firearms in
American society. After all, "no other modern Western nation in the
same time span has had as many heads of state killed as has America."
Consequently, the country had divided, with some groups advocating
the use of force to achieve rights and equality, while, on the other side,
appeared "danger signs of a rising vigilantism; of preoccupation with
tanks," machine guns, and other weapons of destruction, of "private
rifle clubs urging all civilians to be armed." The Vietnam War had
come home.[21]

President Johnson and many political pundits in early 1968 focused
narrowly on Vietnam, perhaps not surprisingly after the shock of the
Tet offensive. McCarthy only moderately dissented on the war, but he
offered a sweeping explanation (of which the war was only one part),
to explain why Americans feared they were facing a breakdown of
their society. On different political wavelengths than McCarthy, the
so-called experts in Washington downplayed the danger he and his

message posed to Johnson's reelection plans. "Senator McCarthy's campaign still shows no sign of sparking," British Ambassador Sir Patrick Dean wrote back to London on March 1, 1968, after taking political soundings in Washington. "It will be surprising if he makes a good showing" in New Hampshire, even if he was the only candidate challenging the president—and even though Johnson's organization in the state did not have the president's name on the ballot and thus had to organize a campaign to write in his name.[22]

Dean's views were echoed by others who noted that the relaxed McCarthy had once more reduced his campaigning in New Hampshire. Of course there were thousands of Clean for Gene students going house to house with the senator's moderate message on the war and his less moderate attack on the Johnson administration's refusal to deal with fundamental problems that were tearing the country apart. The president's camp meanwhile committed serious political errors, for example, taunting McCarthy with Cold War clichés. "The communists in Vietnam are watching," Johnson's supporters proclaimed. "Don't vote for fuzzy thinking and surrender." New Hampshire voters considered themselves too independent and informed to be bought off with such sloganeering.[23]

On March 12, those voters transformed the 1968 election by humiliating the president. He won 49 percent of the vote, not bad for an essentially write-in candidate, although he did have the state Democratic Party political organization backing. McCarthy took 42 percent when experts were predicting he would be lucky to win 15 percent. When all the write-in votes were counted as well, McCarthy actually defeated the president by 230 votes. In separate polling, the senator, despite having every leader of the state organization against him, took twenty of twenty-four Democratic convention delegate contests away from Johnson. New Hampshire's Democratic governor, a close friend of LBJ's, had earlier smeared McCarthy by saying that in the highly unlikely event the senator won, his victory would be "greeted with great cheers in Hanoi." Instead, the outcome was greeted with great shock in Washington.[24]

The shock struck not only the president's campaign, however, but also McCarthy's. Poll results were to show that the Minnesota senator—run by Lowenstein and the Clean for Gene students as a peace candidate who would end the war—actually received more votes from those (the hawks) who wanted to take a harder military line against the Vietnamese communists than from those (the doves) who wanted the United States to withdraw. Among the New Hampshire voters who selected McCarthy over Johnson, the hawks outnumbered the doves by a 3-to-2 margin. One poll revealed that more than half the Democrats in the state did not even know McCarthy's position on Vietnam. It was good enough for the voters that the senator was simply running against Johnson. Nor was it lost to observers that a supposed hard-liner, Richard Nixon, won the Republican primary with more votes than were given to all the other candidates combined, Republican and Democratic. Given these figures, New Hampshire voters actually supported the war in Vietnam—but apparently not the way Johnson was fighting it.[25]

These striking statistics indicated that when McCarthy talked about the war, voters accurately did not see him emphasizing the need for a peaceful settlement. They instead viewed him as a candidate who offered an alternative to Johnson, and then went beyond the war itself to analyze the general breakdown splintering and bloodying American society. When asked later in the spring about issues of social welfare and civil rights, McCarthy supporters turned out to be more conservative than those who wanted Vice President Humphrey or Senator Robert Kennedy of New York to head the Democratic presidential ticket. A number of New Hampshire citizens, along with many other McCarthy backers, simply wanted to end the war (they apparently did not care how), so Americans could address the growing problems in their streets, on their campuses, and in their inner cities.[26]

Four days after the primary, another shock hit both Johnson and McCarthy. Robert Kennedy announced he was a candidate for the presidency. The New York senator had previously refused to put his political career on the line. No Kennedy had ever lost an election, and taking on a sitting president could end that winning streak. New Hampshire voters, however, had dramatically demonstrated the depth of the opposition to Johnson. McCarthy was understandably bitter by Kennedy's late entry. Besides not caring for the Kennedys personally, in 1960 he had worked hard, but unsuccessfully, to obtain the Democratic presidential nomination for Adlai Stevenson (the governor of

Illinois and a fellow intellectual in politics), so John F. Kennedy could not have it. McCarthy's dislike of the family stretched from the personal to the religious to the political.

Robert Kennedy publicly offered to work in "harmony" and support McCarthy in the upcoming Wisconsin and two other primaries (because it was too late for Kennedy to enter those contests). The Minnesota senator coldly replied, "I can win in Wisconsin alone as I won in New Hampshire without any outside help." He viewed Kennedy as a wealthy, spoiled Johnny-come-lately who wanted to take over a cause that the Clean for Gene team had pioneered. With Kennedy's announcement, the Democratic Party antiwar forces became badly divided. It did not help McCarthy's mercurial temper when several top aides quit his campaign so they could join the Kennedy camp. Nor did it help when polls of mid-March showed Democrats preferring Kennedy over Johnson by a 44 percent to 41 percent margin, but who chose Johnson over McCarthy by a whopping 59 percent to 29 percent. New Hampshire seemed to be the exception. But it turned out to be a historic exception.[27]

No one read polls and election results better than Lyndon Johnson. He realized that the New Hampshire vote was a stinging embarrassment for a sitting president. He also understood that McCarthy had defeated him by tapping into something beyond the Vietnam War. *Time* magazine caught this in its comments on the primary:

> In an era when many young Americans are turning away from involvement in the democratic process by dropping out either to psychadelia or the nihilism of the New Left, the cool, crisply executed crusade of Eugene McCarthy's "ballot children" provides heartening evidence that the generation gap is bridgeable—politically, at least.[28]

Dealing with McCarthy's challenge was going to be bad enough for Johnson. As *U.S. News & World Report* recorded in late March, "It now is being taken for granted" that Johnson would "receive another blow from the voters of Wisconsin in the primary . . . on April 1. Many Democrats suggest that it will be more severe than that of New Hampshire."[29] And as the polls already revealed, once Kennedy was able to enter primaries in May and June, the situation would become even more grim for Johnson. The president despised and feared the New York senator even more than did McCarthy, if that were possible. He knew that the Kennedys returned the hatred and were now revving up their well-bankrolled political machine to drive him from office. All the while he was haunted by a seemingly endless war that did not allow him to sleep at night. Johnson was about to be forced to make a historic decision.

President Lyndon B. Johnson shrinks in the presence of three ghostly enshrouded skeletons wearing helmets labeled "Vietnam"
Courtesy of the Library of Congress

3

LYNDON JOHNSON: "PEOPLE GROW TIRED OF CONFUSION"

Jack Valenti, long an intimate adviser of Lyndon Johnson's, recalled that he once cited a passage from Alexis de Tocqueville's *Democracy in America* while helping LBJ write a major speech. The speech was a response to the growing condemnation of the president's Vietnam and Great Society policies. Valenti quoted Tocqueville's insight that "the [American] people grow tired of a confusion whose end is not in sight." "Johnson buried his head in his hands," Valenti remembered, "and said, 'That's sure as hell right.'"[1]

By late winter 1968, the president, who had stood so tall politically in 1964–1965, was bent and exhausted. Despite Eugene McCarthy's stunning showing in New Hampshire, despite Robert Kennedy's much ballyhooed entrance into the race in mid-March, Johnson would no doubt have been renominated for the presidency. Even if McCarthy and Kennedy won all the primaries, LBJ, with his ties to state political bosses and his control of patronage, would obtain the number of convention delegates needed to win at the Chicago convention scheduled for August. But it would not be easy. Indeed, it could be deeply humiliating for the president to suffer primary losses, while begging for support from people who not long ago had begged him for help and the payoffs from his Great Society programs.

Johnson's dreams, shaped and made possible by his 1964 landslide win, had turned into nightmares. He had, for example, dreamed of leading the nation's young people on a liberal crusade. "I have visited many campuses," he declared in 1965, "and I can tell you that this generation of young Americans is a generation of which I am deeply proud. . . . This is not the lost generation [of the 1920s] or the silent generation [of the 1950s]. . . . This is the concerned and the committed generation." Many in that generation in early 1968 now refused, in shocking numbers, to fight in Vietnam, while others marched on Washington chanting, "Hey, hey LBJ, how many kids did you kill today?" He was proud of the openness in the American system as compared with communist societies: "We have always welcomed dissent. We have never muzzled disagreement," he overgeneralized in 1964. But dissent now took the form of burning inner cities, attacking police and bystanders, and condemning such liberal fundamentals as racial interaction and the containment of communism anywhere. The world of Johnson and Vice President Hubert Humphrey was collapsing, despite their vast power. The more they spent on Vietnam and the Great Society, the faster that world seemed to splinter. "I get no comfort . . . that the defense budget this year [1968] is roughly equal to the gross national product of all of Latin America," observed Secretary of State Dean Rusk, a southern liberal and leading hawk on the war. But not even such a gigantic defense budget could turn around Johnson's misfortunes.[2]

"It is hard to imagine . . . the atmosphere in Washington in the sixty days after Tet," Secretary of Defense Clark Clifford recalled. "The pressure grew so intense . . . I felt the government itself might come apart at the seams." Johnson had been the ultimate inside Washington player, but now at times he seemed lost. George Reedy, the president's press secretary and close friend, later noted that LBJ "had never in his entire life learned to confess error, and this quality— merely amusing or exasperating in a private person—resulted in cosmic tragedy for a President." Among other tragedies, Johnson believed "he had no alternative . . . to feeding more and more draftees into the [Vietnam] meat grinder," Reedy believed. Locked into a set of failed policies, LBJ and many other liberals and conservatives determined to fight a war whose original objectives —forcing the North Vietnamese communists to retreat from South Vietnam and thus to weaken Chinese power—now seemed well beyond their reach.[3]

By February and March 1968, when nearly 80 percent of Americans believed that Johnson's Vietnam policies were going nowhere, it was easier to condemn the messenger rather than the policies. Thus the president and his advisers criticized Walter Cronkite of CBS news for declaring that Tet demonstrated the weakness of Johnson's approach, or they questioned the *New York Times* journalists' reporting from Vietnam.

As a definitive study of the media and the war concluded, however, Americans were actually not turned against the conflict by the media, but by the hard, horrible statistics of battlefield casualties. Public support inevitably dropped 15 percentage points when total casualties increased by a factor of ten. Johnson and his advisers had no idea how to deal with this iron law of public opinion, except, as several of his military leaders unfortunately suggested, to increase the number of U.S. troops who could become more casualties. As Clark Clifford later wrote, "The bulk of the reporting from the war zone reflected the official position. Contrary to right-wing revisionism, reporters and the antiwar movement did not defeat America in Vietnam." Instead, the former secretary of defense concluded, "Our policy failed because it was based on false premises and false promises."[4]

The military's frustrations boiled over on February 6, 1968, at Johnson's regular Tuesday luncheon meeting held to discuss the war with his closest advisers. General Earle Wheeler, Joint Chiefs of Staff chairman, exploded. He had led the failed drive to persuade Johnson to send over some 205,000 more troops. Now he demanded—the media be damned—that U.S. planes and other firepower be allowed to strike more civilian areas:

> I am fed up to the teeth with the activities of the North Vietnamese and the Viet Cong [the Viet Minh communist troops in the South]. We apply rigid restrictions to ourselves and try to operate in a humanitarian concern for civilians at all times. They apply a double standard. . . . In addition, they place their munitions inside of populated areas because they think they are safe there. In fact they place their SAMS [surface-to-air missiles] in civilian buildings to fire at our aircraft.[5]

A weary Johnson finally agreed to reduce some limits on U.S. bombing. But he knew that Wheeler was simply venting his increasing frustration, not offering anything new that would somehow end the war.

Some ten days later, news leaked that the U.S. Army had sponsored a study (neatly named Pax Americana), which concluded the country had to be prepared to intervene around the world, for an unlimited amount of time, to contain dangerous conflicts. The study emphasized the need for more soldiers to deal with such an endless task. Several senators, led by J. William Fulbright (D-AR), Foreign Relations Committee chair and now Johnson's most eloquent enemy as regards the war, demanded the report be made public so it could be debated. The administration refused with the excuse that publication might "produce serious repercussions abroad." Even as U.S. officials proved unable to prevent Vietnamese communists from being able to "romp at will over much of the landscape of that miserable country" as one of Secretary of State Rusk's top aides bitterly phrased it, Johnson's military advisers seemed to be considering creating new Vietnams.[6]

Outgoing Secretary of Defense Robert McNamara, once a prime architect of the war and now more deeply fatigued, frustrated, discouraged, and despondent than Johnson, used his last days in office to try, somehow, to turn around the administration's policies. On February 20, 1968, he publicly testified that the incidents leading to the 1964 Gulf of Tonkin congressional resolution—the resolution that Johnson and McNamara had long claimed gave them all they authority they needed to wage the war—had been in considerable part thought up by the U.S. government. In shocking testimony before Fulbright's committee, McNamara admitted, for the first time, that the North Vietnamese attacks on U.S. destroyers in the Gulf of Tonkin had been provoked: the Americans were helping South Vietnam conduct intelligence and other operations against the North. The administration's case in 1964 for passing the resolution came crashing down. But McNamara was not done. In top-secret discussions on the military's need for 205,000 more troops, he called the request "madness." He had enough of honoring "the requests from the Wheelers of the world," McNamara declared privately, because it was now clear the military had "no plan to win the war."[7]

The U.S. forces that had defeated the Japanese empire, helped destroy Nazi Germany, and in 1950–1953 fought China to a standstill now seemed to be disintegrating. Soldiers openly protested in favor of peace, created a small antiwar press, and, on one occasion, even let loose a moan of protest against their commander in chief when Johnson called on them to be prepared to fight and die for freedom in Vietnam. U.S. troops participated in antiwar demonstrations in Japan and Europe. Stories began to surface of increased drug use and defiance of orders by the infantry "grunts" who put their lives on the line in Vietnam's jungles.[8]

Again, however, Vietnam was only a piece of the general crisis. The danger of a breakdown in the U.S. military reflected a more general breakdown in the larger U.S. community unable to withstand (as Tocqueville had warned 130 years earlier) the bloody and economic demands of a long war. British Ambassador Sir Patrick Dean told his superiors in London: "It is an unhappy commentary on the country's state that these two terms [civil rights and crime] should have to be conjoined." In other words, the perception was growing among Americans that the riots, black nationalist demands, and growing violence in the cities had been shaped by Johnson's attempts to protect the civil rights of minorities, especially African Americans. But no matter how much he legislated and promised, the realities of poverty and discrimination did not disappear fast enough, or at all. Dean recorded that Johnson produced a flurry of reaction when a group of visiting students asked him whether the upcoming summer would again be bloody and he answered, "We can't avert it." He mistakenly thought the remark would not be reported.[9]

The strains caused by the war and domestic violence were bad enough in the mid-1960s when the economy boomed. In 1968, just as Americans were reeling from the Tet offensive, their economy faced a crisis. It would now become much more difficult to deal with either the war or domestic threats with the usual American solution of throwing more money at them. Kennedy and Johnson had escalated the war during an era when the economy was perhaps the healthiest in American history. Unemployment and inflation were low, and economic growth rocketed upward. In a 1966 speech he perhaps later regretted, Vice President Humphrey sounded the liberals' mantra that Americans could now afford both waging war and reforming their own country: "It is not a matter of guns or butter, foreign aid or domestic education," he declared. "They are tied together. You cannot separate them, because the only way you can have guns at prices that you have to pay is to have an economy that can afford them, and the only way that you can have foreign aid is to have an economy that is productive enough to pay the bills."[10]

The "guns and butter" speech sounded logical, as long as the economy kept expanding to pay for both. Johnson believed it would. He told Congress that "we can continue the Great Society while we fight in Vietnam." So he had recommended an all-time-high budget and more spending on the war, but no tax increase. Above all else, LBJ did not want to have to propose a tax increase—to ask Americans for further sacrifice. "If I proposed it," he admitted to a close aide, "the [conservative] hawks will vote against the Great Society as an excuse, and the doves will vote against the war." Johnson "really did believe," the aide recalled, "that he could have it all ways, that we could have it all ways."[11]

The false belief he could "have it all ways" led to the false conclusion that ideology no longer mattered. Ideology was for communists and socialists. American capitalists and democrats were, as the national tradition had it, pragmatic—they were the tough minded who cared only about practical consequences and results, not theory. The end of ideology craze that swept American politics in the early 1960s was roughly equal to the rock-and-roll craze that struck American teenagers at the same time. But it turned out that this end of ideology faith actually rested on ideology: the longtime American theory that problems could best be averted not by more fairly distributing what happened to be available but by producing more—an ideology neatly captured in the popular phrase, "A rising tide raises all boats."

"When the cost of fulfilling people's aspirations can be met out of a growing horn of plenty—instead of robbing Peter to pay Paul—ideological roadblocks melt away," declared Walter Heller, a top economic adviser to both Kennedy and Johnson. They followed Heller's advice that nothing worked better to unleash American ingenuity than tax cuts, advice that Johnson no doubt later wished he had not accepted. There were, however, two other less happy sides of such piping prosperity. Pockets of poverty, especially in the inner cities and rural South, where a lack of education and opportunity worked against minorities and poor whites, proved to be immune to Heller's economics. As two historians of the era summarized, moreover, a good economy ironically "underwrote the decade's radical insurgency. Prosperous times made possible wide detours from careers into dissenting politics and alternative lifestyles that college students took. . . . If you dropped out, you could later painlessly drop in."[12]

By early 1968, however, the economy had begun to sour. Vietnam costs shot up to $20 billion annually. No end was in sight. Humphrey's faith that Americans could have both guns and butter became questionable as costs rose to pay for the Great Society, and also to rebuild burned-out inner cities. But another problem, a problem that would vex Americans into the twenty-first century, also began to appear. Ten years before, six West European nations led by the financial powerhouses Germany and France had created a Common Market, then started to integrate their economic systems and surround them with a single tariff wall. Their economies took off, total production rose 50 percent (compared with a U.S. rise of 45 percent over ten years), and their trade more than tripled. U.S. corporations accelerated their investments to take advantage of the Common Market's new opportunities inside the tariff wall. A leading French journalist, J. J. Servan Schreiber, warned in his best-selling book, *The American Challenge* (1968), that some $10 billion of U.S. investments since 1958 were turning Western Europe into an American economic appendage. "Is Belgium in danger of becoming a colony of America?" a Belgian official was asked. "We already are," he replied.[13]

From Johnson's perspective, the problem with such colonization was the billions of dollars that left the United States, as well as American jobs, most notably inner-city manufacturing jobs. Gone also was the possibility of collecting taxes from these funds. Since 1945 the United States had built an entire, and highly successful, international commercial system by making the dollar the dependable and accepted international currency. Business communities everywhere were willing to use the dollar because it rested on a U.S. promise to redeem it, if necessary, in gold. This promise looked good in 1945, when Americans held 60 percent of the world's gold.

By 1968, however, growing U.S. investments abroad and the increasing costs of Cold War policies in Vietnam and elsewhere had cut U.S. gold holdings in half. Since Americans no longer had the gold to guarantee the dollar, its worth suddenly came into question. And since the dollar was the foundation for world as well as U.S. prosperity, Johnson admitted in February 1968 that he faced a mushrooming problem "that could touch off an international financial crisis" within the year.[14]

Secretary of the Treasury Henry Fowler had earlier blamed the Vietnam War for the crisis. Not only were the costs of the conflict rising, Fowler worried, but by creating demand for U.S. goods the war raised prices, created dangerous inflation that drove those prices still higher, and therefore made it more difficult for many U.S. businesses to compete for markets abroad. Senate majority leader Mike Mansfield (D-MT), warned Johnson in mid-March 1968 that expanding U.S. efforts in Vietnam would result in "more inflation, more balance of payments complications, and possibly financial panic and collapse." Even ardently prowar Secretary of State Dean Rusk began to back away from sending in hundreds of thousands more troops: "We have . . . got to think of what this troop increase would mean in terms of increased taxes, the balance of payments picture, inflation, gold, and the general economic picture." *Time* magazine summarized the crisis by announcing in March that the nation was threatened with "the largest gold rush in history, a frenetic speculative stampede that . . . threatened the Western world."[15]

The growing economic crisis thus went far beyond Vietnam, although the war formed a central part of it. The American corporate and political elite, already shaken by the Tet offensive, now faced the disintegration of the international system they had led in building out of World War II's rubble. For many of these elite, Vietnam was becoming an unwelcome distraction, a sideshow, to the most vital issue of economics. At the apparent end of a long postwar expansion, how could the U.S. multinational corporation, the backbone of the American economy and the engine for much of the global economy, deal with the new crisis?

At a private meeting of the New York City Council on Foreign Relations, top members of this elite met in January 1968 to discuss the problem. The meeting was chaired by George Ball, an international lawyer and business leader who, as the number two State Department official during 1964–1965, had warned Johnson (behind tightly closed doors) about the extraordinary dangers of escalating the Vietnam conflict. "The international corporation which is a quasi-political institution pointing the way toward the most effective use of resources and toward a new concept of the world economy will have a major impact on moves toward unity," Ball emphasized to the New York City group, "since it is essential that it find a way to operate efficiently within the

world economy." He warned: "Sooner or later it is going to collide
with world political authorities who, unable to control [private] economic decisions, will try to take political reprisals." Another participant (who was a professor, not a business leader) skeptically asked Ball
"whether economic factors have ever controlled political"—that is,
haven't economics always been shaped by politics? An incredulous
Ball lectured the professor that "economics will influence the political
shape of the world since politicians can go [only] so far in interrupting
profit before strong pressure develops for a more suitable set of political rules."[16]

President Johnson was learning this lesson about profit's power
firsthand. In mid-March he lunched with Dean Acheson. As Harry
Truman's undersecretary and then secretary of state, Acheson had
overseen the creation of the building blocks of U.S. Cold War policy.
An outspoken cold warrior, he had supported LBJ's effort in Vietnam.
Now, however, Acheson was questioning that effort. The economic
crisis, especially the run on U.S. gold, was a major reason. "The gold
crisis has dampened expansionist ideas," he wrote privately after the
luncheon. "The town [Washington, D.C.] is in an atmosphere of crisis." The president stood at the center of the crisis. When he met with
his top military leaders, he bluntly declared they were colliding with
larger forces than their own and would have to retreat. "Our fiscal situation is abominable," Johnson declared. It was impossible to give the
military what it wanted, save the dollar, obtain needed new taxes from
Congress, and also protect the Great Society at home. "I will go down
the drain. I don't want the whole alliance and military pulled in with
me." LBJ then demanded, "We must have something," meaning
something new. Military officials could not provide it.[17]

Johnson's fears were also creeping into unlikely places in Congress.
George Aiken (R-VT) was a longtime power in the Senate who had
grown skeptical about the war, but, resembling most members of
Congress, remained quiet. The early 1968 crises raised his doubts
considerably. When White House officials tried to convince him the
Tet offensive had been a failure, Aiken replied, "If this is a failure, I
hope the Viet Cong never have a major success." In closed-door debates of the growing economic problems, Aiken had announced two
years before that "I am not happy about the war at all. . . . But the

sooner the people find out that wars are not free, the sooner there will be more people unhappy about wars."[18]

Johnson was certainly learning that wars were not free. One of his early biographers, Doris Kearns, who came to know him well, concluded that the Texan fervently believed that "success or failure was determined entirely by the individual himself; structural barriers simply did not exist. . . . All his life Johnson retained the belief that any problems could be solved by personal force." By March 1968, however, he was discovering that not even his vaunted Johnson treatment could tear down the "structural barriers" raised by the economic crisis. George Ball was being proven right: economics could force the making of unwelcome political decisions, even by someone as powerful as the U.S. president. The chief executive could order a half million Americans into battle in an instant, but he could not stop a small number of bankers and speculators from taking away America's gold supply on which the dollar and the nation's economy rested.[19]

Most Americans had insufficient knowledge of economics and international affairs to understand what was happening in March 1968. But, as the old saying had it, do not overestimate Americans' knowledge of the facts or underestimate their intelligence about what is going on. Elmo Roper, a leading analyst of U.S. public opinion, noted that Americans were "confused" about the dollar's sudden weakness but understood the dangerous implications. "Not only is the thought of the American dollar being deprecated by foreigners new and repugnant" in people's minds, Roper wrote, but "there is a vague uneasiness that we must have been doing something wrong, something that might eventually hurt the average American personally."

Many "average Americans" had been shaken in February by the report of the National Advisory Commission on Civil Disorders, led by Governor Otto Kerner, Democrat of Illinois. Johnson had appointed the Kerner Commission to investigate the massive inner-city riots. The commission finally blamed white racism and issued 150 recommendations for handling the problem. LBJ estimated it would cost an astronomical $75 to $100 billion to pay for putting the recommendations into effect.[20]

Several advisers close to Johnson began to understand the complexity and depth of the growing danger in early 1968. Above all,

Clark Clifford, the new secretary of defense, whose judgment the president deeply trusted (in part because Clifford had long supported the war), began to learn from his many business contacts across the United States that they now saw the war as unwinnable, too expensive, and a major reason for the unrest and violence. Clifford also discovered to his surprise that even outspoken warhawks in Congress were having second thoughts. Senator Stuart Symington, long a powerful promilitary voice, "thinks we should get out," Clifford told the president. "He thinks the dollar will depreciate." Faced with General Wheeler's request for hundreds of thousands of more troops, the new secretary of defense decided to use the request as the reason for a bottom-to-top reevaluation of the war effort.[21]

Clifford asked the Pentagon to be specific about its plans to win the war. He was astonished when the military leaders essentially replied that the plan was more of the same: "I was told that there was no plan for victory in the historic American sense. . . . I was appalled: nothing had prepared me for the weakness of the military case." He was convinced that the Vietnamese communists would match any U.S. buildup person for person with, as Clifford directly told Johnson, "no end in sight." Such an expensive buildup, moreover, could force Congress to cut back domestic spending as much as 20–30 percent, especially given the economic pressures. A cutback of that size was a certain recipe for more unemployment, antiwar protests, and, of special importance, inner-city social unrest and deaths. Clifford's survey confirmed his advice to the president in early March: LBJ had to look past continuing military demands for more troops and examine "the overall impact on us, including the situation here in the United States. We must look at our economic stability, our other problems in the world, our other problems at home; we must consider whether or not this thing is tying us down so that we cannot do some of the other things we should be doing."[22]

Vietnam was thus part of a large set of problems. Clifford suggested to Johnson that he reconvene the so-called Wise Men who had, since 1965, given the president advice about the war. The Wise Men had strongly supported his military escalation, which was not surprising because as a group they stood unsurpassed as tough-minded warriors against communism. By March 1968, the Wise Men consisted of fourteen private citizens, including Acheson, General Maxwell Taylor, and

McGeorge Bundy, Johnson's former National Security Council adviser. Both Taylor and Bundy had been intimately involved in the earlier military escalation. Others were John J. McCloy (a banker and an architect of late 1940s Cold War policies), and, for the doves, George Ball. After a series of briefings, Acheson spoke for the majority when he told Johnson on March 26 that the United States "could no longer do the job we set out to do in the time we have left and we must begin to disengage." The president was stunned. He angrily charged privately that the Pentagon and State Department briefing team must have misled the Wise Men—that "somebody had poisoned the well."[23]

The group, however, stood its ground. Many of them now concluded the price for the effort in Vietnam had become much too high: continued disruptions at home, too little money for growing domestic needs, major threats to the dollar, and a fear that Americans would become so sour on the war that they would demand a more general withdrawal from the world, including from Western Europe, which the Wise Men considered the top priority for U.S. foreign policy. "The establishment bastards have bailed out," Johnson supposedly railed in private. In the next several days, Clifford pushed the president to accept the advice. "These guys who have been with us and who have sustained us so far as we are sustained are no longer with us," he reportedly told Johnson.[24]

The president was preparing a major policy speech on the war to be given over national television on Sunday, March 31. The advice he received for the speech was not all from doves. His National Security Council adviser, Walt Whitman Rostow, had long pushed for a greater effort in the war. His mind was not changed by the Wise Men. Rostow, unlike the tough-minded Acheson, was not one to admit he had been wrong for nearly fifteen years about Vietnam. "If we lose our heads at this critical moment and listen to extremists," Rostow told Johnson in mid-March, "we might" lose all of Southeast Asia to "aggression . . . open the way to a new phase of Communist expansion; . . . and bring us all much closer to a Third World War." Clifford and others close to Johnson, including his longtime Texas friend and speechwriter, Harry McPherson, thought Rostow had gone off the deep end. He seemed to have closed his eyes to the growing dangers at home. "Walt has a kind of rugby player's view of . . . international events. It's sort of a 'pull up your socks—let's get going, let's put our shoulders to the wheel . . . and it's going to be okay' point of view," McPherson recalled. But it was totally unrealistic by March 1968. Rostow was "utterly neglecting Good Friday and only talking about Easter," was the way McPherson phrased it.[25]

Early drafts of the March 31 speech reflected Rostow's advice more than Clifford's. With the assistance of the Wise Men, however, the secretary of defense began to change the tone of the speech. He received surprising help from Secretary of State Rusk, who was concluding that the bombing was not paying off, and that a new peace plan might attract the communists if the carrot of a bombing cutback was held out. Another key adviser, Assistant Secretary of State William Bundy, was starting to see that military escalation could produce only more bad consequences for the United States. As the analyst of the Pentagon's documents in March 1968 later phrased it, "two major considerations" began to reshape Johnson's policy: the belief that sending in more forces would not make victory more likely and "a deeply felt conviction of the need to restore unity to the American nation."[26]

More personal reasons began to appear. Those close to the president, including his wife, Lady Bird, were becoming deeply concerned about his health. Having some years before suffered a severe heart attack as well as being hospitalized for recent illnesses, LBJ was being ground down by the pressures of an unwinnable war, collapsing home front, and now defection among men he had long trusted. Mrs. Johnson let it be known she hoped he would not run for reelection. Nor could he find help from the Democratic Party. He had risen to ultimate power within this party of his revered Franklin D. Roosevelt, but after 1965 Johnson had weakened it by centralizing the party's focus and finances around his own political demands. The surprising weakness of the party's apparatus was a major reason why Eugene McCarthy, who had little to do with Democratic leaders, could successfully challenge both the party and the president.[27]

On March 31, Johnson went to church and then to the vice president's home so Hubert Humphrey could read the speech the president planned to deliver that evening. According to LBJ's chief of staff, James R. Jones, Humphrey without comment read through the sections that said the United States wanted to negotiate with North Vietnam. To show his good faith, Johnson would halt all naval and air attacks on that country, except in a volatile area just above the northern demilitarized zone. Then Humphrey read the final paragraph that, as *Newsweek* later phrased it, "shook the world." In order to pursue peace without distractions, LBJ planned to declare, "I shall not seek, and I will not accept, the nomination of my party for another term as your President." Jones recorded that Humphrey's "face flushed, his eyes watered, and he protested that Mr. Johnson could not step down." Johnson replied, "You'd better start now planning your campaign for President." Humphrey, his shoulders hunched and looking "pathetic," said quietly, "There's no way I can beat the Kennedys."[28]

Johnson electrified the nation and much of the world with his announcement of the peace plan and withdrawal from the presidential race. The next morning prices on the New York Stock Exchange shot upward as the market traded more shares than ever before. The following day, McCarthy swept the Wisconsin primary to win all the state's delegates. Along with some McCarthy and Kennedy supporters, delighted college students took to the streets chanting, "The hawk is dead." It did not seem, however, that Johnson quit the race because he feared losing to McCarthy or Kennedy. Jones argues that a private poll commissioned by the White House several days before the speech concluded that the president could defeat any challenger. Given the small number of primary elections in those days, as well as his own power of the presidency, which he delighted in wielding, he could have lost the primaries and still obtained the party's nomination through his relationships with state party machines and city bosses who actually controlled many of the delegates. But for the proud, prickly president, it would have been a most humiliating—and, perhaps, on election day, useless—political journey.[29]

Johnson later commented on his thinking when he decided to quit the race: "My biggest worry was not Vietnam. It was the divisiveness and pessimism at home." That divisiveness and pessimism, however, infected Vietnam policies as well as everything Johnson had hoped to do with his Great Society legislation. In this limited sense, his March 31 withdrawal worked. Public opinion approval of his war policies rose in early April from 38 to 57 percent. British Ambassador Sir Patrick Dean reported to London that LBJ was "a consummate tactician who usually operates in such a way as to leave himself with a number of options open. . . . This he has now once again done. He has embarked on the 'father of the people' line so he can call for patriotic support while following his own plans on Vietnam."[30]

Although he offered to limit the bombing, Johnson expanded other military operations. U.S. troop levels went up from a pre-Tet number of 486,600 to 535,500 by late summer. More Americans were killed after March 1968 than had died in any other comparable period of the war. U.S. fighting to pacify the countryside and kill communists operating in the villages accelerated. The president limited the bombing in the North in part because, as General Wheeler secretly told U.S. Pacific commanders, weather in the area was "unsuitable for air operations" anyway. Meanwhile, air strikes in other areas intensified, especially in neighboring Laos, where communists had built support bases from which they could infiltrate South Vietnam. Laos's Plain of Jars had once been home to 50,000 people, but by late 1968, a United Nations observer recorded, "The intensity of the [U.S.] bombing was such that no organized life was possible in the villages." The number of missions carried out by the huge, deadly B-52 bombers grew by three times in 1968.[31]

Johnson never gave up his commitment to keeping South Vietnam independent and noncommunist. Shortly after his March 31 speech, he wrote South Vietnamese President Thieu that if negotiations with the communists did begin, "nothing will be more important for their success than continued aggressive military operations inside South Vietnam." LBJ emphasized, "We must make time our friend." To his and Thieu's surprise, the North Vietnamese declared on April 3 they would talk with the Americans about preconditions for peace negotiations. Those early talks quickly stalemated as Hanoi demanded a complete bombing halt and the participation of the National Liberation Front (the communist faction in South Vietnam) in the negotiations. The United States insisted that the North must first stop attacking the South. Meanwhile, the war roared on through the summer and early autumn of 1968.[32]

By ending his own incredible political odyssey, Johnson gained some maneuvering room in the war. But he would not have peace at home. Two political assassinations horrified Americans and ended the president's hope that the 1968 election campaign could move ahead in a more united, less violent, America. Johnson continued to learn that Tocqueville's warning about the dangers of taking Americans into an endless "confusion" was "sure as hell right."

President Lyndon B. Johnson and Rev. Dr. Martin Luther King Jr. in the Cabinet Room, March 18, 1966

Photo by Yoichi R. Okamoto, Courtesy of the LBJ Library and Museum

4

MARTIN LUTHER KING: THE DREAM

Two days before Martin Luther King Jr. was assassinated on a motel balcony in Memphis, Tennessee, Ambassador Sir Patrick Dean secretly told his superiors in London that politics in the United States appeared heading for drastic change. He had been warned by the most distinguished U.S. journalist, Walter Lippmann, that "the American political structure is likely to undergo some fundamental transformation before very long." Dean added that Lippmann's view that the system was going to be shaken "is spreading, not only among the pundits" such as Lippmann but "in the grass roots too." Something else also had to be noted: "If one adds to this cauldron the heady brew of negro discontent, one is entitled to wonder if there may not be some remarkable changes."[1]

Such "remarkable changes" had already begun to occur with the 1964 Civil Rights Act and the 1965 Voting Rights Act. President Johnson took credit for passing this historic legislation, but it had been the growing civil rights movement of the late 1950s and 1960s that forced its passage. The two measures did little to undercut African American anger. Rioting and death plagued inner cities during 1967–1968, as major branches of the movement turned increasingly radical and demanded not merely racial integration, but a war on the institutions that perpetuated white domination.

The most famous African American leader did not join that particular war. Martin Luther King Jr. won the 1964 Nobel Prize for peace
because he shaped a civil rights movement based on nonviolence. By
1965, and especially in 1967, King followed that logic to come out
against the Vietnam War. His opposition shocked many Americans,
including other black leaders, and deeply angered Lyndon Johnson.
When King was murdered on April 4, he had helped reshape the political campaign by eloquently arguing how minorities in the United
States would never enjoy their God-given and constitutional rights until the killings stopped in Southeast Asia. Domestic events, he argued,
were tightly linked with U.S. foreign policies. His assassination, however, triggered a new round of inner-city riots that led frightened
Americans to search ever more frantically for security—for some kind
of relief and safety from what seemed to be a murderous, disintegrating society.

King and heavyweight boxing champion Muhammad Ali were the
two most famous African Americans in the world. Ali achieved fame
by his brilliant boxing abilities, his conversion to Islam, and, in 1967,
a headline-making refusal to be drafted into the U.S. Army. King
reached his pinnacle by a quite different route: by becoming the
charismatic leader of peaceful civil rights movements, then explaining
his beliefs with some of the most memorable and eloquent speeches
in American history. But in early 1968 both men had reached a common destination. By opposing the Vietnam War, they profoundly influenced the debate over both the conflict and the policies needed to
end it.

Born Michael King Jr. on January 15, 1929, he was the oldest son of
a noted minister who headed the large, influential Ebenezer Baptist
Church in Atlanta, Georgia. After a visit to Germany in 1934, his father changed his own and his son's name to Martin Luther King and
Martin Luther King Jr. The change honored the early sixteenth-
century German theologian Martin Luther, who had condemned the
corruption in the Roman Catholic Church and became founder of
Protestantism. King's father and grandfather (also a minister at
Ebenezer Baptist) were deeply involved in the NAACP and the
NAACP's efforts to obtain equality for African Americans. Martin Jr.
attended Morehouse College, where he studied the relationships be-

tween Christianity and social change, while also writing his first public letters to demand "basic rights and opportunities" for African
Americans. He did his doctoral studies in theology at Boston University. In 1953, while in Boston, he married Coretta Scott, who was
studying at the prestigious New England Conservatory of Music. As a
student of pacifist principles and a highly effective speaker in her own
right, she went on to influence her husband's evolving views of the
Vietnam conflict.

A year after their marriage, the young minister became the pastor of
the Dexter Avenue Baptist Church in Montgomery, Alabama. Consequently, the Kings were on the spot when Rosa Parks was arrested after she refused to give her bus seat to a white person. Martin became
the head of the year-long bus boycott that supported Parks and, ultimately, changed Montgomery's race relations. As he focused on mobilizing black churches, the most important institution in the African
American community, he emerged as a major civil rights leader. King
took care to work with white community leaders who might listen to
him, a tactic he employed with success throughout his life. Influenced
by his wife and the nonviolent leadership of Mohandas Gandhi during
India's successful struggle against British colonialism in the era leading
up to Indian independence in 1947–1948, King began to base his strategy on peaceful principles that, he believed, were an integral part of
Christianity. "We will match your capacity to inflict suffering," he told
whites, "with our capacity to endure suffering. We will meet your physical force with soul force. We will not hate you but we cannot in good
conscience obey your unjust laws. . . . We will soon wear you down by
our capacity to suffer. And in winning our freedom," King concluded,
"we will so appeal to your heart and conscience that we will win you in
the process."[2]

In 1957, he helped found, and became the first president of, the
Southern Christian Leadership Conference (SCLC). The SCLC became his major springboard for national change and one of the most
potent political organizations in the country. King's power was recognized in October 1960. Having moved to Atlanta to copastor
Ebenezer Baptist Church with his father, King was arrested in a civil
rights demonstration. As he sat in jail, a phone call came from John
F. Kennedy, the Democratic nominee running in one of the tightest

presidential contests in the nation's history. Kennedy's expression of concern made national headlines and helped him defeat Richard Nixon in an extremely close race.

It did not, however, lead to a close King–Kennedy relationship. The president moved cautiously on civil rights. He was not notably warm to the idea of the August 1963 march on Washington of 200,000 people who demanded equal rights for African Americans and other minorities. King, on the other hand, became the symbol of this march. Just four months before, he had been on national television as the leader of the antisegregation march on Birmingham, Alabama. That event became indelibly etched in American memory when, with television cameras rolling, the police turned loose vicious dogs on the marchers. King spent five highly publicized days in the Birmingham jail. Now, in Washington, he stood before the Lincoln Memorial to deliver a speech that climaxed the August march. It made him a household name. Proclaiming "I have a dream," he urged integration and freedom not just for African Americans, but for "all of God's children—black men and white men, Jews and Gentiles, Catholics and Protestants." His inclusive, nonviolent message led *Time* magazine to name him Man of the Year. In 1964, he became the youngest winner in the history of the Nobel Prize for peace.

Meanwhile, President Kennedy and his brother Robert, attorney general of the United States, heard from informants that a close white adviser and friend of King's was, or had been, a member of the Communist Party. The Kennedys authorized the FBI to tap phone lines used by King and the SCLC. The taps remained in place until mid-1966. No evidence ever surfaced that King or the SCLC was influenced by communists, nor was the adviser ever prosecuted. The wiretaps did lead the FBI to circulate lies about the Nobel Prize winner—such as the CIA message issued just before King was murdered in 1968: "According to the FBI, Dr. King is regarded in Communist circles as 'a genuine Marxist-Leninist who is following the Marxist-Leninist line.'"[3]

Far from being a communist, King was a relative conservative within the civil rights movement, which encompassed organizations that were turning increasingly militant and separatist out of frustration and desperation. The growing popularity of these groups, especially for young blacks; King's glaring failure when he tried to carry his campaign into the North, notably into heavily segregated Chicago; and his frustration with President Johnson's faltering Great Society Program—all led him to realize that his own popularity and power to effect change was ebbing. During 1966–1967, he began a fundamental reassessment of his position and ambitions.

Until early 1967, King handled white liberals, led by President Johnson, with great care. They had dominated American politics for thirty-five years. In contrast to black radicals such as Stokely Carmichael, who condemned "Whitey" for exploiting African Americans for many centuries and demanded total control (not simply integration) over their own livelihood, King courted the white power structure to find the economic and political help necessary to improve African Americans' situation. He did play hardball in seeking that help. King and his top aides, notably Andrew Young and Jesse Jackson, quietly threatened white power structures with massive demonstrations, lawsuits, and economic boycotts if desegregation and aid to impoverished black neighborhoods were not forthcoming. Often such threats were enough to end segregation in southern business districts and schools. In waging this nonviolent war, King was helped by sympathetic liberals (often, but certainly not always, from the North), who often put their lives on the line in marches and demonstrations.

When King moved into the North to fight housing discrimination, however, he encountered a different type of opponent. In large urban areas of the Midwest and Northeast there were fewer white liberals who could effectively help him, and many more white ethnic groups who were deeply suspicious of blacks. Well organized, these groups often formed the backbone of smoothly functioning political machines. Sometimes, as was the case with the Chicago Democratic Party operation of Mayor Richard Daley, such groups enjoyed close relationships with the Kennedy and Johnson administrations. The machines skillfully threw up obstacles to King's plans. When he led marches into ethnic neighborhoods where people of Central and Eastern European descent lived, he and his followers were stoned by mobs and driven out. He quietly retreated from Chicago and left what remained of his operation to a young Jesse Jackson to try to rebuild.

At the same time, King was reluctant to alienate northern liberals, whom he had considered his natural allies, and was highly unwilling to anger Lyndon Johnson. The president had, after all, passed major civil rights legislation that King strongly supported in 1964–1965. A man with a national mission to reform the country's race relations would take on the powerful president of that country only after a great deal of thought—and frustration. By 1967, King's frustration was growing because of his failure to mobilize the SCLC campaign in the North, but also because Johnson was dragging the nation ever deeper into the Vietnam quagmire instead of dealing with raging inner-city needs. When King told a group of angry young African Americans that they should be nonviolent, one shouted, "I had a dream . . . Craaaaap. We don't want dreams. We want jobs."[4]

After long, prayerful consideration, King concluded that African Americans could never obtain enough jobs or enjoy their full rights until poorer white Americans were mobilized to fight for their own rights as well. In other words, he began to move away from policies based on race to policies based on class. This was an explosive turn. Race was the terrible chasm separating Americans for centuries, but at least it was recognized and hotly debated—and even, in part, an explicit cause of the Civil War in 1861. Debating class differences, however, was deemed by most people in the United States to be un-American. Marxists, such as those who ruled the nation's great enemy, the Soviet Union, emphasized class—the division between rich and poor—as central to human affairs. But many who viewed themselves as real, red-blooded Americans had long declared class irrelevant because they believed a huge, all-encompassing middle class was central in their nation's development. They further believed the American poor could move into the middle class through discipline and hard work. The United States, most of its people assumed, was the land of opportunity, not the land of class divisions that had triggered radical revolutions in France (1789) and Russia (1917).

King's growing emphasis on the need to help all poor people, regardless of race, and to portray the problem of poverty in class terms, thus threatened Americans who wanted to believe they enjoyed both limitless opportunity and obvious differences from the class-ridden, poverty-ridden, revolution-ridden Old World from which so many of their families had fled. But King's next conclusion equally unsettled many Americans, black as well as white, and moved Lyndon Johnson to fury. King argued that nothing fundamental could be done to help poor blacks and whites until the Vietnam War ended. Only then could the economic resources (the war was now blotting up $30 billion a year) and political resources (the president and Congress were consumed by a bitter battle over the war) be freed up for a campaign to effectively fight poverty in the world's richest nation.

King's popularity fell in 1966–1967, as younger African Americans joined black nationalist, separatist organizations led by charismatic, self-styled revolutionaries. But he never surrendered his belief in the principles of nonviolence. He condemned growing demands of black nationalist groups for reaching their goals through force. Some of these groups proclaimed that power in American society only came out of a gun barrel. Or, as one black leader, H. Rap Brown, phrased it in 1967 during riots in Maryland, "Burn this town down. But don't tear down your [African American] own stuff. When you tear down the white man, brother, you are hitting him in the money. Don't love him to death. Shoot him to death."[5] Even as he emphatically opposed such rhetoric, King failed to win back support from Johnson and other white leaders, especially as he turned against the war.

His concerns about the Vietnam conflict appeared as early as 1965. In a Howard University speech in Washington, King believed the war was "accomplishing nothing." His prescription, however, was remarkably moderate. He did not, for example, demand a unilateral American withdrawal. King told the SCLC annual convention that U.S. officials should stop bombing and instead negotiate directly with the communists. Americans could next help Vietnam rebuild "some of the villages which have been destroyed." Moderate as they were, such words brought down on his head the wrath of fellow SCLC leaders, who wanted nothing to do with criticism of President Johnson. Whitney Young, head of the National Urban League (a leading African American political organization), warned that "Johnson needs a consensus. If we are not with him on Vietnam, then he is not going to be with us on civil rights." Young's remarks were an interesting comment on the degree of Johnson's commitment to civil rights and how easily it could be replaced by his growing commitment to the war.

King, however, was moving along a separate, broader, and historic path. Contrary to Young and other black leaders, he concluded the entire society needed fundamental reform. But change could not begin until the war ended. In early 1967, King moved into the front rank of the antiwar movement. His most important speech was given on April 4 at New York City's Riverside Church. Condemning "the apathy of conformist thought," he declared bluntly that the "Vietnam war is an enemy of the poor." King condemned the policies that led African American soldiers to die in "extraordinarily high proportion to the rest of the population." These soldiers, he once noted, were being sent off to die to "guarantee liberties in Southeast Asia which they hadn't found in America."

He had broadened his vision beyond the black community to "the poor at home." Now, at Riverside Church, King was direct: "The Great Society has been shot down on the battlefields of Vietnam." He warned, moreover, that further expansion of the war could bring a Chinese response and then world war. Finally, King declared he could not advocate nonviolence at home but then agree to killing and mutilating "thousands and thousands abroad." He later told journalists that if he were draft age, he would "not even serve as a chaplain" in the military, but be a conscientious objector. Believing that the United States was "the greatest purveyor of violence in the world today," by early 1968 King condemned "this cruel, ceaseless, unjust war." Again he moved from that specific belief to a broader lesson: "Somewhere along the way we have allowed the means by which we live to outrun the ends for which we live."[6] That pronouncement could have served as an epitaph for the 1960s.

Three months before his death, King confronted Johnson and the Democratic-controlled Congress that had passed civil rights legislation. "We need to make clear in this political year to Congressmen on both sides of the aisle and to the President of the United States," he declared in January 1968, "that we will no longer vote for men who continue to see the killing of Vietnamese and Americans as the best way of advancing the goals of freedom and self-determination in Southeast Asia." He combined this call with another for "a radical redistribution of economic power." At the University of Kansas on January 19, King charged that American "values" were "corroded and destroyed every day as a result of the war in Vietnam. It has diverted attention from civil rights. It has strengthened the military-industrial complex. . . . It has placed us in a position of being what [Senator J. William] Fulbright has called 'arrogant,' of being victimized with the arrogance of power."[7]

Such words, of course, further alienated Johnson and many white liberals. The Riverside Church declaration brought broad condemnation. *Life* magazine called it a "disservice to [King's] country." *U.S. News & World Report* accused him of "almost lining up" with the communists. Notably, only 25 percent of African Americans polled said they agreed with King's views on Vietnam. For the first time in several years, the Nobel Prize winner was not chosen as one of the ten most admired Americans. Johnson's press secretary helped shape such opinion by spreading false stories that King had been associated with communists.[8]

Such extraordinary responses did nothing to prove King's charges wrong. Indeed, his case was strengthened in early 1968 when the war accelerated with the Tet offensive, and again during the first three months of the year when ten times as many race-related outbreaks occurred in the United States than had erupted in the first three months of 1967. Washington officials no longer simply had to calculate how many American soldiers were required in Vietnam, but how many of those soldiers could be spared from the ever growing job of restoring order in American cities. When Johnson let it slip that a "bad summer" lay ahead, perhaps even worse than the bloody summers of 1965–1967, he merely expressed most Americans' daily fears.[9] Such fears, and King's warnings, became headlines in March 1968 when a special commission appointed by the president to investigate the riots issued its report.

Chaired by Democratic Governor Otto Kerner of Illinois, the commission of eleven distinguished whites and African Americans offered their work four months earlier than the deadline imposed by Johnson to help the country prepare for a summer that promised to be the worst yet. The report's widely quoted "basic conclusion" was stark: "Our nation is moving toward two societies, one black, one white— separate and unequal." Unintentionally echoing King's themes, the report warned that "reaction to last summer's disorders has quickened the movement and deepened the divisions. Discrimination and segregation have long permeated much of American life; they now threaten the future of every American." The commission then clearly placed the blame: "What white Americans have never fully understood—but what the Negro can never forget—is that white society is deeply implicated in the ghetto. White institutions created it, white institutions maintain it, and white society condones it." *Time* magazine summarized its own reading of the report: "never before has the U.S. been so imperiled by the threat of open racial warfare."[10]

Then followed hundreds of pages of evidence to support such conclusions. No conspiracy, communist or otherwise, triggered the riots, the Kerner commission emphasized. The upheavals were caused by conditions deeply rooted in American history—a history most Americans were ignorant of or chose to ignore. As whites (and their tax money to pay for city services) fled to the suburbs, 14.8 million of the country's 21.5 million African Americans crowded into the cities, where crime rates were 35 times higher than in some white neighborhoods, and where infant mortality was 58 percent higher. Most of the estimated 14,000 rat bites reported annually in the United States occurred in black neighborhoods, largely because cities let garbage collection and other sanitation measures decline in those areas. Over 40 percent of nonwhites in the country lived below the poverty level, defined as a family of four trying to survive on an income of $3,335 or less each year. Unemployment and underemployment in areas populated by African Americans ran as high as an unbelievable 33 percent (especially unbelievable because the 1960s had been prosperous years)—or nearly nine times worse than the national unemployment figure.

If Johnson and other white leaders became uncomfortable reading such figures, they turned incredulous when they saw the commission's recommendations: 2 million jobs had to be created in just three years, half by the private sector, half by the government. The complex problems required fresh tax increases, not least tax money for a series of welfare measures to ensure family incomes could rise above the poverty level so children could be adequately fed and housed. Entire cultures had to be transformed. More black people had to be included in police departments. More police were to be committed to African American neighborhoods. Police would also have to learn restraint in dealing with rioters: "Weapons which are designed to destroy, not to

control, have no place in densely populated urban communities."
Federal money and leadership were to be committed to schools on an
accelerated schedule, and adults were to be enrolled in new programs
to reduce illiteracy.[11]

The national reception to the report was cold. Many Americans
wanted to pay no more taxes for either the Vietnam War or to help
black neighborhoods. Analysts quickly noted that the commission
placed little or no blame on African Americans themselves, but on
whites—an emphasis that whites could not reconcile with black radical leaders who urged burning cities and shooting whites, including
police. Johnson himself was deeply angered. The report gave his
Great Society little credit for trying to improve conditions in three
years, and, in the president's mind, threw far too few compliments his
way for pushing historic civil rights legislation. The White House, not
surprisingly, provided little guidance or publicity to the general public. The administration only released a dry statement commenting that
"the report will be carefully evaluated." Johnson personally refused to
say anything about the commission's work for six days. When he finally
did comment, he mostly bragged about his own civil rights record.[12]

Republican front-runner Richard Nixon summarized the feelings of
many: the report "in effect blames everybody for the riots except the
perpetrators." Vice President Hubert Humphrey publicly doubted
the report's thesis that the country was becoming more, not less, divided by race. Such a false thesis might too easily turn into a "nightmare reality," he warned.[13]

The commission's emphases, however, were actually more subtle—
and frightening. In studying 164 disorders in 1967 that erupted in no
fewer than 128 cities, the report revealed how Americans, and especially their police, were on hair-trigger alert. The national tempera-
ment seemed to be revved up to the breaking point. In Newark, a
prankster set off firecrackers, and nervous national guardsmen and
state police opened fire on a housing project. They killed two moth-
ers and a grandmother. A Newark police authority recalled that "it was
so bad that, in my opinion, guardsmen were firing upon police and police were firing back at them." In Detroit, a soldier accidentally shot
his rifle, and the army then sent a barrage of bullets into a building
that was, fortunately, empty. An African American guard fired a shot

in the air to drive off looters and was himself quickly killed in an out-pouring of police bullets. Americans were having grave doubts about the very authorities—their president, military, and police—who were supposed to keep them safe and their society orderly.[14]

Just how widespread these doubts were became clear in the report's amazing sales: 100,000 copies sold in just the first three days it be-came available. Americans in March 1968 seemed to be trying to take a crash course in rioting so they could somehow avoid what was shap-ing up to be a firestorm of a summer. "Ominous harbingers of sum-mer violence were already evident last week in several cities," *Time* magazine noted on March 15. Among other indications was "a strike by garbage collectors in Memphis" that "escalated into scattered dis-turbances and threats of rioting." The Memphis strike was one of Martin Luther King Jr.'s top priorities by late March. His involvement was not widely welcomed by Tennessee's white power elite, even though King was considerably more moderate, not to mention more pacifist, than other African American leaders.

King had decided to initiate a Poor People's Campaign to protest peacefully, but massively, in Washington, D.C., and elsewhere. Its purpose was to show Americans the black community was able to force civil rights legislation through on a national basis much as Rosa Parks, King, and others had been able to change segregationist laws in a few southern states a decade earlier. The campaign put up a shanty-town close by the Lincoln Memorial in Washington. The display dis-gusted many whites and angered black radicals who deemed King hopelessly out of touch with political realities—realities they believed could be dealt with only through force, not peaceful demonstrations.

By March 28, 1968, his popularity thus seemed to be sliding further as he led a march through Memphis to support the sanitation work-ers. When African Americans, especially young people, began to loot stores, King again was bitterly criticized. He refused to give any ground, however. In an April 3 sermon, he declared that "difficult days" lay ahead. "But it doesn't matter with me now because I've been to the mountaintop [and] I've seen the Promised Land." He added, "I may not get there with you. But I want you to know tonight that we, as a people, will get to the Promised Land." The next day he was killed as he stood on the balcony of the Loraine Motel. A racist, James Earl

Ray, was captured and sentenced to life imprisonment for the killing. As his nonviolent hero, Mohandas Gandhi, had been in 1948, so too was King assassinated. A decade earlier he had been stabbed and later targeted by a bomb that missed. But amid the bloodshed and upheaval of 1968 in both Vietnam and the United States, this assassin did not miss.[15]

Some 110 cities across the country erupted in violence. Tens of millions of dollars in property damage was accompanied by 46 deaths and 200,000 arrests. Nashville endured five days of urban war. In Chicago, Mayor Daley ordered his police to "shoot to kill" arsonists. But nothing surpassed what seemed to be a battlefield in Washington, D.C. A visitor walked out of the Library of Congress, looked up the Mall past the U.S. Capitol toward the Washington Monument, and saw dark clouds streaming northward from the African American neighborhoods to the north and east. Directly ahead lay a scene few had imagined: U.S. armored vehicles and military forces deploying on the Capitol grounds to prevent a possible assault on the great domed center of American democracy. Fire and smoke seemed to surround the White House and other government buildings. Rioting was rampant. Public transportation broke down. It seemed impossible to escape the American version of Dante's hell.[16]

A revealing analysis emerged from Ambassador Sir Patrick Dean's cables and letters to London. The Memphis sanitation workers' strike, he believed, was "symptomatic" of more ominous American troubles. When the Memphis mayor refused to recognize a large African American labor union, protest marches resulted, then the "moderate Negro leaders" such as King lost control "of their people, especially their young." Within twenty-four hours after King's death, radical black leaders symbolized by Stokely Carmichael "described the assassination as the biggest mistake white America has made, and as killing all reasonable hope for the future," Dean reported. "No white man, including Robert Kennedy, was exempt from responsibility, and the time has now come," Dean continued with his paraphrase of Carmichael's words, "for the Negro to retaliate by getting guns and carrying out executions in the streets."[17]

Another of Dean's comments was equally disturbing. Mayor Daley's order to shoot arsonists was not copied in other cities where police

Photograph showing a soldier standing guard in a Washington, D.C., street with the ruins of buildings that were destroyed during the riots that followed the assassination of Martin Luther King Jr., April 8, 1968
Courtesy of the Library of Congress

were held back. "But the notion that black life is worth more than property, whether white or black" the British ambassador reported, "is a new one to many people. . . . Thus [this order of] Mayor Daley . . . a great many people agreed with him, and just in case it does not work out that way they are making sure their homes are well supplied with guns." Dean then indicated why President Johnson might have second thoughts about increasing troop strength in Vietnam: "The U.S. Army has been quietly preparing for further troubles, by various training measures, and has doubled the number of troops assigned and available for duty in the cities."[18]

The assassination of King and Johnson's resignation from the presidential race five days earlier accelerated a fundamental shift in American political debate during the fateful spring of 1968. Vietnam was becoming less the central problem and more a part of a series of highly explosive issues that were interrelated. These linked problems began to resemble a terrible spectre that, instead of shrinking in the light of spring and early summer, grew ever larger and more dangerous. Or, as King had phrased it, the "black revolution" was "forcing America to face all its interrelated flaws—racism, poverty, militarism and materialism."[19]

Americans were becoming unsettled by what they saw in this mirror of "flaws." "The effect of the riots has been to bring home forcefully to the American people the state of insecurity which they face at home as well as abroad," Dean emphasized to the British government, "and with the subsiding of polemics about Vietnam [because of Johnson's withdrawal from the race], there is no longer any doubt that the racial issue and above all, law and order is the top preoccupation of the average American elector." Dean summarized: "By any standards April has been an historic month in the United States."[20]

For the growing number of Americans, both black and white, who were preoccupied with law, order, and insecurity, however, there would be no relief. As the long Vietnam War ground on, American democracy was—necessarily?—coming under growing pressures that threatened to rip apart the thin fabric holding the society together.

Robert F. Kennedy in the Cabinet Room of the White House, January 28, 1964
Photo by Yoichi R. Okamoto, Courtesy of the LBJ Library and Museum

5

ROBERT KENNEDY: THE "NATIONAL SOUL"

On the April night when Martin Luther King Jr. was assassinated, Robert Kennedy was campaigning for the Democratic presidential nomination in large Indiana crowds. After hearing the horrible news, he remarked to a friend, "That could have been me."

Kennedy and King shared several important characteristics. They both came to condemn Lyndon Johnson's policies in Vietnam with great reluctance. They both arrived at a broad, fundamental political analysis that revolved around poverty and class, not race alone or the war. They both lost their lives to assassins in 1968, a catastrophic year. In a larger sense, King and Kennedy were less the victims of murderers than of a society that resembled a compartmentalized cooker under terrific pressure from war abroad and inequality at home that weakened its most vulnerable seams. It finally began to explode piece by piece.

The two men reached their final moments in 1968, however, by different routes. King came out of a deeply religious background in a minority American community. He reached international fame by creating new political rules (nonviolence and desegregation). Kennedy emerged from a more secular background. His father, Joseph P. Kennedy, had made millions in banking, importing whiskey after Prohibition ended, as a Wall Street operator, and in the movie business. As Irish Roman Catholics, the nine Kennedy children, spurred on by their ultracompetitive father, often saw themselves as outsiders in a political world seemingly defined by Protestants and Anglo-Saxons. But with wealth, grassroots political power in Massachusetts, homes in Palm Beach (for the winter) and Cape Cod (for the summer), and education in elite colleges and law schools, the Kennedy children exemplified those who had made it in America, rather than those, like King, who faced a continual battle for equality and opportunity.

From their different paths, both men began their political wars early in their lives. The wars they chose to fight, however, differed. By the mid-1950s, King, as minister of a large church, was involved in the often bloody struggle for equal rights to use transportation and schools in the South. Kennedy was the twenty-seven-year-old manager of his brother Jack's successful run for the U.S. Senate in 1952. Robert then worked for Senator Joseph McCarthy's Permanent Subcommittee on Investigations. McCarthy, a friend of the Kennedy family, was making "McCarthyism" a household word for a ruthless search to uncover communists in the United States. It turned up no important communists but ruined many lives when people were accused of being sympathetic to the Soviet Union. In 1957, Robert became a kind of household name himself, at least among some labor unions and crime families. As chief counsel for a Senate committee, he publicized the corruption found in the powerful Teamsters Union that dominated, among other sectors, the nation's trucking industry.

By 1960, a broad tradition of American liberalism that dated to the New Deal-World War II era reigned supreme in American politics. This liberalism seemed so dominant that observers (who had more talent for coining catch phrases than for catching the central themes of the times) concluded the nation was experiencing an "end of ideology." Communism and threats to liberalism seemed to be on the decline. Big political and economic questions in the United States now could be settled in a broad liberal, anticommunist consensus. John and Robert Kennedy, with their Democratic, liberal backgrounds, political abilities, and personal charisma, seemed to be superb examples of that consensus.[1]

King and the two Kennedys emerged from different parts of that broad American liberalism. The Baptist minister represented nonviolent, fundamental change in race relations and a new kind of politics. Indeed, he was about to lead a fundamental challenge against liberalism and its consensus ideology. Robert Kennedy represented a hard-knuckle approach, less concerned for broad liberal social change, and the old politics practiced so successfully by Kennedys back in Massachusetts. Both John and Robert (especially Robert) held deep suspicions of "professional liberals" who seemed to have a "sort of death wish" in that they would prefer to "go down in flames" on behalf of a cause than win, as Robert phrased it. The Kennedys cared about winning first. Liberal social change seemed at times to be a distant second.[2]

In 1960, Senator John Kennedy—his campaign managed with uncommon discipline by his younger brother—outmaneuvered Senator Lyndon Johnson to gain the Democratic presidential nomination. Johnson, over Robert Kennedy's opposition, was asked by John to be the vice presidential nominee. A major turn in the campaign against Republican Richard Nixon occurred when King was arrested in Atlanta for trying to integrate a snack bar, and John Kennedy called Coretta King to offer his sympathy. Black leaders, led by King's father, who had long been suspicious of the Kennedys, now came out publicly in favor of the Democratic nominee. Given that Kennedy won the election by the smallest popular vote margin in American history, and given that he won two-thirds of the African American vote, the call to Coretta King may have put him in the White House.

At the time, however, Robert Kennedy condemned the call and blasted adviser Harris Wofford, who had suggested to John that he make it: "Do you know that three southern governors told us that if Jack supported Jimmy Hoffa [head of the corrupt Teamsters Union], Nikita Khrushchev [the Soviet Union leader], or Martin Luther King they would throw their votes to Nixon?" "This election may be razor close," he screamed at Wofford, "and you probably just lost it for us." Robert mellowed as he saw the results, but he remained closer to southern segregationists, with whom he had closely worked in the Senate during the 1950s, than to King and the civil rights movement.[3]

In 1960 the hatred between Robert and Lyndon Johnson became deeply rooted. The younger Kennedy finally agreed to offer the vice presidential spot on the ticket to Johnson in the hope and belief that the proud Texan would not accept. When he did, Robert's pained reaction was "Oh, my God!" Johnson probably delivered several southern states that enabled John to become president, but Robert, a world-class hater, especially if he thought his brother's interests were endangered, never changed his mind about LBJ. For his part, Johnson jealously believed, rightly, that the young attorney general— "punk kid" or "snot-nosed brother," as Johnson called him—was considerably more influential than the vice president. LBJ agonized over even the small slights, such as his office receiving only one White House parking space while the attorney general's had three.[4]

Robert's views of Johnson never mellowed, but he did change on civil rights. Through the early 1960s, he mistrusted liberals who stirred trouble on civil rights marches in the South. He also had reservations about King and the giant 1963 rally in Washington. But as Kennedy saw firsthand the brutal treatment African American protesters received in the South, began to understand King's nonviolent philosophy, and witnessed the terrible poverty that swallowed up black families in both north and south, he started to criticize the racial situation.

John's assassination in November 1963 brought a crisis in Robert's life—the despised Johnson took over his brother's office. Robert had found his personal mission in protecting his brother, even though the two were very different. As a close observer of the Kennedys noted, "Jack's conduct [in conducting his life] was ironic detachment; Bobby's was humorless loyalty. Jack's Catholicism was nominal; Bobby's fervent. Jack was the [Kennedy] clan's prince; Bobby its foot soldier." The younger brother's personal agony was profound. A friend heard him cry out the night after the assassination, "Why God?" a question the deeply religious survivor could not answer. Robert soon left the attorney general's office to run for the Senate from New York, where he had taken up residence. Kennedy had to admit that he won his 1964 race on Lyndon Johnson's coattails. The president carried the state by two million votes, while the new senator won by 719,000. "Listen," Kennedy joked to Johnson in a phone call election night, "I guess I pulled you through up here."[5]

Within a year his worsening relationship with the president was a prime topic of American politics. The central issue first dividing the two, other than their sandpaper personalities, was Vietnam. As Johnson escalated the war in 1965, Kennedy began to question the policies cautiously. His brother, after all, had greatly intensified the American involvement by increasing the number of U.S. "advisers" from 600 to 16,000. Nor, in Robert's later view, had John ever thought seriously about retreating from Vietnam. As LBJ told Kennedy to his face, he was following the advice of "your State Department"—the advisers he inherited from the Kennedys. By 1966, after 100,000 U.S. troops had been committed, Robert was breaking with his brother's and Johnson's policies. He was notably influenced by George Kahin, a Cornell University professor who was probably the nation's leading expert on Southeast Asia. Kahin argued that the driving force of the war was not communism (as Johnson kept preaching), but Asian nationalism. Given their own history, Kahin believed Americans should naturally cooperate with nationalists, even if the Vietnamese kind called themselves communist. Kahin further believed that if, as Johnson and his advisers kept saying, Chinese communists were the greatest threat in Asia, then the best way of containing China was to work with the Vietnamese nationalists who had been hating and fighting Chinese attempts to influence their country for a thousand years. Only a negotiated political solution, not a military victory, was possible, Kahin concluded, and it was in the U.S. interest to pursue such a solution as rapidly as possible—especially before tens of thousands of American and Vietnamese lives were needlessly lost.[6]

Kahin had provided a road map for opposing the conflict, but Kennedy was most cautious in following it. He criticized the war effort for taking resources away from Great Society programs, but carefully did not ask for a unilateral retreat from Vietnam. He argued that a negotiated settlement was preferable and had to involve South Vietnamese communists (the National Liberation Front, or NLF).

Since the U.S.-supported South Vietnamese government absolutely refused to deal with the NLF, his proposals went nowhere. The idea of including communists in any government drew fire from Vice President Hubert Humphrey, who declared it amounted to putting "a fox in the chicken coop" or "an arsonist in the fire department." Moreover, challenging a sitting president who had won election in a political landslide was dangerous, even for a Kennedy. Taking him on when the president was passing civil rights and other reform measures, with which Kennedy largely agreed, would have been stupid. As late as June 1967, Kennedy introduced Johnson at a New York City Democratic fund-raising dinner with fulsome praise for the president and his program: "He has led us to build schools, to clean the water . . . to educate children and to heal the sick and comfort the oppressed on a scale unmatched in history."[7]

Despite urgent advice from close friends and advisers to break openly and cleanly with Johnson over Vietnam, Kennedy refused to do so into early 1968. When Allard Lowenstein asked him to lead an antiwar challenge to the president, Kennedy backed away. Lowenstein finally recruited Senator Eugene McCarthy. Kennedy, however, was slowly but surely becoming an increasingly vocal critic of the administration, even if he was not a "profile in courage" (to use the title of his recently assassinated brother's best-selling book about American leaders who courageously took difficult stands). Robert was more a profile in hesitation. He was clearly aiming for the 1972 presidential race when Johnson could not run again. Nor did he want needlessly to anger Johnson, whose support he would need in 1972.

Three series of events finally turned Kennedy into an avowed presidential candidate in 1968. The first emerged from trips to the riot-torn area of Watts and homes of terribly impoverished farmers and workers in the South. During a journey to California, he became a close friend of Cesar Chavez. Against tremendous and often brutal opposition from the state's farmers and landowners, Chavez had organized the United Farm Workers to obtain living wages and decent working conditions for the laborers, including many immigrants, who harvested much of the nation's fruits and vegetables—in this particular case, grapes. Kennedy began to understand that the Great Society was inadequate and, in the case of Chavez's large group of laborers, even irrelevant. Then what remained of Johnson's domestic program began to be cut to shift funds to the war effort. These experiences changed many of the conservative social views Kennedy had held as attorney general. He emerged as a politician viewed by minorities, especially African Americans and Hispanic Americans, as a last, best hope of the possible candidates.[8]

A second reason for Kennedy's change was the transformation of the U.S. political landscape in late January 1968 by the Tet offensive. On the day it began, Kennedy publicly supported Johnson's reelection. His words began to change as the administration, while attempting to turn Tet into a U.S. victory, declared that the communists had failed to trigger a general civilian uprising against the American-propped-up South Vietnamese government. Kennedy's response was bitter: "How ironic it is, that we should claim a victory because a people whom we have given sixteen thousand [American] lives, billions of dollars, and almost a decade to defend, did not rise in arms against us." A famous, widely distributed photo showed the chief of the South Vietnam National Police blowing the brains out of a suspected communist agent who had been stopped on a Saigon street. Millions of stunned Americans watched an NBC television film of the killing. The Johnson administration defended the shooting as something that happens in a fight with communists. Kennedy, however, condemned the act and, by implication, the U.S. government's defense: "we are not fighting the Communists in order to become more like them—we fight to preserve our differences. . . . The photograph of the execution was on front pages all around the world—leading our best and oldest friends to ask, more in sorrow than in anger, what has happened to America?"[9]

It was that precise question—what was happening to America (not merely what was happening in the war)—that in early 1968 began to haunt the nation and shape the election process. Kennedy, however, was in no position to take advantage of his insight because he continued to refuse to challenge Johnson—until a third event turned him around: Senator McCarthy's surprising humiliation of the president in the New Hampshire primary. Kennedy had apparently planned to enter the race before the primaries began but, again hesitating, decided to wait. That decision turned out to be a terrible error. With Johnson wounded by McCarthy, it now appeared that Kennedy was arrogantly and unfairly moving in on the kill. Beginning to believe, as admirers told him, that he was the crown prince of the Democratic Party, the rightful heir of the glamorous Kennedy legacy, the senator declared four days after the New Hampshire primary that he would run for the presidency.

McCarthy and his supporters were furious. Actor Paul Newman said, "It's a shame Kennedy chose to take a free ride on McCarthy's back." "Hawks are bad enough," said one student who worked for McCarthy, "we don't need chickens." Pro-McCarthy columnist Mary McGrory wrote acerbically, "Kennedy thinks that American youth belongs to him as the bequest of his brother. Seeing the romance flower between them and McCarthy, he moved with the ruthlessness of a Victorian father whose daughter had fallen in love with a dustman." In mid-March, when Kennedy paraded up New York City's Fifth Avenue in the annual St. Patrick's Day celebration, there were the usual screaming teenage girls, but observers were stunned to hear the senator booed as well.

Kennedy sent his brother, Senator Edward (Ted) Kennedy, on an overnight mission to tell McCarthy that Robert was about to enter the race, while hinting to the Minnesota senator that he might consider withdrawing from the contest, an act that the often arrogant McCarthy thought was remarkable and quickly dismissed. "What did you two talk about?" a reporter asked McCarthy after the meeting. "Well, we didn't talk about anything very important," he replied with a straight face. "I don't think people do at three o'clock in the morning." But he angrily told others that it had been "lovely in New Hampshire" and he had waited for the Kennedys to help, "but they didn't come in. They just threw messages over the fence." A blood feud was developing between the two camps that threatened to split and neutralize the antiwar opposition.[10]

Kennedy, however, cared less about McCarthy (whom he did not take seriously as a no-holds-barred political challenger) or splitting the antiwar vote than he did about driving Johnson from office—a "mean, bitter, vicious" person, he privately called the president, "an animal in many ways." Johnson fully returned the hatred, but, more importantly, he began to see he had been humiliated in New Hampshire and might well lose the Wisconsin primary in early April. LBJ began to have nightmares that, as he remarked to close friends, in the history books his presidency would be "trapped forever between the two Kennedys." But he also feared he would be remembered only as the architect of a ruinous war. So on March 31, 1968, he took himself out of the race to concentrate on bringing the conflict to an honorable close. Kennedy's new campaign, with decisive help from McCarthy, claimed a prized political victim.[11]

Kennedy, finally in the race, now focused on Vietnam. In a major speech at the University of Kansas on March 18, he called the president's policy "bankrupt," then declared that U.S. policies of bombing and political insensitivity were "creating more Viet Cong [communists] than we are destroying." He implied that Tacitus's description of Roman imperialism fit Johnson's policies: "They made a desert and called it peace." But Kennedy did not want to retreat from Vietnam. He instead urged entering into negotiations with the communists in South Vietnam, the Viet Cong—a negotiation the U.S.-supported South Vietnamese government bitterly rejected. Meanwhile, U.S. troops should, he argued, "concentrate on protecting populated areas, and thus save American lives and slow down the destruction of the countryside." (Johnson and his advisers had long considered such an "enclave policy," but finally rejected it in the belief that the war would be won or lost in the countryside where the majority of Vietnamese lived and that surrounded the cities.) As Kennedy understated his plan, "This is no radical program of surrender. This is no sell-out of American interests." In other words, the senator was not about to march in the streets with the antiwar groups to demand an immediate end to the conflict.[12]

Kennedy entitled his speech "Conflict in Vietnam and at Home." It was the "at home" theme that he soon began to emphasize. "We are in a time of unprecedented turbulence of danger and questioning," he told the Kansas audience. "It is at its root a question of the national soul." McCarthy, also a devout Roman Catholic, was as disturbed as Kennedy about what was happening to that "soul," and both men understood that the sources of the danger now went well beyond Vietnam. Although McCarthy maintained a kind of distant, poetic detachment from the disintegrating soul, Kennedy moved in to assess and repair it with all the energy he had demonstrated in tracking down communists and racketeers in the 1950s or in organizing his brother's election victory in 1960. McCarthy, moreover, had shown remarkably little excitement about specific American disasters that were appearing, such as the sliding economy or the continued impoverishment of minorities. Kennedy became passionate about these problems, which went well beyond the war. The war's costs prevented Americans from facing them properly. What were the "causes" of the crisis in the "national soul"? Kennedy answered, "Some are in the failed promise of America itself: in the children I have seen starving in Mississippi; idling their lives away in the ghetto; committing suicide in the despair of Indian reservations; or watching their proud father sit without work in the ravaged lands of Eastern Kentucky." Then, too, "we seem equally unable to control the violent disorder within our cities—or the pollution and destruction of the country, of the water and land that we use and our children must inherit." In his mind, Vietnam was "a third great cause of discontent" after these first two crises that were tearing apart American society.[13]

Two weeks later, Johnson quit the race. Four days after that, Martin Luther King was assassinated. That night Kennedy was scheduled to speak in a black Indianapolis ghetto to a large audience who had not yet heard of King's death. When an aide gave him the news, Kennedy was badly shaken: "Oh, God. When is this violence to stop?" The police asked him not to give the speech. He went ahead anyway. Kennedy told his audience about the assassination, then eloquently referred to his own loss when his brother was killed. Emphasizing that rage and riots were not the answer, he concluded, "Let us dedicate ourselves to what the Greeks wrote so many years ago: to tame the savageness of man and to make gentle the life of the world. Let us . . . say a prayer for our country and for our people." The next night in Cleveland he condemned violence, then asked, "What has violence ever accomplished? . . . We calmly accept newspaper reports of civilian slaughter in far off lands. We glorify killing on movie and televi-

sion screens and call it entertainment." Violence, Kennedy emphasized, went beyond the use of guns. There is also "the violence of institutions," the "violence that afflicts the poor, that poisons relations
between men because their skin has different colors," and there is "a
slow destruction of a child by hunger." "Violence," he emphasized,
"breeds violence."[14]

The 1968 campaign was turning into an examination of the national
soul that went far beyond Vietnam. The divisions in that soul even appeared in the split between Kennedy and McCarthy supporters. The
New York senator's popularity spread among African Americans and
other minority groups who saw him, correctly, as sympathetic to their
problems. "The hatred and contempt that rained down on Kennedy
from McCarthy's (almost all white and middle-class) supporters would
be hard to credit unless one felt it oneself," recalled an aide to the new
candidate. Meanwhile, this observer continued, Kennedy, as the heir
of his murdered brother, suddenly found himself in "a howling, deaf-
ening wind tunnel" of crowds. Tragically for the campaign, "the near-
hysteria of his supporters, and the candidate's own emotionalism, re-
minded voters of the disorder in the streets, which exploded after
Martin Luther King was murdered on April 4th."[15]

Disorder seemed to be multiplying everywhere. Some one hundred colleges endured extensive demonstrations after King's death.
At New York City's Columbia University, radicals took over buildings, occupied the president's office, and destroyed the life's work
of faculty until a thousand police ended the occupation. Fire
burned down Stanford University's ROTC building, and a bomb
blast struck Selective Service offices in Berkeley, California. Under
the weight of the protests, organizations such as Students for a
Democratic Society and the Student Non-Violent Coordinating
Committee, that had spearheaded protests earlier in the 1960s, now
publicly fought each other over questions of race, ideology, and
how much force to employ in the street. In January 1968, the weird
counterculture appeared poised to bring on more mayhem. Jerry
Rubin and Abbie Hoffman led the Youth International Party, or
Yippies, that pledged the "politics of ecstasy." They promised to
deliver a number of well-drugged supporters to the Democratic

National Convention in August, where they would nominate a pig for the presidency, then eat it. The entire society seemed not only to be falling apart, but doing it with considerable pride and out on the streets in full view.[16]

Kennedy's campaign at times appeared to add to the growing chaos. Few Americans felt neutral in the 1960s (or later) about the Kennedys. When an enthusiastic crowd of African Americans nearly tipped over the senator's car, a reporter told one of the candidate's close friends, "You've got to turn it down." The friend replied, "We can't. It's too late." Kennedy continued (quite unlike McCarthy or Republican candidate Richard Nixon) to give highly emotional speeches that whipped up the campaign's enthusiasm, while deeply angering opponents. This became the underside of the Kennedy mystique: the fear that hatred would overcome reason in a murderous individual who wanted to kill a member of the famous family. Aides constantly warned him against walking into crowds. He rejected the advice. Kennedy wrote down a line he found in a work by Albert Camus: "Knowing that you are going to die is nothing."[17]

In Vietnam, the communists tried to unleash another Tet-type of offensive during May and June. They were driven back with heavy losses. U.S. military leaders told Secretary of Defense Clark Clifford that now "the United States is bargaining from a position of strength." But fewer and fewer Americans seemed to believe it or to care. Their eyes were less on Vietnam than on their streets or campus buildings. With Johnson out of the race, Vice President Humphrey became a front-runner for the Democratic presidential nomination. Clifford privately noted in May that the Paris peace talks had to be kept going because if they were wrecked, "Bobby shoots up" in the presidential polls. But again, many Americans seemed to care about neither Humphrey nor the slow progress of the peace talks. At the inner sanctum of the U.S. elite, the New York City Council on Foreign Relations, corporate leaders and foreign policy experts secretly wrung their hands over possibly "the worst international financial crisis since 1931." The war was alienating the newly emerging nations, damaging relations with Europe, and undermining the United Nations. One council analyst feared less a U.S. retreat from Southeast Asia than the retreat's consequences inside the United States that might make it impossible for any President to conduct effective foreign policy in the foreseeable future. In other words, the question was now less about restoring order in South Vietnam and more about restoring some order and sanity before American society rocketed out of control.[18]

The Kennedy–McCarthy clash intensified in the primary elections of April, May, and early June. McCarthy easily won in Pennsylvania and Massachusetts because Kennedy announced too late to have his name on the ticket. The New York senator picked up convention delegates in Massachusetts and triumphed in Indiana. In Oregon, however, he became the first Kennedy to lose an election. But McCarthy could not celebrate his victory. Both men had to focus on the important June 5 California primary. Much of the campaigning was sound and fury signifying little other than the rising temperature of the American people. Behind the scenes, Humphrey quietly rounded up convention votes from the Democratic Party organizations in each state that actually controlled delegate selection.[19]

Kennedy hoped to overcome Humphrey's power within the party by putting back together parts of Franklin D. Roosevelt's New Deal political juggernaut: African Americans, big-city bosses (although Humphrey already had many of these in his camp), and blue-collar union workers. He was easily the choice of the large majority of black voters because of his empathy with them and the overromanticized memory of his assassinated brother. African Americans believed, on the other hand, that Humphrey represented an administration that, despite its civil rights legislation of 1964–1965 (which now seemed so long ago), could not restore order and protect lives and property in their neighborhoods. Kennedy had less luck with the city bosses, although he courted them with an intensity that sometimes embarrassed his younger, more idealistic advisers.

The core problem was in the white neighborhoods of union laborers and ethnic groups. Kennedy hoped to create a black–white coalition to act as a bridge between races, which seemed to be separated by an ever widening chasm. The Indiana primary was a test case. He failed. A remarkable 86 percent of blacks supported him, as did some ethnic Roman Catholic groups. But the white neighborhoods in the great (and declining) steel city of Gary went for McCarthy. Polls showed that Kennedy's position on the war made little difference. Voters judged him on the basis of whether he could restore order in the streets and, in the eyes of many whites, whether he was too closely tied to blacks whom those whites too easily blamed for the disorder. As two of his closest advisers later noted, the lesson of the Gary results "was that the more personally involved the white voters were with racial struggle, the more they identified Kennedy with the black side of it, and turned to his opponents as an outlet for their protest." In the Oregon primary, observed a congresswoman who supported Kennedy, he lost because "there are no ghettoes in Oregon."[20]

The New York senator was approaching the same point that Martin Luther King occupied in the last years of his life. The problem of race, they both finally concluded, could not be dealt with until first the problem of poverty was solved. "We have to write off the unions and the South now, and replace them with Negroes, blue-color whites, and the kids," Kennedy told a friend. "Poverty is closer to the root of the problem than color," and this meant poor whites and African Americans had to see "that they have common interests." As the Indiana primary demonstrated, however, the senator could not piece such a coalition together.[21]

The reasons why Kennedy failed to create such a coalition goes to the heart of American politics and, indeed, the nation's history. Some eighty years before, a third-party populist movement attempted to deal with the poverty that engulfed whites and blacks in the South and West by attempting to bring both races into a radical economic reform program. Within a generation, white political demagogues had played on both white economic fears and white racism to turn populism into a whites-only movement that shed much of its radicalism. Populism disappeared, mostly into the fold of a conservative (and in the South whites-only) Democratic Party. Kennedy had no chance of averting a similar fate for his new class-based coalition unless he could find enormous economic resources to offer both lower-class blacks and whites to help them while, at the same time, not alienating higher-income Americans. These middle-class and wealthier Americans tended to vote in much larger numbers than the poor.

But the long and increasingly costly war, the growing drain of rising military costs and overseas corporate investments, the gold flooding out of the United States to meet the nation's growing debt abroad—all these made Kennedy's plans a pipe dream unless he could pull off truly radical reform in both military and corporate policies. And Kennedy, for all his rhetoric when urged on by large, worshipful crowds, was neither radical enough nor sufficiently politically adept to deal with all of these challenges. At the same time, he had an immediate problem of winning the Democratic presidential nomination. To accomplish this, he had to court big-city machine bosses who controlled many delegates and also ruled over segregated cities in which African Americans were isolated in ghettoes. When blacks protested in the streets, their actions alienated poor whites—who believed that the Democrats in the Johnson administration were passing civil rights legislation to protect these rioters but doing little or nothing for poor whites.

Alabama Governor George Wallace seized on this white anger to form a political base that made him a presidential contender in 1968. Kennedy tried to do it another way: by uniting, rather than dividing, whites and blacks and by defining the problem as one of class and economics rather than one of race. At a high point of the longest war in American history, he stood little chance of succeeding. The costs of an expensive war do not allow politicians to find the kind of money needed to provide for the vast needs for the lower economic classes in America.

Kennedy's apparent opportunity to succeed, if success were possible, came in the California primary election. The victor could win 174 convention delegates, or about one-eighth of the number needed to gain the nomination. California, moreover, was unlike Oregon in that it had large numbers of politically active African American and Hispanic groups. It also had a state party boss, Jesse Unruh, who was pro-Kennedy. On the other side were middle-class whites who disliked Kennedy's courting of blacks and browns, and also labor leaders who were prowar and thus tied to Humphrey. Prowar Democrats, it turned out, preferred voting for McCarthy over endorsing Kennedy's concern for minority voters.[22]

Kennedy defeated McCarthy 46 percent to 42 percent. The slate supporting Humphrey finished a distant third at 12 percent. McCarthy carried middle- and upper-class white areas, especially in northern California. Kennedy overwhelmingly won in the black, Hispanic, and machine-controlled neighborhoods. He did not, however, obtain a majority of the vote. The army of college students who had switched to support him in March had largely dropped out of the campaign by June. They were alienated by Kennedy's dependence on party hacks in the Unruh machine and his refusal to offer a fundamental criticism of the war effort. He would only suggest a negotiated settlement that could include the communists in a South Vietnamese government, a plan the U.S.-shaped regime in the South rejected out of hand. In his effort to win poor white votes, Kennedy even spoke out against welfare, job preferences (that might favor blacks), and school busing so schools could be integrated. California's highly conservative governor, Ronald Reagan, noted with some surprise that Kennedy was talking "more and more like me."[23]

The New York senator was now grateful for any kind of victory, regardless of the margin. At his triumphant announcement in Los Angeles's Ambassador Hotel, he told cheering supporters that the next step was the New York primary, the state he represented, and with a victory there they would be on their way to winning the nomination. New York, however, was not a sure thing. McCarthy's supporters were well organized and well financed.

What might have happened in New York, however, will never be known. As Kennedy left the hotel through a kitchen exit (his security guards believed the large crowds made the regular hotel exits too dangerous), he was shot by Sirhan Sirhan, a Palestinian who might have been angry because he had watched Kennedy court Jewish voters. Or perhaps he pulled the trigger merely because he recently bought ammunition for his pistol. Kennedy died hours later.

This time no riots erupted, no urban outbreaks wrecked neighborhoods. There was instead a weird calm, even quiet, as Americans of all races tried to understand what was happening to them. "I am sure," Ambassador Patrick Dean reported to his London superiors after

Kennedy had died, "that not since the 1860s has the questioning of most of the basic tenets [of U.S. society] ever been so widespread and profound." "The first reaction of most Americans," Dean emphasized, "has been to call for the reinforcement of the means of maintaining law and order." They then were demanding a "re-examination of national priorities."[24] Richard Nixon, resurrected from the political dead, would lead that supposed reexamination.

Richard M. Nixon campaign, 1968
National Archives

6

RICHARD NIXON: THE CANDIDATE
FROM SQUARESVILLE?

After the September 11, 2001, terrorist attacks on the United States, the *Atlantic Monthly* concluded that "the modern terrorist era—in which acts are directed at civilian and international targets—is said to have begun in 1968. Since then, terrorism has evolved in two main phases: initially low impact and politically motivated attacks, and, more recently, indiscriminately lethal and religiously motivated attacks."[1]

The killings of Martin Luther King Jr. and Robert Kennedy within two months in 1968 seemed to be politically motivated, but they were certainly not low impact. They shook Americans' usually unshakable confidence in their institutions and future. Several months before, the Tet offensive had raised grave questions about the nation's course in Vietnam. The two assassinations, then the urban rioting and deaths that resulted from, most immediately, King's murder and, in the longer perspective, centuries of slavery and discrimination—all these in mid-1968 drove the country to its lowest point in the twentieth century. For nearly four hundred years Americans had believed they were God's chosen people. Some were now wondering whether, because of the bloodshed in Vietnam and racial hatred, that blessing had been withdrawn.[2]

The danger Americans faced by 1968 went well beyond the increasingly costly fighting in Southeast Asia. Americans were a people of immigrants from many nations spread across a vast continent. They had been held together by an ever rising economy, belief (not always practiced) in equality and opportunity, and a written Constitution. In 1968, the economy was endangered by inflation and doubt. Equality and opportunity were under attack by doubters, often violent, who took to the streets. The Constitution, especially its provision for free speech, was appealed to by those in the streets who seemed to be the enemies of the law and order the Constitution supposedly ensured. It was a strange, upside-down kind of world that was interesting to study from a safe distance, but seemed to be extraordinarily dangerous up close. For Americans coming of age in the supposed safety and endless economic abundance of the 1950s and early 1960s, it was quite new.

In their book on U.S. society during the 1968 political campaign, some visiting British journalists took note of something extraordinary. All could not be well, they concluded, with a people whose television industry in the first quarter of 1968 took its advertising revenue in this order—Anacin headache tablets, $4,618,500 of advertising; Alka-Seltzer stomach remedy, $3,993,400; Salem Menthol Filter cigarettes, $3,552,700; Winston filter cigarettes, $3,321,600; American Telephone and Telegraph, $3,295,200; Bayer aspirin, $3,110,500; Bufferin headache tablets, $2,929,500; and Listerine antiseptic, $2,401,000.[3] Americans had developed a horrible headache and severe addictions as a result of crises in Vietnam and at home—and driving them to frequent trips to the medicine cabinet and cigarette machines.

The American dream was not supposed to work this way. A leading politician who saw himself as a shining example of that dream stepped forward to run for the presidency with the promise that if he reached the White House, he would end the terror in the streets so the dream could be revived. He said much less during his campaign about what he would do to stop the terror in Vietnam.

Born in 1913 at Yorba Linda, California, Richard Nixon grew up in nearby Whittier. His mother was a Quaker, devoted to her religion and family. His father was an itinerant jack-of-all-trades who moved the family often while teaching his sons severe discipline and the belief that hard work had to pay off—a belief his own life did not prove to be true. Nixon later recounted that late at night he often listened to train whistles and planned how he could escape to realize that American dream through grit and discipline. This approach paid off when his good high school and Whittier College grades gained him admission to the Duke University Law School. In 1940, while practicing law, he married Thelma (Pat) Ryan, and they went briefly to live in Washington, D.C. He soon left for a four-year hitch in the navy, mostly in the South Pacific, where he rose through the ranks and put together a small nest egg because of his talent at poker.

That was the only real talent Nixon demonstrated until 1946, when he gained election from California to the U.S. House of Representatives. Four years later he won a U.S. Senate seat. In both 1946 and 1950 Nixon defeated a widely known Democrat (in the Senate race it was the Hollywood actress and activist Helen Gahagan Douglas), in part by waging a low-level campaign that insinuated his opponents sympathized with communists and other left-wing causes. In 1949–1950, he gained national headlines by leading the case against Alger Hiss, a former State Department official and graduate of elite northeastern schools, who had been accused of being a member of the Communist Party. Hiss seemed to be winning his argument that he was innocent until Nixon, by sheer perseverance, dug deeper into the official's background. Evidence finally surfaced that was hotly debated, but sufficient to put Hiss in jail for perjury (he was convicted for lying under oath that he had not been a Communist Party member).

Nixon suddenly became a national figure and a hero to those like the headline-seeking Senator Joseph McCarthy (R-WI), who believed that the nation's Cold War problems must be due to traitors inside the government. McCarthy never uncovered a communist, although he did ruin many lives of those he falsely accused. Nixon, therefore, seemed to anticommunist conservatives to be heaven-sent, given the role he played in putting Hiss behind bars. In 1952 Republican leaders sought to ride Nixon's popularity and balance the national ticket (in both ideology and age), by naming the thirty-nine-year-old as the vice presidential nominee with the sixty-two-year-old former general Dwight D. Eisenhower, a middle-of-the-road Republican.

Nixon's career nearly ended during the 1952 campaign. He was charged with creating a personal slush fund from political contributions. The Californian dramatically recovered by giving a nationally televised speech in which he first disavowed the fund. Nixon then successfully appealed to Americans' sense of forgiveness by claiming that his wife, Pat, wore only an inexpensive cloth (not fur) coat, and that although his little dog Checkers was a gift from friends, he would never surrender it, regardless of the political price he might have to pay, because his two daughters so loved the pooch. This Checkers speech, declared the distinguished journalist Walter Lippmann, was "the most demeaning episode in American political history." That claim covered several centuries. The speech revealed Nixon as both a hard-fighting, shrewd survivor, and a politician who knew how to use the new medium of television.

Eisenhower grew to mistrust (and apparently dislike) Nixon, but during his two terms the vice president traveled the world to become an expert on foreign policy. He also served the Republicans at home by continually lashing out at Democrats for being weak-kneed on the communist danger. In 1960, despite Eisenhower's lack of enthusiasm for him, Nixon gained the party's presidential nomination. He lost to John F. Kennedy, in part because he did not prepare himself properly for the first televised debates in U.S. presidential history. Nixon swore that next time he would master, rather than be mastered by, television.

In 1962, however, when he tried to revive his political fortunes by running for the California governorship, he lost again. His political life seemed to be over. Many reporters distrusted and sometimes hated the man who had become known as "Tricky Dick." The press "won't have Nixon to kick around any more," or so the defeated politician told his postelection press conference with a rigid, to-hell-with-you smile. He returned to practicing law and patiently began one of the most remarkable political comebacks in American history by traveling tens of thousands of miles to speak and work for Republican candidates (who then owed him). In June 1964, he stumped for the right-wing Republican presidential nominee, Senator Barry Goldwater, while other moderate members of the party kept their distance from the outspoken conservative who stood little chance against President Lyndon Johnson. Nixon meanwhile polished his foreign policy credentials to become the major Republican voice on Vietnam and other overseas issues.[4]

He was soon leading the Republican condemnation of Johnson's Vietnam policies that were not winning the far-away war. In a famous response, the worn-down, embattled president publicly slammed Nixon. "I do not want to get into a debate . . . with a chronic campaigner like Mr. Nixon," Johnson told reporters in late 1966. "It is his problem to find fault with his country and with his Government during . . . October every two years."[5] Nixon quietly took over the Republican Party while moderating and honing his old anticommunist proclamations. In an influential 1967 article, he outlined a global foreign policy that actually seemed to push Vietnam down his priority list. He instead emphasized the need to come to some understanding with the two great communist powers, the Soviet Union and China. His attitude toward China seemed surprisingly moderate, given his loud anticommunism over the years and the eighteen-year U.S. refusal to recognize diplomatically that mainland China even existed. (In retrospect, the 1967 publication anticipated Nixon's historic trip to Beijing in 1972 that finally began to restore U.S.-Chinese relations.) The article seemed to be a turning away from the long-held American idea of sending U.S. men and women to fight anywhere in the world if it were necessary to contain communism. Nixon was saying, apparently, that as president he would send them only to the most vital areas—while helping allies fight the Cold War so Americans could devote their energies to restoring order to the chaotic streets at home.[6]

As his 1968 campaign began, Nixon grew increasingly vague about his plans for Vietnam. Through the mid-1960s he had helped shape the Republican warhawk line that only a military victory would suffice. The shocking Tet offensive changed the elites' view that a military victory was possible, and Nixon moved with that elite. By March he was telling New Hampshire voters not about possible military triumphs, but only that "new leadership" would "end the war and win the peace in the Pacific."[7] Sticking to this line throughout the campaign, Nixon never had to offer a more explicit, detailed position— one that would be open to easy criticism by both the Johnson administration and Republican challengers for the nomination. Nixon had his party's nomination virtually locked up quite early.

He believed, moreover, that for most voters the issue they wanted to hear about was not the war, but how to end the bloodshed and disorder the war seemed to ricochet back to American streets. He is "hotting up the campaign, encouraged by several recent polls," the British embassy in Washington reported to London in December 1967. "Though Nixon has been very cagey about committing himself on . . . Vietnam" he has declared publicly that the country "faces 'internal war' between the races," while the cities take on "all the aspects of guerilla war."

The British report emphasized that other Republican candidates were coming to agree with Nixon's approach. California Governor Ronald Reagan "has also read the signs of the times. He said a week or two ago" in a public speech "that the Republican Party would be wise to refuse to discuss solutions to the war in Vietnam." The party should instead attack Johnson, Reagan declared, for lying about the war's progress. After the election, the California governor added, the new Republican president should "end the war as quickly as possible." After all, Reagan stressed, "Vietnam was 'a little 16th rate, water buffalo kind of country.'" He intended to devote his time to attacking inflation and Johnson's Great Society domestic program.[8]

Led by Nixon, the Republicans were thus beginning to tap into the huge, growing reservoir of fear and disgust engulfing American voters. Historian Charles DeBenedetti discovered the middle American town of Millersburg, Pennsylvania, where the citizens talked more about war protesters than about the war. They saw protesters as another form of countercultural hippies who aimed to use drugs and rock music to overthrow traditional American life. An antiwar protester was viewed as "a hairy youth with needle marks in his arm, wearing a blanket and flowers, who is more likely also a Communist." This un-American did not believe in "God, family, private property, good grooming . . . Bing Crosby, Bart Starr [quarterback for the champion Green Bay Packers], or anything else that Millersburg believes in." Interestingly, however, the town's citizens, while damning the protesters, did not mind those who evaded the draft, as long as their hair was fairly short and they did not march in the street. Some even said they supported the war simply because "the war protesters were against it."[9]

Because he understood these feelings, which were rapidly spreading in early 1968, and because he had systematically collected support for the Republican nomination since 1964 (if not since 1952), Nixon made short work of his challengers. The major danger threatened to come from New York Governor Nelson Rockefeller, obviously well-funded but also a member of the party's liberal wing who had infuriated many Republicans by refusing to work for Goldwater in 1964. Rockefeller, however, could not make up his mind whether he wanted to take on Nixon. Since 1965, he had declared he would not run for the presidency so he could concentrate on problems in New York. Critics claimed that the rich, sometimes arrogant Rockefeller was waiting to be appointed to the presidency so he would not have to bother with the indignity of campaigning.

As he hesitated, George Romney, who had won three terms as Michigan's governor, became Nixon's main challenger. Romney had been a successful chief executive of American Motors, one of the Big Four automakers, where he produced the first American compact car. When he moved from the state to the national stage, he turned out to be an amateur and not ready for prime time. After making clumsy and contradictory remarks about Vietnam in 1967, he finally clamed he had been "brainwashed" by U.S. military officials during a visit to the country. (Senator Eugene McCarthy, who did not have a high opinion of Romney's intelligence, joked that "a slight rinse" would have been sufficient.) Critics lit into him for being both naive and unpatriotic. Romney's support in the polls slid so rapidly that he pulled out of the race two weeks before the first primary vote.[10]

Rockefeller had endorsed (and given $250,000 to) Romney. The New Yorker detested Nixon, so when Romney withdrew, Rockefeller again indicated interest in running—then again backed off. His role as the Hamlet of 1968 finally drove away major supporters, such as Governor Spiro Agnew of Maryland, and pushed them into Nixon's camp. In New Hampshire, Nixon won an overwhelming victory, despite Rockefeller's hope that neighboring New Hampshire Republicans would write in his name on the ballot. In the end, reports spread that he probably spent $10 million in his failed effort to win the nomination. One journalist joked that Rockefeller would have done better if he had simply bought four hundred Republican Convention delegates at $25,000 each.[11] The governor's fading was unfortunate for the debate over Vietnam. While other candidates, notably Nixon, refused to be specific about their plans, Rockefeller (aided by his private foreign policy adviser, Professor Henry Kissinger) issued a detailed policy statement for a military disengagement from the conflict. It drew little attention.

Meanwhile, a third challenger appeared. California Governor Reagan had been a successful B-movie actor (the one in the cowboy films who never got the girl). During the 1950s he moved his allegiance from the Democratic Party to the Republicans largely because he was devoting more and more of his time to fighting union power and left-wing influences in the world's film capital. Highly successful as a pitchman on television, he was the first American politician who understood how to translate acting skills and an understanding of the new communications technology into political power. The handsome Reagan, who later claimed he was the only candidate who knew which side of his profile to turn to the television camera for maximum effect, was also carefully schooled by California public relations gurus and political insiders. To the surprise of many, he defeated the popular incumbent governor, Edmund C. Brown, in 1966. While having great appeal for southerners, Goldwater followers (for whom he effectively stumped in 1964), and his television and film fans, Reagan had nevertheless been in politics too short a time to stop the Nixon steamroller.[12]

In late May, Nixon took 73 percent of the vote in the Oregon primary against Rockefeller and Reagan. For one of the first times in a presidential primary campaign, Rockefeller spent millions to buy Madison Avenue and mass media advertising so he could overcome Nixon's lead. The attempt failed, but future candidates employed this incredibly expensive tool—and were forced to raise the tens of millions of dollars needed to utilize it. After his Oregon triumph, Nixon correctly concluded the nomination was now safely his unless he made an error. Observers were betting that would indeed occur. After all, the old Nixon had often lost his cool, most notably in that 1962 press conference. "Everyone is waiting for Nixon to blow his stack or confront Rockefeller directly," Nixon remarked privately (he often referred to himself in the third person). "Well, it hasn't happened up to now, and I think it's too late to start."[13]

Instead, he became the so-called new Nixon who either ignored opponents or treated them with condescending respect. This new Nixon, confident of the nomination and seeing a clear road to the presidency itself, also blurred issues, including Vietnam, so as few voters as possible would be mad at him. "Nixon's positions are so purposely vague that to attack him is much like attacking a cloud," an adviser to Vice President Humphrey observed in June 1968. The adviser believed that the range of people to whom Nixon had to appeal was so broad that he "will have to remain vague."[14]

The adviser was mostly correct. Nixon deliberately sought to blur many issues. He and his own advisers knew, as one of them candidly observed, "for years Nixon was one of those men it was fashionable to hate." His aides also believed he was plagued by a "likeability gap" best exemplified by the 1960 Democratic question: "Would you buy a used car from this man?" A particularly sharp analysis of the candidate was made by Roger Ailes, a talented public relations adviser to Nixon, a genius when it came to using television, and in the 1990s a creator of the Fox television network. "Let's face it, a lot of people think Nixon is dull," Ailes commented during the 1968 campaign. "Think he's a bore, a pain in the ass. . . . Who was forty-two years old the day he was born. They figure other kids got footballs for Christmas, Nixon got a briefcase and loved it." Perhaps worst of all, he was the kid who always had "his homework done and never let you copy."[15]

To fix the image, Ailes and other advisers carefully arranged to have the candidate appear on television only in highly controlled situations in which Nixon felt comfortable and looked relaxed, rather than (as he sometimes did) appear to be a stiff robot or, as occurred during his 1960 televised debate with John Kennedy, having beads of sweat break out on his face. Nixon changed not by becoming a new Nixon, but by becoming a new image. As one of his top advisers explained, American voting was not based on reality, but is

a product of the particular chemistry between the voter and the *image* of the candidate. . . . *We have to be* very clear on this point: that the response is to the image, not to the man, since 99 percent of the voters have no contact with the man. It's not what's *there* that counts, it's what's projected—and . . . it's not what *he* projects but rather what the voter receives. It's not the man we have to change, but rather the *received* impression.

A reporter who noted this quote concluded: "Nixon had become so thoroughly repackaged that he became, in a sense, the first President to win the office by suicide."[16]

Such packaging could win the presidency. It would not sharpen the debate over Vietnam, but an unsharpened debate was a result Nixon preferred. One of the few exceptions to this general strategy of mere image and vagueness was his direct appeal for southern conservative votes. His constant emphasis on the need for law and order was part of this appeal, although that particular message attracted increasing numbers of voters all across the country. More directly, Nixon moved to take southern states away from his main competitor in the region, Alabama Governor George Wallace, by quietly making deals with southern power brokers, such as the longtime segregationist Senator Strom Thurmond of South Carolina, as well as Senator Howard Baker of Tennessee and Senator John Tower of Texas.

Thurmond and his fellow conservatives understood that the southern white reaction to Johnson's civil rights legislation was shifting large numbers of people out of the Democratic Party and in the Republican camp. They would come in ever larger numbers, Thurmond reasoned, if Nixon stressed law and order—code words, in the minds of many Americans, for the need to deal harshly with civil rights marchers, inner-city rioters, and antiwar protesters. Nixon promised these southerners they would have his ear as president. He worked out a strategy that appealed to the South and countered Wallace's campaign by coolly emphasizing law and order without explicitly stressing race. This approach allowed Wallace and his antiblack, prosegregationist past to become the lightning rod for those who were appalled by, and fighting against, racial hatred.[17]

Nixon put together a distinguished group of advisers. Some of this was merely for show, especially since Nixon was becoming famous for being a loner and keeping his own counsel. In announcing the team who would work with him on race relations, observers identified highly knowledgeable experts. Most notably, however, there was 7-foot 1-inch Wilt Cham-

berlain, a basketball legend who in Nixon's campaign literature was identified as a "black capitalist." As one of Nixon's top aides, John Ehrlichman, recalled, the hoops star towered above crowds and "was the ultimate visible black support." Then the Nixon camp began to receive
"horrified reports of Mr. Chamberlain's appetites, requests, tastes, demands and insatiable requirements," Ehrlichman remembered. One example was his hotel bill at the Miami Republican Convention, "which included thousands of dollars of charges from the men's haberdashery at
the Hilton" hotel.[18] Chamberlain was less in evidence during the rest of
the campaign. Front and center were respected Washington insiders.
These included economic adviser Alan Greenspan, Patrick Buchanan (a
gifted twenty-nine-year-old speechwriter), and two leading economists,
Arthur Burns and Paul McCracken. The Nixon team was appealing, confident, and formidable.[19]

On August 1, just as the Republican nominating convention was to
convene, Nixon for the first time provided a few details about his plan
for Vietnam should he move into the White House. Promising to be
fully honest with the American people about the war, he declared he
would talk with the Russians (apparently hoping they would pressure
their Vietnamese allies to negotiate). He would also put "greater emphasis" on pacification (whatever that meant), give "urgent attention"
to Vietnamization, and gradually phase out American troops. He
pleased many doves by promising to end the highly inequitable military draft and replace it with a volunteer force—but only after the war
"is behind us." Finally, Nixon foresaw "eventual conversations with
China," although he was unclear about what "eventual" meant or
whether the "conversations" might also relate to the war.[20]

Many observers were not impressed. Nixon was laying out a plan
for once again trying to Vietnamize the war (turning it over to reinforced South Vietnam forces). Such a plan had not worked when it
had been tried over the past decade because of the corruption and
lack of fighting spirit among those forces. After Nixon provided these
few details on August 1, he again retreated to safe generalizations
about the war while emphasizing instead how his presidency would
somehow restore law and order inside the United States.

(It later turned out that Nixon did have another idea for ending the
war, and it was a stunner. He revealed it to at least two of his top aides

in 1967 and during the 1968 campaign. While relaxing after working on a speech, he told his top assistant, H. R. Haldeman, that he could end the Vietnam War because he had a theory: "I call it the Madman Theory, Bob. I want the North Vietnamese to believe I've reached the point where I might do *anything* to stop the war. We'll just slip the word to them that, for God's sake, you know Nixon is obsessed about Communism. We can't restrain him when he's angry—and he has his hand on the nuclear button." With the communists believing they were dealing with a "madman," the former vice president concluded, "Ho Chi Minh himself will be in Paris in two days begging for peace." He discussed the "madman theory" again later during his presidency, but neither Ho nor his successors responded by rushing to Paris to make peace, and Nixon never got around to telling American voters that they should vote for him because he was a "madman.")[21]

The Republican Party Convention that met in Miami during early August witnessed a coronation. The only real threat to Nixon's nomination occurred when Reagan began to win the hearts of some southern delegates. Senators Thurmond and Goldwater quickly doused the move and reclaimed the delegates. The front-runner obtained the nomination on the first ballot.

His forces controlled the platform committee. The Republican campaign platform thus had as its centerpiece, "We will not tolerate violence!" Planks on the war were remarkably moderate, if tantalizingly vague. If elected, the Republicans promised a "de-Americanization" of the conflict but pledged no "camouflaged surrender." Reagan had wanted a much tougher stance on the war; he even wanted to make a point of not ruling out the use of nuclear weapons. Nixon, with Rockefeller's help, faced Reagan's demands down. In addition to pledging to build up the South Vietnamese so they could fight their own war, the Nixon-shaped plank emphasized "a program for peace" that would "offer a fair and equitable settlement for all." Instead of demanding total military victory, Nixon was moving the Republicans toward the negotiating table. Exactly how he would make deals for an "equitable peace" (i.e., keep South Vietnam noncommunist) was unclear, given the strength of the communists and the weakness of the South Vietnamese regime. But at least he did not imply that nuclear weapons would be the way to win friends and influence peace negotiations in Southeast Asia.[22]

In his acceptance speech, Nixon zeroed in with remarkable instinct on the most important theme of the 1968 campaign. He applauded the "forgotten Americans, the non-shouters, the non-demonstrators" who were "good people" and "decent people." *Time* magazine nevertheless commented, "Somehow Nixon manages to sound more forceful and specific in emphasizing the need for law and order than in pleading for social justice." As the Republicans debated, a bloody riot erupted across Biscayne Bay in Miami's black ghetto. It went on for three days and three lives were lost. Six hundred soldiers finally brought it under control. Few outside the African American community seemed to notice.[23]

The most surprising news coming out of the convention was not who received the presidential nomination or the terrible riot, but the vice presidential candidate: Governor Spiro Agnew, the forty-nine-year-old Maryland governor. The overwhelming first response was, "Who?" As Agnew immediately admitted in an interestingly constructed sentence, "Spiro Agnew is not a household word." Colorado Senator Peter Dominick exclaimed, "There are 2 million people in my state who have never heard of Agnew. It's a terrible choice."

But Nixon had his reasons. One, certainly, was that the unknown, rather plodding governor would never outshine Nixon. He was a "political neuter," as the phrase was used at the convention, possessing neither strong principles nor impassioned followers. A second reason for the selection was that Agnew happily agreed to be an attack dog against the Democrats, while Nixon could take the vague high road. The governor would be Nixon's Nixon. Importantly, Agnew, as a Rockefeller Republican, had appealed to the Democratic voters in the 1966 election and especially to African Americans in Maryland. He repealed racist laws that had long been on the books, and for the first time blacks were appointed to important positions on the governor's staff. As Rockefeller continually hesitated to enter the race, Agnew switched his support to the more conservative Nixon.

And then the Martin Luther King Jr. assassination triggered riots in Baltimore. Agnew called in federal troops as well as the national guard. One of his public statements was interpreted to mean that looters should be shot. He summoned, then tongue-lashed, one hundred African American leaders for allowing such outbreaks to occur. Most of

the leaders angrily walked out on him. In Miami, liberals also threatened to walk out in rebellion against Agnew's nomination, but as Republicans they had no place to go. With the choice of the Maryland governor, Nixon underlined his commitment to law, order, and the
conservative South. As for the war, Agnew had a son serving in Vietnam.
The two candidates could be as vague as they wanted about the conflict
and it would be difficult to charge them with being unpatriotic.[24]

Thus, the Republican candidates opened the final stretch of the
campaign with their hands free to deal with the subject of Vietnam. As
polls showed that Americans wanted a "de-Americanization" of the
war, Nixon said he wanted no more soldiers sent to fight but also opposed an immediate pullout from the country. He urged, along with
virtually everyone else in the United States, that the Vietnamese take
on more of the fighting and dying, but he refused to say how he would
pressure the weak South Vietnamese regime to do so. Demanding a
negotiated settlement and self-determination for South Vietnam, he
did not specify how these would be brought about.

In late July, Nixon had met with Johnson to discuss the crisis. He
urged the president not to undertake a bombing pause, which the communists demanded as a precondition for meaningful negotiations, because that was the "one piece of leverage you have left." Johnson
agreed. He came away from this and another meeting admiring Nixon's
toughness. Those close to the president feared that he was beginning to
favor Nixon over Vice President Humphrey, whom Johnson considered
weak and unpredictable in carrying out vigorous policies in Vietnam.
One of the last things Nixon wanted was a halt to the bombing and the
beginning of serious talks that might lead to the "de-Americanization"
of the war. If this occurred during the campaign, Humphrey would
greatly profit. It was in Nixon's interest for the war to continue as a
bloody ghost hovering over the Democratic campaign to remind voters
the mess the Johnson–Humphrey team had created in Vietnam.[25]

Blurring the war issue while emphasizing law and order, Nixon and
Agnew roared out of Miami at full speed. Polls indicated that before
the convention, Nixon had been even with the probable Democratic
nominee, Vice President Humphrey. But afterward the Republican's
margin suddenly jumped six to sixteen points.[26]

In the New Hampshire snows of February and March, Nixon had emphasized to his largely middle-class audience the many sins Lyndon Johnson had committed in not winning the war in Vietnam. One observer recorded that the few blue-collar workers who came to see the candidate applauded "only when he talks of law and order and an end to violence." Later, that theme dominated his speeches, especially after the Oregon primary. During his victory in that state, he privately noted that on the Democratic side Robert Kennedy was gaining attention by stressing that when he was attorney general he took the hard line against corruption and other lawlessness. After talking with Oregon voters, Nixon remarked to aides, "Do you know a lot of these people think Bobby is more a law-and-order man than I am!" An acute journalist concluded, "From then on, law and order became the prime theme of his [Nixon's] campaign, and was to remain so to the end."[27] On Vietnam, of course, he determinedly remained vague.

The war, meanwhile, was not only ruining the nation's foreign policy but also helping reshape the political system itself. Most Americans had patriotically supported what was becoming the longest war in their history, only to discover that it was coming home to their streets. And as it did, they searched for leaders who promised to restore peace and stability to those neighborhoods, however vague their plans might be for solving such a complex problem. But Nixon and his advisers had apparently concluded that Americans were too busy or too ignorant politically to look below either the image or the generalizations his campaign was producing about the war. After enduring years of riots and sending a half million of their sons and daughters to a distant war, Americans wanted peace (an honorable settlement, if possible), law, and order. "The U.S. is Squaresville, and Nixon is the quintessential square," nationally syndicated columnist Stewart Alsop told Ambassador Dean in October 1968, "and it may be the main reason why he will win."[28]

Americans wanted to put Vietnam, antiwar protesters, and inner-city riots far behind them so they could return to Squaresville, the place where they could imagine the promises of train whistles while dreaming the centuries-old American Dream. Nixon pledged to take them there.

September 6, 1968, Time *Cover depicting Hubert Humphrey and Edmund Muskie with Mayor Daley in the background*
Getty Images

HUBERT HORATIO HUMPHREY: THE ISOLATION OF THE POLITICS OF JOY

Resembling a giant surrounded by attackers intent on mutilating and then ejecting him from the scene, American liberalism entered the 1960s as the nation's main political ideology, but at the end of the decade weakened and, in some quarters, was left for dead. The American liberal tradition had been proud, pivotal, and lengthy. It had emerged after the American Revolution under the tutelage of no less than Thomas Jefferson and Andrew Jackson, who preached (but did not always practice), the centrality of protecting individual freedom from governmental power. During the presidencies of Theodore Roosevelt and Woodrow Wilson in the early twentieth century, however, liberalism underwent a surprising transformation.

The two men led the Progressives of the late 1890s to the 1920s who redefined the federal government as a protector of individualism—whether it was in using federal (and the states) powers to break up monopolistic corporations who gouged consumers, to control the railways whose few owners overcharged customers, to establish national parks in which many citizens rather than a few logging companies could enjoy nature, or to help the person whom Wilson called "the little man on the make" (the small entrepreneur who needed governmental protection against the corporate robber barons who tried to drive competitors into oblivion).

By the 1930s, liberalism no longer meant that men and women would be left to compete in a supposedly free and open marketplace. Precisely because enormous corporations dominated the market-place, liberals viewed government as the only hope of restoring some competition and maintaining individualism. The terrible economic depression following the 1929 stock market crash, in the minds of many liberals, had been triggered by uncontrolled greed and corruption in the banking system, stock markets, and businesses generally. Under Franklin D. Roosevelt's New Deal, liberals used government not only to clean up the mess but also to provide jobs and badly needed new infrastructure (such as modern bridges, roads, and dams for electrical power). The New Deal also created sources of governmental capital to help the ambitious expand into overseas markets.

World War II stopped the further expansion of liberal reform, as wars usually do, but it also helped fasten tight the changes brought about earlier by the New Deal. Several billion dollars of government spending on the war finally brought the nation out of the depression and helped set off a wartime and postwar economic boom. The New Deal and its liberal followers enjoyed the glory of helping to win history's greatest war. With sufficient government involvement, all things seemed possible by the late 1940s, the time when Lyndon Johnson, with reverence for his hero Franklin D. Roosevelt, first reached the U.S. Senate. Now with the globe's greatest economy (other competitors in Europe and Asia had been reduced to rubble by the war), Americans and their government could march together abroad to fight the good fight against a communist empire that believed in neither God nor private property.

Liberalism was triumphant at home. Not even the enormously popular Republican President Dwight D. Eisenhower wanted to touch social security, government oversight of banks and stock markets, and other New Deal creations. Nor could Eisenhower, much to his frustration, significantly reduce the mammoth defense budgets. He might warn, as he did in his farewell address, against what he termed the military-industrial-academic complex. (Leading universities made millions of dollars designing weapons and planning how to use them to maximum effect.) But taking these government dollars out of the economy could trigger another economic crisis. And be-sides, this military-industrial-academic complex was the front line of the global war against communism.

Hubert Humphrey emerged from Minnesota progressive politics as a national star in the late 1940s, just as American liberalism took on the double task of using government to keep the country pros-perous and the rest of world anticommunist. As a U.S. senator be-tween 1949 and 1964, moreover, Humphrey became nationally known because he insisted on adding another dimension to liberal-ism: using governmental powers to protect and provide jobs for the nation's poor, especially minorities such as African Americans. At the 1948 Democratic Convention, he made national headlines by leading the forces that drove the South Carolina segregationist leader, Strom Thurmond, and his many followers out of the convention hall and into a third party. The Humphrey speech that triggered the famous walk out was one of the most effective ever given at a national polit-ical convention, although President Harry Truman, the convention's nominee, did not appreciate that the Minnesotan had split his party just before the start of the campaign. With Humphrey's help, Truman nevertheless scored one of the great political upsets in the nation's history.

Humphrey's passion for civil rights, better race relations, and pro–labor union legislation should be kept in mind, for the passion was to turn bitter in his 1968 election campaign. His outspoken anti-communism, a large part of the liberal ideology in the 1950s and 1960s, also should be remembered, for it too helped drag him down in 1968. Before the mid-1960s, Humphrey had little reason to believe these enthusiasms would one day destroy his presidential ambitions. Until that point, he rode the crest of liberal power in midcentury America to the Senate and, in 1964, the vice presidency.

Humphrey was even less able to anticipate the terribly difficult, draining days he endured in 1967–1968 because of his ever present optimism, wide smile, and the belief that the country's greatest days lay ahead of it. All of this he gloriously defined as the "politics of joy." A backslapper and hail-fellow-well-met who seemed to remember the name of every voter whose hand he had ever shaken, he was also a speaker whose words cascaded out of his mouth with great, gleeful speed (and sometimes with too little sense that his audience might have something else to do than listen to him). As novelist Norman Mailer wrote, Humphrey, when wound up before a large audience, "had a formal slovenliness of syntax which enabled him to shunt phrases back and forth, like a switchman who locates a freight car by moving everything in the yard." During the 1968 campaign, a top adviser congratulated Humphrey for his answers in a television interview and then added, "but cutting them in half would have doubled their effectiveness."[1]

In the mid-1950s, Lyndon Johnson ruled the U.S. Senate in which Humphrey served. Late one night a conservative bill came to the floor guaranteeing farmers much less for their work than Humphrey thought just. As one of Johnson's top aides recalled, Humphrey was bone tired and in a passionate, hoarse-voiced, and angry tone he began to lecture the few who remained on the Senate floor:

> "Hubert Humphrey did not come to the United States Senate to vote for sixty percent of living wage." And it was such a powerful speech that Dick Russell [conservative Democrat from Georgia] who had started out of the chamber, turned around, came back and sat in front of Humphrey, reached around and grabbed Olin Johnston [conservative Democrat from South Carolina], and some others, and pointed at Humphrey. . . . And they all began pounding the table with Humphrey. It was a damned revival. You could see the relationship between Humphrey and those guys who had mostly come up in the depression.[2]

The Minnesotan's passionate liberalism set him about as far apart from Richard Nixon as any two people in the same line of work could be. Both, however, shared an ardent anticommunism, at least between the late 1940s and early 1960s. Again, Humphrey's perspective came out of a rich tradition in the country's liberalism. Woodrow Wilson had refused to recognize the existence of the Soviet Union when it replaced the Russian empire in 1917. His nonrecognition policy remained in place sixteen years until Franklin D. Roosevelt, despite some reluctance and tough opposition from members of his administration, faced reality—and the need for Soviet markets amid the economic depression—to open diplomatic relations in 1933. But liberals

blasted any threat of communism, overseas or at home. In a blistering 1919 speech, Wilson told Americans to beware of communism,
which he defined as "the poison of disorder, the poison of revolt, the
poison of chaos" that now, he warned ominously, "has got into the
veins of this free people." One result of such frightening speeches after World War I was a "red hunt" for communists, a hunt that mostly
ruined lives and forced innocent recent immigrants to return to Europe. In 1947, President Harry Truman carried on the anticommunist theme of American liberalism. In his Truman Doctrine message
to Congress, he demanded a U.S. commitment, and large sums of
money, to fight communism abroad. Within weeks, he also initiated
the nation's first peacetime loyalty program in which the FBI and
Congress searched for communists within the government. The liberal search turned into McCarthyism's witch-hunts between 1950
and 1954.[3]

Humphrey moved into the Senate during these years. In the 1950s,
he, along with most politicians, liberal and conservative, condemned
Communist China as well as the Soviet Union. Resembling most liberals, he not only despised communism for what it was, but also hoped
to ensure that voters would not confuse his left-of-center domestic politics with his foreign policy views. Not wanting to be open to charges
from the right wing that being a liberal might mean he was soft on left-
wing activities, Humphrey and other liberals made it a point to be
more outspokenly anticommunist than many conservatives.

The 1962 Cuban missile crisis, which threatened to engulf the world
in nuclear war, led the Minnesota senator to rethink relations between
the two superpowers. In 1963, when President Kennedy made the first
major breakthrough in arms control by agreeing with the Russians to
limit testing of nuclear weapons, Humphrey was a Senate floor leader
who pushed the treaty through to ratification against strong opposition
from the U.S. military and conservative political forces. Along with
nearly all of his congressional colleagues, however, he did not question
the early U.S. military escalation in Vietnam.

Nor did he question President Lyndon Johnson's demand for more
liberal legislation to help improve schools, minority rights, and the
poor. In deciding on his vice presidential running mate in 1964, Johnson played games with several candidates, but Humphrey emerged as

a logical choice. He and Johnson had entered the Senate together in early 1949. They agreed on what they saw as the many virtues of the New Deal and ardent anticommunist policies. Humphrey could bring along millions of northern liberals in the 1964 election, while Johnson swept his South and West. After their smashing triumph, they worked together to pass the president's Great Society program that aimed to update the New Deal, especially for the poor, the elderly, and African Americans. But they also escalated in Vietnam until the administration had invested 500,000 troops and an annual $30 billion in this particular anticommunist commitment.

By 1967, as the two men prepared to run for reelection, massive government spending at home and abroad was launching an inflation that drove up prices. All of the Great Society's spending, however, did not stop riots that erupted in Newark, Detroit, Los Angeles, and other cities. Johnson remarked that he felt so besieged that he wanted to hunker down like a rabbit in a hailstorm. Hunkering down ran contrary to every fiber in Humphrey's body (or Johnson's). But even the Minnesotan was puzzled by the enemies who now bombarded the administration's liberal programs. That Richard Nixon, Senator Barry Goldwater, and others on the right would attack them was not surprising. Humphrey, however, was stunned by the rapid growth of opposition on his left—those who condemned the Great Society for not going far enough to help the poor and minorities, and those who condemned the policy in Vietnam for sending U.S. troops there at all.

American liberals for decades had been happy to fight attackers on their political right, the "malefactors of great wealth," as Theodore Roosevelt first tagged them. But liberals were not used to strong, organized opposition on their left. In the 1890s to 1930s, such opposition usually came from socialists or a rather pathetic Communist Party, both of which could be largely dismissed as political threats. Now, under the impact of a growing antiwar movement and its belief that the Great Society program was inadequate, the left launched all-out attacks on Humphrey's liberalism on the streets and in university teach-ins. "An early fighter for civil rights and federal aid to cities," one close observer wrote in mid-1968, "Humphrey is the epitome of old-style liberal politics." But "that is his problem, and he has approached his need for a new identity by deemphasizing massive federal spending and stressing," with few specifics or apparent passion. As for Vietnam, the left saw the vice president as a sellout, as Johnson's puppet. "Nothing would bring the real peaceniks to our side," a Humphrey friend observed, "unless Hubert urinated on a portrait of Lyndon Johnson in Times Square before television—and then they'd say to him, why didn't you do it before?"[4]

As he entered the presidential race in the spring of 1968, therefore, Humphrey's lifelong political identity was under blistering attack. Johnson worsened, not helped, his vice president's agony. Johnson and Humphrey had been friends since the early 1950s, but in the same way a grave digger is friends with his shovel. Johnson, ambitiously aiming to be king of the Senate as its majority leader, systematically manipulated Humphrey to make the Minnesotan believe he was the Texan's friend and would deliver the northern liberal Senate votes Johnson needed to gain the Senate throne. Humphrey served the same purpose when the president chose him as his running mate in 1964.

Johnson trusted him no more, and probably a good deal less, than he did other northern liberals. That trust melted down to nothing in 1965 when Humphrey publicly and gently began to suggest he favored a negotiated settlement in Vietnam. The angry president cut him out of nearly all important foreign policy meetings. The vice president was not consulted before Johnson dispatched thousands of troops to the Dominican Republic in 1965. Nor did LBJ let Humphrey know about secret intelligence briefings regarding the communist buildup that climaxed with the Tet offensive. The vice president learned about the offensive by watching television.

"LBJ treated him like a staff sergeant might treat a private," one top administration official observed. "I was embarrassed." Through most of the 1968 campaign, Johnson gave Humphrey few funds and no enthusiastic endorsement. Close aides believed Johnson saw Humphrey as weak, Nixon strong, and preferred the Republican—especially since Nixon would probably stay the course in Vietnam with more toughness than the Minnesotan. "After four years as Vice President,"

Humphrey recalled, "I had lost some of my personal identity. . . . It would have been better had I stood my ground." But he could not, in part because of Johnson's overpowering personality, in part because Humphrey believed he needed the Texan if he hoped to have a chance at winning the 1968 election.[5]

Increasingly isolated in the administration and ignored by the president, Humphrey tried to return to Johnson's good graces by loudly supporting the war. In early 1966, when critics urged a political coalition between the northern communists and South Vietnam, the vice president said that putting the communists in such a coalition would be like putting "a fox in a chicken coop. . . . Soon there wouldn't be any chickens left." It was, quite inadvertently on Humphrey's part, a highly accurate commentary on the great weakness of the U.S.-supported South Vietnamese government. As the war continued to go badly, the vice president fell back on his politics of joy: Americans must pay the price to stay in Vietnam to perform "big tasks . . . But I say . . . that unless you reach for the stars in this day, you will find yourself in the swamp." Such remarks were not policy but empty cheerleading.[6]

Although Johnson no longer consulted him, the vice president's prowar rallying cries drove away his former liberal supporters who had become harsh critics of both the war and the Great Society. Humphrey found himself in a highly unusual place for a person who was the front-runner for his party's presidential nomination: neither his president nor many of his longtime political friends wanted much to do with him.

Johnson had never been one to worry about party politics, unless, of course, he was running for office himself. After March 1968, that would never again be the case. His interest in Humphrey and Democratic Party officials rested on one simple principle: stop Robert Kennedy, whom the president despised. Johnson even secretly pushed a Republican, Nelson Rockefeller, to enter the race in the belief he was the best hope to defeat Kennedy in November. After the New York senator was assassinated in June, the president no longer seemed to care about Humphrey at all. He only cared that his vice president be an unwavering supporter for whatever the White House was deciding about Vietnam. Humphrey later sorrowfully understated the truth: "Legend to the contrary not withstanding, when it came to party politics he [LBJ] was not good."[7]

Humphrey's isolation—from the president, liberals, conservatives, those in the streets, even his own personal political identity and what had once been his strong beliefs—was so complete, so obvious, that leading party power brokers doubted him from the start. Mayor Richard J. Daley of Chicago, a powerful Democrat, groused, "He's a lousy candidate. If we're going to have another Lyndon Johnson, let's have the real thing."[8]

The vice president's dilemma was defined by two letters he received in June 1968. In the first, a longtime Minnesota friend, Secretary of Agriculture Orville Freeman, warned him that given the country's dark mood, perhaps Humphrey was going "a little far on the happiness kick." Polls showed that a big issue was law enforcement and order. Surveys also revealed that

> you come through soft on this. The best reason seems to be that inevitably one who expresses concern for inequities, for poverty, for discrimination, for slums, thereby unavoidably comes through soft on law enforcement. . . . Surveys . . . show overwhelming pro-police support.[9]

Freeman said nothing about Vietnam as an issue, only about the social upheaval it had helped ignite.

A second letter further tightened the trap in which Humphrey now found himself. An old friend wrote the vice president, "I fear a Humphrey campaign keyed to strident pleas for 'law and order'— a phrase which now clearly connotes to many audiences: 'let's keep the minorities and the poor in their place.'" The war, assassinations, and administration errors were undermining American justice: "I'm worried about the increasing mood of political candidates that 'justice' now carries such negative connotations among the peaceful white majority that it's risky even to mention the word." The friend quoted a remark made to him by a California liberal: "'Justice?' Can't use that word much in a campaign this year. It's become almost as dirty a word as 'peace.'"[10]

Ensnared as he was in a political bear trap, Humphrey was lucky that once he announced for the presidency in April, he did not have to enter primaries to win the nomination. This was the last time in American presidential politics that such a thing happened. After party reforms in 1970–1972, no candidate could win without entering all or nearly all the state primaries. In 1968, however, Humphrey could play it the old-fashioned way, and while McCarthy and Kennedy attacked each other in a number of states, the vice president gathered delegates controlled by state and city Democratic organizations. The chairman of the Democratic National Committee, John M. Bailey, noted that if McCarthy won every delegate in every primary he entered, he would end up with only 15 percent of the convention vote. This was good for Humphrey. When he made public speeches, such as those at Kent State University, Bucknell University, or in major cities, he was screamed at, interrupted by demonstrators, and embarrassed by massive walkouts of antiwar groups.[11]

Humphrey desperately searched for a policy on Vietnam that would please the antiwar groups but not displease Lyndon Johnson. So he departed from his long hatred of Communist China to declare the need to build bridges to mainland China. But when Robert Kennedy proclaimed "no more Vietnams," Humphrey felt he had to condemn the senator for being irresponsible and even insinuated Kennedy was unpatriotic. Pleasing both the president and the protesters was a bigger task than squaring a circle.[12]

Understanding this contradiction, a fellow Minnesotan, Eugene McCarthy, unleashed bitter attacks on Humphrey that went far beyond the issue of Vietnam. He accused the vice president of being an ally of the "Bosses," a mere machine politician and a friend of segregationist Georgia Governor Lester Maddox (with whom Johnson had once forced an unhappy Humphrey to pose in a picture in 1967 just so the president would not lose support in Georgia). Humphrey held his own, but throughout the summer, he and his advisers felt the vice president had to focus on McCarthy and virtually ignore Nixon, while using hundreds of thousands of scarce dollars for television ads. That money was later badly needed in the race against Nixon. As the dollars and key parts of his old liberal support disappeared, the vice president of the United States was reduced to begging. Because "of the more recent attacks upon me in the . . . press," Humphrey wrote to an

African American leader in Washington, D.C., "would you feel free to
write a Letter to the Editor" explaining the Minnesotan's long commitment to "the Negro, the disadvantaged, the poor, the young." The
letter was written, but neither liberal support nor cash flow improved.[13]

Humphrey thus went to the Chicago nominating convention in
late August virtually assured of a nomination on the first ballot, but
it promised to be worthless. The state Democratic organizations,
especially in the large states of New York, California, Pennsylvania,
Michigan, Ohio, and even Humphrey's home state of Minnesota,
were divided by the war, riots, and racial backlash. The peace
groups splintered the vice president's liberal support. This was
ironic, since over the spring and summer, as Secretary of Defense
Clark Clifford recalled, Humphrey privately supported the antiwar
group inside the administration (led by Clifford and the ambassador to the Paris peace talks, Averell Harriman) against the
warhawks led by Secretary of State Rusk. He expressed that support, however, only "when he was consulted" by Johnson, Clifford
added, and that "was not very often." Other than a bitterly divided
Democratic Party, the Chicago convention would be remembered
for another reason: the appearance of a countercultural, antiwar
left whose activities climaxed in a brutal, nationally televised confrontation with police. The war came home to Chicago streets in
August 1968.[14]

The confrontation had begun early that year when Johnson refused
to switch the convention away from Chicago to a safer location in the
South, perhaps Miami. The president took Mayor Daley's word that
the Windy City would be calm in August. Daley's police would see to
that. With the site chosen, antiwar leaders Dave Dellinger and Tom
Hayden began planning to protest the conflict during the convention—in an orderly, legal fashion. Their attempt to obtain a permit
from Daley's officials, however, failed. Word began to circulate that
the police were willing to crack heads, if necessary, to keep protesters
far away from the convention facilities.[15]

Now another group appeared, the Yippies (sometimes standing for
Youth International Party, but a play on the word "hippie"). They were

led by Abbie Hoffman, active in the civil rights movement, and Jerry Rubin, a product of Berkeley's antiwar and free speech movements. Yippies set out to ridicule the U.S. government with comical acts, such as when they threw money from a balcony onto the floor of the New York Stock Exchange, then watched gleefully as the traders below fought each other to pick it up. The Chicago convention became their major target. Perhaps, as one Yippie said, they would even enliven the city by putting LSD into the water system. They also intended to make fun of the Democrats by nominating their own candidate, Pigasus, a 150-pound pig.

Again, word spread that Daley and his police severely lacked a sense of humor and would employ force to keep the Yippies away. Several thousand nevertheless showed up. Hayden and the more mainstream antiwar leaders disliked the Yippies for their flippancy but welcomed their presence—especially their music and appeal to the young. "Without the musicians," Hayden said, "you couldn't get the youth base." If true, that was a devastating comment on American youths and their lack of seriousness about the war that was killing thousands of their own number.[16]

British reporters covering the convention found everything surreal. It "took place in the International Amphitheater, a huge, ugly building in the stinking stockyards," the London-based correspondents recorded. "It had been provided with a perimeter defense that would have graced Khe Sanh [the Vietnam battlefield of the moment]: barbed-wire fences, armed troops, circling helicopters, and a restricted air zone in which other planes were forbidden to fly below 2,500 feet." "To reach the hall" the reporters noted, "the delegates had to travel four miles by special buses. Along the route newly erected strips of brown wattle fencing failed to hide the ugliness that they were supposed to disguise. The only color was in the red, white, and blue posters proclaiming 'WE LOVE MAYOR DALEY' from almost every window."[17]

The opening battle occurred not in the streets but in the platform committee even before the convention officially started. The context was tragic. Some 27,000 Americans, and hundreds of thousands of Vietnamese, had already died in the war. During the days the Democrats met, 308 more U.S. troops were killed. Johnson was nevertheless de-

*Protest at the Chicago Convention, where the Counterculture,
tear-gas, and police billy clubs became political symbols.*
Courtesy of the Chicago Historical Society

termined that two of his fundamental policies—no halt to the bombing of North Vietnam until the communists made key concessions and no inclusion of the communists in a new South Vietnamese government—must be upheld in the party platform. Antiwar factions, led by Senators Eugene McCarthy, George McGovern of South Dakota, and Edward Kennedy of Massachusetts (Robert's youngest brother), took opposite positions. They urged an unconditional bombing halt as a necessary first step toward a negotiated settlement and U.S. withdrawal. They also wanted the South Vietnamese regime to recognize reality by broadening the government to include communists. Humphrey privately did not disagree with these two positions. He especially quietly favored an immediate end to the bombing. But when Johnson, back in Washington, learned of these developments, he berated his vice president: "This plank [of the antiwar group] just undercuts our whole policy and, by God, the Democratic Party ought not to be doing that to me and you ought not to be doing it, you've been a part of this policy." Humphrey backed down. Johnson's planks were nailed into the party platform.[18]

Two of the most effective speeches on the issue came from Senator Edmund Muskie of Maine, who supported the president, and Kenneth O'Donnell, who argued for the antiwar group's plank. Muskie declared that "free elections" could be held in South Vietnam only if there were "safeguards"—no communists involved in overseeing them. A bombing halt, he warned, without any communist assurances that they would not take advantage of it by moving in fresh soldiers and supplies, could only endanger "our troops." O'Donnell, a former top aide to President John Kennedy, laid out the broader, bleaker picture. In the last Congress, he noted, $6 billion was cut "out of all the programs affecting the lives of every single American, out of the programs in health, in education, and the problems that face our children." That badly needed money would not be available unless "we . . . disengage ourselves from the expenditures not only of our best treasure, the young men, but the fact that we are spending $30-billion a year in a foreign adventure in South Vietnam. It must end."[19]

On August 28, the antiwar forces took their fight to the convention floor. After a bitter three-hour debate, Johnson's (and now Humphrey's) planks were passed by a vote of 1,567 to 1,041. Singing "We Shall Overcome," the losers vowed to continue their fight after the convention, which meant they were in no mood to support Humphrey. He nevertheless easily won a first-ballot nomination with 1,760 votes. McCarthy received 601, McGovern 146. Reverend Channing Phillips, a Kennedy delegate, received 67 votes; he was the first African American ever to be nominated as a major party presidential candidate. The vice presidential nominee was Senator Muskie, a serious, respected liberal who had delivered powerful support for the Johnson war plank. All this arrived for Humphrey, who had been waiting decades for the moment, with great bitterness. As he watched his nomination, television pictures switched back and forth between the convention and the struggle erupting in the streets.[20]

The Battle of Chicago, as it has been called, started on August 25, the day before the convention opened. Police used tear gas and mace as well as billy clubs to break up an encampment of antiwar groups in Lincoln Park. As fighting between police and protesters continued in scattered areas of the downtown, 5,000 U.S. Army troops moved in. The Illinois governor had already ordered 6,000 national guardsmen to encamp close by. These forces should have been enough to contain the protesters peacefully, but on August 27, as the antiwar groups held an "unbirthday party" in honor of Lyndon Johnson, police took off their badges (so they could not be identified) and used night sticks and mace to disperse the party.

On August 28, Humphrey was nominated. All hell broke loose. Protesters had moved into Grant Park, directly across from the main convention hotel. When a person took down an American flag, the police charged, freely swinging their clubs. The conflict grew until by that night the suffocatingly sweet fumes of tear gas seemed to surround the delegates staying in the hotel. As protesters taunted and threw anything they could pick up to defend themselves, the police continued to beat and arrest anyone they could reach. Over 1,000 people, including 192 policemen, were injured over four days, and 662 arrested, including Jerry Rubin and Abbie Hoffman. The famous antiwar journalist I. F. Stone concluded, "The war is destroying our country as we are destroying Vietnam."[21]

In his hotel room, Humphrey watched the growing conflict with horror, and no doubt a premonition that he was watching his chances for the presidency disappear among the clouds of tear gas. In the convention hall, Senator Abraham Ribicoff of Connecticut (a former member of John F. Kennedy's cabinet) was nominating Senator McGovern for the presidency when he suddenly declared that with "McGovern as President . . . we wouldn't have these Gestapo tactics in the streets of Chicago." The stunned convention let out a roar of approval. Mayor Daley leaped to his feet, shook his fist at Ribicoff, and shouted words that few could hear, although his lips clearly said, as Norman Mailer recorded, that Daley was telling Ribicoff "to go have carnal relations with himself." Humphrey did nothing to damp down the hatreds. During his acceptance speech he was booed for including Johnson with Franklin D. Roosevelt, Harry Truman, and John F. Kennedy as great presidents. He infuriated many delegates by declaring, "And tonight to you, Mr. President, I say thank you. Thank you, Mr. President." As Mailer noted, this assumed Johnson was even watching. In any case,

Humphrey was effusively thanking a person who had done as little as possible on his behalf.[22]

An official investigation termed the conflicts in the streets a "police riot." The authorities had certainly been provoked by the protesters, the report concluded, but the police used "unrestrained and indiscriminate . . . violence . . . often inflicted upon persons who had broken no law, disobeyed no order, made no threat." Polls revealed, however, that as many as 70 percent of Americans approved the way Daley and his police handled the situation. Senator Barry Goldwater, the Republican presidential nominee in 1964, was quoted as saying he was amused by television pictures showing news reporters being beaten up. Shortly after the convention ended, Humphrey declared it was time to "quit pretending that Mayor Daley did anything that was wrong." Hearing this, an angry Eugene McCarthy vowed never to endorse Humphrey.[23]

The vice president thus began his campaign as a symbol for antiwar riots on the streets, while Richard Nixon continually talked about law and order. Nominating conventions usually give candidates a quick lift in the polls, but Humphrey received none. He ran as many as twelve points behind Nixon, and only twelve points ahead of third-party candidate George Wallace. And, as if the administration's troubles in Vietnam and on the streets were not enough, a second foreign policy blow hit Humphrey.

Throughout 1967–1968, Johnson (and then his vice president) planned to run in part on the claim they had remarkably reduced Cold War tensions by working out a new relationship with the Soviet Union. Such a claim might help offset the foreign policy disasters in Vietnam. In July 1968, two landmark events occurred: direct commercial jet service began between New York City and Moscow; and U.S.-USSR leaders brought 57 other nations along to sign the Treaty on Non-Proliferation of Nuclear Weapons (in which most nonnuclear states promised not to build the weapons). Happier times finally seemed to lie ahead in the Cold War.

Then on August 20, as Democrats began to arrive in Chicago, thousands of Soviet troops invaded Czechoslovakia. The country was already communist, but its reformers were trying, slowly, to evolve a more open system. As he destroyed the Czech reform movement, So-

viet leader Leonid Brezhnev further stunned Washington by announcing a new doctrine: Russia reserved the right to use force at any
time to preserve a rigid and faithful communist empire. Over the next
two months, stories surfaced that both Americans and Soviets were
developing new weapons, including chemical and biological weapons
of mass destruction. The Cold War had turned much colder.
Humphrey's hope of claiming his administration had created a safer
world was destroyed.[24]

But the major foreign policy topic was, of course, Vietnam. Here
again the vice president found himself in deepening trouble, partly
by his own doing. In his first campaign trip after the convention, he
talked to a surprisingly small Philadelphia crowd dominated by antiwar protesters. Trying to rescue the situation, he claimed U.S. forces
in Vietnam could safely begin to pull out in late 1968 or early 1969.
Within twenty-four hours both Secretary of State Rusk and President Johnson publicly repudiated Humphrey's statement. Later in
September, Nixon trapped the vice president on Vietnam. Until
then the Republican had promised "an honorable peace" but refused to give many details. Humphrey decided to smoke out Nixon
by declaring that if elected he would "move toward a systematic reduction in American forces," regardless of what happened in the faltering, on-and-off Paris peace negotiations between the United
States and North Vietnam. Nixon quickly called Humphrey's words
a turn-tail-and-run policy. Without pressure from U.S. forces, the
Republican stressed, the communists would never agree to a just
peace. Johnson and Rusk were no happier than Nixon with
Humphrey's statement.[25]

Again, however, the war was only one of the vice president's problems. Like a monster, it had grown far outside itself to reshape the
hopes and, above all, the fears of Americans. "Every poll—Gallup,
Harris, Quayle, those taken for Humphrey in individual states—make
clear that safety in the streets, crime, riots, hecklers, etc., is one of the
two, if not the major issue in this campaign," a political adviser privately told the Humphrey camp in early October. "In every state in
which issues have been tested, Crime Prevention and law and order
top the list of issues. . . . In every state the great majority (around 75
percent) want to use massive force short of shooting or with shooting

to stop riots and looting." The adviser continued: "Nixon is seen as substantially closer to the voters' position than is Humphrey. This issue is costing Humphrey votes." But, the adviser went on, the Democratic candidate had an even greater problem. As Vietnam and law and order are the two top issues, "on both . . . a substantial majority of voters . . . take a 'tough' line." And on both issues, Humphrey was seen as "less 'tough'" than Nixon.[26]

The vice president was trapped between the fear that if he did try to appear as "tough" as Nixon on this issue, it would be seen by African Americans as a code word for keeping them in their place, and he would lose many of his most important supporters. Antiwar groups would interpret such a "tough" stance as his commitment to keeping them from protesting the war. Meanwhile, he and his staff could not escape hecklers who frequently drowned out his speeches. Advisers considered using "labor teams" to manhandle the hecklers, but the real issue, as one aide phrased it, was whether amid such chaos Humphrey could even appear to be able to deal with the problem: "People will ask themselves, 'Is this a man who can handle the problem of law and order?'" In the border states particularly, law and order were "the words commonly used to describe reaction against demonstrators and racial unrest," so had become the "dominant issue." Thus, in Kentucky, Nixon was far ahead, Wallace second, and Humphrey falling below 20 percent approval in a longtime Democratic state. Some party members even were asking for Humphrey's resignation so a less isolated politician, perhaps vice presidential candidate Muskie, could run instead.[27]

Not surprisingly, money contributions dried up, especially in California, where the party was badly divided. The vice president hoped to raise millions to buy television time but received hundreds of thousands of dollars instead. Larry O'Brien, the campaign's chief of staff, privately commented that "you can get people to stand up for bows, but nobody is going to stand up for the boos," especially if these people had large bank accounts. Pathetically, Humphrey begged every Democrat who held a meeting anywhere to "take up a collection," no matter how small it might be.[28]

But obviously the problem went far deeper than money. "I feel for you in this," Bill Moyers, Johnson's former press secretary, had writ-

ten Humphrey in midsummer, 1968. "You are on a tightrope. But so
is the country. . . . I think we are on the verge of some kind of national
nervous breakdown."[29] The vice president was in no position to take
political advantage of this challenge. The politics of joy was out of
fashion in the United States of 1968. George Wallace, however, was in
a position to take advantage. He mounted one of the most significant
third-party challenges in American political history.

October 18, 1968, Time *Cover depicting Curtis LeMay and George Wallace*
Getty Images

8

GEORGE WALLACE: THE POPULISM OF THE VIETNAM WAR ERA

As the campaign entered the homestretch on October 1, 1968, Ambassador Sir Patrick Dean closely analyzed the polls and then reported to London that "Nixon has not pulled ahead, but Humphrey has lost support to Wallace," who worried both parties equally. "If the election was held today he [Wallace] could well win more electoral votes than Humphrey, though not enough to deny Nixon the outright victory." Nixon, however, was worried that "these proportions may well change." Clearly, former governor of Alabama George Wallace was mounting the most important third-party challenge in a half century against the Republican and Democratic candidates.

Dean then outlined the issues that were catapulting Wallace into the rare air of American politics. "They are still blurred," Dean reported, but "law and order stand out as an easy first." Regardless of who won the presidency, he concluded, the war and four years of protests and riots had pushed Americans considerably to the right: "Given the attitude of Southern Democrats and the temper of the times, the next President . . . is certain to face as conservative a Congress as any in the last thirty years."[1]

Once again—as in both world wars and the Korean conflict—when Americans found themselves involved in a long overseas military struggle, they reflexively became more conservative, less interested in reform. And if the poorer and marginalized Americans protested loudly against this trend, middle- and upper-class whites only moved farther to the right in their desperate attempts to find order and security against such protests.

George Wallace, even more than Richard Nixon, tried to exploit this search for security so he could scramble the presidential race. Perhaps if he obtained enough electoral votes to deprive any candidate of a majority, he could throw the final decision, as the Constitution provided, into the House of Representatives. Or, perhaps, he could bargain his support, if sufficiently impressive, with the winner to obtain what he wanted: strong curbs on the federal government's right to intervene in the states to end segregation and enforce equal rights laws for minorities. This unjust federal power, as Wallace and many other Americans saw it, arose out of the Supreme Court's historic *Brown v. Board of Education* decision in 1954, which ordered an end to segregated schools and other facilities. The South particularly dragged its heels in enforcing the decision, but then, in 1964, with southerner Lyndon Johnson driving it, Congress passed Title VI of the Civil Rights Act, which provided enforced guidelines to desegregate the schools. If desegregation did not occur, federal funds, on which the states depended, would be cut.

These demands hit a South that continued to undergo more rapid, disorienting change than any part of the country, except possibly the booming West Coast. The civil rights marches that began in the late 1950s and accelerated during the 1960s brought racial warfare to the streets of southern cities. The effects were magnified, moreover, because such urban areas as Atlanta, Memphis, Miami, and Montgomery represented a New South that attracted industry, technology firms, and millions of fresh arrivals to work in the expanding economy (and warm weather). Thus, traditional southerners faced mounting attacks on their way of life: an increasingly organized African American movement that could exercise majority voting power in many areas and a modernization process that was creating a strange, jarring, ever changing world. The white South once had two reasons for feeling safe and secure: superiority over African Americans and a comfortable, or at least predictable, way of life. Both were rapidly disappearing amid a war that was being fought by many southerners (black and white). Other southerners were the targets of protests, sometimes violent protests, by both black and white civil rights advocates.[2]

In his early years, George Corley Wallace seemed an unlikely candidate for leading the fight to roll back the clock. Born in 1919, he worked his way through college and law school, in part by boxing professionally. After serving in the air force during World War II, he rose through the ranks of Alabama politics, then ran for governor in 1958. He lost to a candidate who, Wallace remarked, "out-segged" him— was more antiblack and prosegregationist than the more liberal Wallace. The loser swore never to allow that to happen again. After being elected governor in 1962, he declared in his inaugural address: "I say segregation now, segregation tomorrow, segregation forever!" The next year he became nationally known when federal courts ordered the University of Alabama to admit its first African American students. The governor dramatically, as he put it, "stood in the school house door" to keep the students out. President John Kennedy obeyed the court orders and finally integrated the university by placing the Alabama national guard under his control, then ordering Wallace to move out of the way. The federal government was changing life in Alabama.

Wallace used his new fame, and new causes, to enter Democratic Party primaries in 1964. To the astonishment of politicians who represented President Johnson in the Wisconsin, Indiana, and Maryland races, the newcomer took between 30 and 40 percent of the vote. He did especially well in ethnic, blue-collar labor areas such as Gary, Indiana. A racial backlash was whipping the political mainstream. Unable constitutionally to run again for the governorship in 1966, he substituted his wife, Lurleen, although she had been ill with cancer. She won, and her husband, who was the real governor, again had access to Alabama money and governmental bureaucrats to help him make another try for the presidency in 1968.

As the wars in both Vietnamese and American streets spread, the political situation was even more inviting for Wallace than it had been in 1964. After claiming "there's not a dime's worth of difference" between the two major parties, he announced his candidacy on February 8. He later declared he would run as the candidate of the new American Independent Party, which was, in reality, only Wallace. Again, to the surprise of professional politicians, the candidate and his advisers (nearly all from Alabama) obtained enough signatures in each state so he could run in all fifty. (Only in the District of Columbia, where a majority of the population was African American, did he fail to get on the ballot.) The Alabama contingent gathered up the hundreds of thousands of signatures despite the complex, time-consuming process that the two major parties had devised. Polls soon revealed that Wallace had as much as 12 percent of the national vote and might well win all the southern states. By late summer, his poll numbers had jumped to 20 percent.[3]

In his stump speeches, Wallace said little about the war. He instead focused on the unsettling, often violent effects of the war and the race revolution on American streets. He appealed to deeply rooted anti-intellectualism by blaming the crisis, especially the federal government's new policies, on "pointy-headed intellectual morons," and also on liberals in government "who can't park a bicycle straight." While he entertained increasingly large crowds with such rhetoric, his campaign surprisingly picked up many of Robert Kennedy's white supporters after the liberal senator was assassinated in June. These people were searching for someone who would make radical changes in a "sick . . . country," as one phrased it—more change than either Nixon, Humphrey, or McCarthy promised. Many of these former Kennedy supporters were not racist and, later in the campaign, made a dramatic turn to Humphrey as they understood the race-baiting, antiunion beliefs that Wallace had stood for as governor. But earlier in the summer of America's raging discontent, Wallace rode high, especially after what he called "the mess in Chicago" during the Democratic Convention. The "mess," he thought, "put us in an excellent position to win the election." He praised the Chicago police (who had beaten up a number of the protesters) for their "restraint." The former governor seized the moment to raise millions of dollars for his campaign from wealthy conservatives, including Colonel Sanders of Kentucky Fried Chicken fame, actor John Wayne, and Texas oil billionaire H. L. Hunt.[4]

Wallace's main enemy, then, was not the Vietnam War or Johnson's handling of it, but the federal government's actions to promote racial desegregation. He nevertheless understood that the war loomed over the campaign, especially as increasing numbers of American troops lost their lives. He also understood that he knew (and cared) little about foreign policy. It was necessary to have a vice presidential candidate who did. Initially he had approached A. B. "Happy" Chandler, the former Kentucky governor and major league baseball commissioner. Chandler, however, was discovered to have unsettling, liberal views about race. Among other things, he was the professional baseball commissioner when the Brooklyn Dodgers brought in the first black player, Jackie Robinson, to play in the modern major leagues. Wallace also considered former Governor Marvin Griffin of Georgia, but he was such a white supremacist that advisers finally warned Wallace to disavow him (although in some states Griffin remained on the ballot with Wallace in November). Finally, the former governor decided to remedy his lack of foreign policy expertise by naming General Curtis LeMay as his running mate.[5]

It turned out that Wallace had made a major mistake. LeMay was a gruff, tough, no-nonsense professional air force officer who was not used to the many hidden traps and close scrutiny of American politics. He believed his commands, and indeed his very presence, were to be highly respected, not questioned. Born in 1906 and holding a degree in civil engineering from Ohio State University, LeMay became famous in World War II by devising the plane formation that most effectively destroyed German industrial plants and cities. Before, the planes had flown in zigzag patterns to escape lethal German antiaircraft fire. LeMay ordered them to fly a straight course so the bombing would be more accurate, damn the heavy aircraft fire. He led the first such attack himself. (The general used the same direct approach as a vice presidential candidate, but with different results.) In 1945, he was a decision maker for the two missions that dropped atomic bombs on Japan, and before that had helped devise the massive firebomb attacks that devastated Tokyo and other cities, which sustained greater loss of life than Hiroshima and Nagasaki did from being struck by atomic bombs.

As head of the Strategic Air Command, whose Cold War mission was to nuclearize parts of Russia if conflict broke out, and as air force chief of staff, cigar-chomping LeMay became known for his fervent hatred for communists and his passionate belief in the utility of nuclear weapons. The former air force sergeant, George Wallace, should have known what his new subordinate, General LeMay, was going to say when he met the press as a vice presidential candidate on October 3, 1968.

The first question inquired about his policy for using nuclear weapons. "We seem to have a phobia about nuclear weapons," LeMay began. He personally saw them as "just another weapon in our arsenal." To drive the point home he added, "I think there are many occasions when it would be most efficient to use nuclear weapons." Oh yes, he declared, U.S. and foreign public opinion "throw up their hands in horror when you mention nuclear weapons," but that was "just because of the propaganda that's been fed to them." Nuclear war would be "horrible," he granted, but then continued: "It doesn't make much difference to me if I have to go to war and get killed in the jungle of Vietnam with a rusty knife or get killed with a nuclear weapon. As a matter of fact, if I had the choice, I'd lean toward the nuclear weapon."[6]

At this point, according to some onlookers and at least one photograph, Wallace pulled on the general's sleeve to signal him to sit down. In 1964, the Republican presidential candidate, Senator Barry Goldwater, had been made fun of—and carefully avoided—by voters because he claimed he would like to drop a nuclear bomb in "the Kremlin men's room" in Moscow. Not ignorant of the antiwar protests but profoundly hating them, LeMay seemed intent on repeating Goldwater's error. Only now he was talking not about a hypothetical war with Russia, but an actual conflict engulfing Southeast Asia. And LeMay seemed blithely to be talking about using nuclear weapons once more against Asians, the only people Americans had already used them against—so far.

Before Wallace could pull LeMay away from the microphone, a reporter asked if the general was suggesting the use of nuclear weapons in Vietnam. "No," he replied. "I don't think it's necessary to use nuclear weapons in Vietnam and I've always said that." A few minutes later reporters asked Wallace about the issue. He responded, "General LeMay hasn't advocated the use of nuclear weapons, not at all. . . . He's against the use of nuclear weapons and so am I." But the general apparently did not understand Wallace's frantic signals. A journalist asked whether he'd use nuclear weapons if it were "necessary to end the war." LeMay answered, "If I found it necessary, I would use anything that we could dream up—anything that we could dream up—including nuclear weapons if it was necessary."

The reporters quickly tagged Wallace and LeMay as "The bombsy twins." From this date of October 3 on, Wallace's campaign went into decline. There were many reasons for it, but LeMay's performance was a major contribution. In the press conference and later in the campaign, the general understandably bragged how proud he was that his air force had "integrated colored units before anyone else, and we did it without any problem," in part by fully working with the "good solid-citizen type" of African American who led the way. But the damage had been done.[7]

Richard Nixon was delighted. He had long wanted to seize southern votes by making the Wallace ticket appear radical and dangerous. LeMay had now done it for him. The former vice president wanted to pose as both hawk and dove on Vietnam by positioning himself between Humphrey and Wallace. The middle was usually the best place to be in a U.S. presidential election. The Republican nominee could appear to be tougher than Humphrey (especially after the Minnesotan began to break publicly from Johnson by taking a more peaceful line in his speech at Salt Lake City on September 30) and more moderate than the belligerent Wallace. LeMay had taken care of that problem for Nixon, too.[8]

Wallace quickly got LeMay away from reporters by sending him on a "fact-finding" trip to Vietnam. The trip was not very educational for the general. When he returned, he again spoke his mind and hurt Wallace's cause. LeMay fretted over communists in universities (he provided no names) and damned treaties signed by the Kennedy and Johnson administrations that checked the spread of nuclear weapons and stopped the testing of those weapons in the hemisphere (testing that had produced dangerous amounts of radioactivity). The general then zeroed in on Vietnam: "I don't think that we have to destroy all of North Vietnam" to achieve a satisfactory conclusion to the war, "but I would certainly act like we had the will to do it and start doing it and then let them determine how much damage they want to take." (These words actually mirrored Nixon's belief that he could pose as a "madman" to scare North Vietnam to the peace table, but at least the Republican nominee had the sense to know he could not say such things aloud—not if he hoped to avoid further scaring Americans who were already frightened that their world was rapidly becoming unraveled.)

LeMay added that "a great deal" of U.S. war protest "is stimulated by the Communists, and I think that is a fair statement to make." Whether or not seventeen U.S. senators who had recently asked Johnson to stop the bombing "get theirs [information] from that area [communism] or not, I don't know. I would be doubtful, however, but certainly if you have been privy to a lot of intelligence reports, even F.B.I. documents . . . you know we are under attack by communism in this country." This was a regular LeMay line. Earlier in October he declared he had decided to help Wallace because Nixon, if he won, planned to pack his cabinet with "left-wingers." Again, he did not name any possibilities.[9]

The Nixon and Humphrey camps gleefully berated LeMay for being dangerously irresponsible, then attacked Wallace for his bad judgment in allowing LeMay's musings both to become public and have the authority of a vice presidential candidate behind them. As soon as Wallace had sent the general 10,000 miles away to visit Vietnam, he mostly dropped foreign policy from his speeches while concentrating on the populist law-and-order message that had earlier made him a contender. These views came together in the American Independent Party platform published on October 13. (The platform was supposedly the party's, but the party was actually Wallace, as indicated by the unusual use in the platform of "I," a first-person reference not found in any other major party platform in American history.)

The platform emphasized the need for a greater use of police to enforce law and order. It also attacked federal courts for enforcing federal laws (such as desegregation) in the states and recommended that the appointments of these federal judges, including those on the Supreme Court, be periodically reconsidered by the Senate. Blasting

"minority appeasement" by Washington officials, the platform reiter-
ated a strong stand for states' rights. Then it included an interesting
section updating traditional American populism to the 1960s.

The platform demanded that the mass of Americans be protected
by *greater* federal involvement for improving transportation, remov-
ing urban slums, fighting air and water pollution, devising new health
services, and even expanding space exploration and scientific research. Wallace urged that the government increase social security
benefits no less than 60 percent, and that senior citizens be helped
with their medical expenses beyond the very considerable aid provided by Lyndon Johnson's Great Society programs. The platform also
asked that federal programs rescue the poor through job training and
large public works projects. Washington officials, in other words, were
only to stay out of the issue of race relations. (Unlike the Republican
and Democratic platforms, this one had no civil rights plank.) Otherwise, Wallace, resembling the Populists of the 1880s and 1890s,
wanted the government to provide enormous help for the mass of
Americans.

The platform's foreign policy sections emphasized the need for the
development of weapons that would give the United States not mere
parity with the Soviets, but superiority. LeMay's influence was obvious here, but not in the plank on Vietnam. That section urged an
"honorable conclusion" to the war through "peaceful negotiations." If
the communists remained stubborn, however, they would have to
suffer a "military defeat" in which the control of military tactics
would be left to the military commanders—who must "act pursuant
to defined national policy." The word "nuclear" was nowhere to be
found.[10]

In an earlier interview with newspaper editors, Wallace had fleshed
out his foreign policy views, or what there was of them. He desired a
negotiated peace in Vietnam, but if it did not soon occur he promised
"a military victory" after becoming president. How he would obtain
this "victory" was foggy. He promised that no more large numbers of
troops would be sent and carefully and completely ruled out the use
of nuclear weapons. Perhaps his most interesting comment was that
he knew that "someday" the United States would reopen relations

with Communist China—a relationship that Nixon and Humphrey were also hinting at, to the surprise of observers who saw all three men as ardent anticommunists.[11]

The real red meat of the Wallace campaign appeared on the same October day its platform was published. Speaking to 11,000 in San Francisco, the candidate was interrupted by hecklers. One Wallace supporter shot unidentified gas into the heckling group. A woman broke her umbrella over a protester. "Kill 'em! Kill 'em!" was heard above the din as fights erupted. Police finally restored order.[12]

Such scenes were not unusual when Wallace spoke, especially outside the South, but he used them to drive home his message that the antiwar protests and the "appeasement of minorities" were rapidly ruining the Great American Dream. "Well," he told one crowd, "it's a sad day in the country when you can't talk about law and order" unless you "want to be called a racist. I tell you that's not true and I resent it and they gonna have to pay attention because [for] all the people in this country . . . the great majority, the Supreme Court . . . has made it almost impossible to convict a criminal." To make the point clear, Wallace added: "if a group of anarchists lay down in front of my automobile, it's gonna be the last one they ever gonna want to lay down in front of!"[13]

He similarly became more direct about Vietnam when he was shouting to supporters rather than talking with newspaper editors. "Many fine people" believe "we should not be in Vietnam," he declared in one speech, and that was all right because those "fine people" were loyal to the United States. But "anyone who raises money and clothes and blood for the Vietcong, and college professors, as some have recently done, who stand and tell student bodies that they long for a victory of the Vietcong Communists . . . in the name of academic freedom, I say to you that it is not academic freedom, that's treason." Wallace could be especially shrewd in beginning to discuss foreign policy, about which he cared little, then slide into a domestic issue about which he cared a good deal:

> To those who say we [Wallace's party] don't know anything about foreign policy, let me ask you this: what do the Republicans and Democrats know about it? We've had four wars in the last fifty years. We've spent

$122 billion of our money. We've got less friends than we had when we
started. We could have built an interstate highway system better than
the one we have now with that $122 billion.[14]

Polls revealed that Wallace's supporters were much more reluctant
than Nixon's and Humphrey's to be foreign policy activists. Their interests were largely in their neighborhoods, towns, and states. When
asked whether "this country would be better off if we just stayed
home and didn't concern ourselves with problems in other parts of the
world," 32 percent of Wallace voters agreed, but only 21 percent of
Nixon's and 17 percent of Humphrey's. A large majority, 62 percent,
of Wallace supporters believed the United States should never have
gotten involved in Vietnam, while 61.7 percent of Nixon's and 55 percent of Humphrey's agreed. On the other hand, 67 percent of Wallace's followers were willing to escalate U.S. military power in the war,
while only 40.5 percent of Nixon's supporters and 28 percent of
Humphrey's wanted to do so. This last set of poll results revealed not
only why General LeMay appealed to many Wallaceites, but also
demonstrated the antiwar feeling that was so troubling for
Humphrey's stumbling campaign.[15]

In an interesting analysis of where he believed power really lay in
American society, Wallace warned that the "proper use of police" was
"the only thing left now to try to curtail anarchy in the country." For
this reason, he went on, "whatever suppression that is necessary"
should be used; otherwise "you are going to have a movement that's
not going to be on the left. It's going to be on the other side and it's
going to stop all of this" upheaval that is going on in the streets of
America. Wallace's reference to the possibility of an American fascism
arising to provide the law and order the Johnson administration was
failing to provide was, on one level, a campaign tactic for justifying the
greater use of police power. But on another level, it was a modern
American populist trying to avoid an American fascism that he believed could result from the antiwar protests and civil rights legislation.[16]

Just as Nixon and Humphrey were attempting to do from their political perspectives, Wallace was dealing with Tocqueville's warning
that American democracy, when trapped in a protracted war, could

hand over its liberties to a government in return for some security. No evidence has been found that Wallace ever read Tocqueville, but given his background he did not need to read the famous nineteenth-century French observer of the United States. The governor believed public protests were dangerous because, from his own experience, they disrupted and jeopardized lives, threatened property along with law and order, and could result in a far-right backlash. He claimed he could avert this with a populist program combined with legitimate police power. That in his formulation African Americans would probably have to surrender most of their recent gains and antiwar protesters would have to be quieted (apparently, if need be, even run over) was in his mind an acceptable price to pay.

Nixon and Humphrey also promised law and order, but they wanted to achieve it without paying that kind of price. Throughout September and early October, however, the major party candidates ran while glancing nervously back at Wallace, who seemed to be slowly but surely gaining on them. The Alabaman was playing most effectively to the racial fears and prejudices of white blue-collar workers—the millions whose votes Humphrey had to have for any chance of winning. Many of these members of organized labor, moreover, had sons and daughters in the military. They wanted to win a military victory now that the United States was so heavily involved, bring their children back home, and in the meantime drive the antiwar protesters off the streets.

All this meant that the labor movement was split top from bottom. In September, the leadership of the nation's largest and most powerful union, the AFL-CIO, endorsed Humphrey for the presidency. The leaders were in part paying back the Democrat for his lifelong support of their interests. Nevertheless, the rank and file seemed to be moving toward Wallace. One poll revealed that one of every six Wallace supporters in the North, and two of every five in the South, belonged to unions. With labor's help, the *New York Times* reported, Wallace could accurately call himself a national candidate, "not because he has abandoned the attitudes of the South but because the rest of the country more and more embraces" his southern values.[17]

An example of Wallace's appeal to labor occurred in mid-October in the Cleveland suburb of Norwood. It was a town of well-maintained small houses populated by ethnic groups who worked in Cleveland's steel and auto plants, then returned home to social lives that usually involved their Roman Catholic faith. On Norwood's southern boundary was an African American district. As muggings, break-ins, and even killings rose in the Cleveland area, Norwood held a town meeting. One woman asked what she should have done when men tried to enter her home. The crowd yelled, "Shoot them! Shoot them!" When it was revealed that a black militant group had built offices close by, there were cries, "Burn it down!" In previous elections, Norwood had voted as much as 90 percent Democratic. Now many women were moving toward Wallace. Others said they preferred him but would vote for Nixon because, as one declared, "if I don't Humphrey will win." Few considered Wallace too extreme. National polls showed that 46 percent of Wallace voters believed whites had the right to keep African Americans out of their neighborhoods, while 22.5 percent of Nixon's supporters and 13 percent of Humphrey's agreed.[18]

Humphrey thus had no problem understanding why Wallace threatened to take these votes away from him. He further knew that the war was part of those reasons. "The blue-collar worker, the lower middle income white feels that the government has no interest in him," the vice president privately wrote a close friend. "They feel the Great Society programs are only oriented to the black man and the poorest of the poor." This "backbone of the Democratic vote is leaving us in droves" because the common worker "just feels that everybody in government has forgotten him. Yet he pays his taxes and his kids fight the war." Democratic union support, one analysis concluded, had been 57 percent Democratic in the 1940s, but now had dropped to 42 percent, with the "defections . . . very largely to Wallace."[19]

In October, as the campaign entered its final weeks, frightened labor leaders, helped along by a last-ditch effort of the Humphrey camp, unleashed a mammoth information offensive to warn union members about Wallace's record. He might sound like a populist on many issues, and his views of civil rights and antiwar demonstrators might coincide with their own, the leaders noted. But his record in Alabama, millions of pamphlets claimed, was strongly antilabor. Alabama "is a low-wage" antiunion state, one pamphlet charged. "Wallace's election will cut your pay $1,000 a year." This information blitz seemed to begin moving rank-and-file laborers toward Humphrey by mid-October. But time was running out for the Democrats.[20]

Nixon also began to target Wallace. The Republican planned to win by taking three or four of the eight most populous and industrialized states (New York, Pennsylvania, New Jersey, Ohio, Michigan, Illinois, Texas, and California). In his 1960 loss, he had won only two of them. But he also needed the New South, the urban areas of Tennessee, Kentucky, Virginia, Florida, the Carolinas, and Georgia. Wallace threatened Nixon in both regions by appealing to laborers in the North and to those who agreed with his antiblack views in the South. In both areas, moreover, Wallace's emphasis on enforcing law and order, forcefully putting down antiwar protests, and prohibiting civil rights demonstrations attracted support. Polls indicated that Wallace supporters in a South that had long voted solidly Democratic now, in the New South, preferred Nixon over Humphrey.[21]

Nixon therefore did not attack Wallace too strongly. He wanted to avoid alienating the former governor's supporters. The Republican nominee instead observed that while Wallace had some interesting ideas, he lacked experience on the national level, especially in foreign affairs. Here LeMay became a useful target for both Nixon and Humphrey. The Republican meanwhile played to southern feelings by parading his supporters from the region, led by Senator Strom Thurmond of South Carolina. The Supreme Court decision banning segregation was correct, Nixon told a southern television audience, but the Johnson–Humphrey administration was wrong in keeping federal funds away from school districts that were slow to desegregate. Nixon thus upheld law and order, while telling southerners (and many northerners) what they wanted to hear about the unjust role of the federal government. In the blue-collar automobile industry town of Flint, Michigan, Nixon posed the challenge to Wallace's supporters that Humphrey was asking as well: "Do you want to get something off your chest or do you want to get something done?"[22] (Translated: do you want to feel good by voting for Wallace, or do you want to get the liberal, soft-on-crime Democrats out of the White House by voting for me?)

Mid-October polls showed that the attacks launched by Nixon, Humphrey, and the labor leaders were working. Wallace's support began to slide. But Nixon's position hardly moved. In the last days of the campaign, Humphrey was suddenly rising from the political dead to run neck and neck with the Republican. In the final weekend, the vice president actually surged ahead in some polls. Then, once more, the Vietnam War reshaped American history.[23]

President Lyndon B. Johnson speaks with President Nguyen Van Thieu in Hawaii, July 19, 1968
Photo by Yoichi R. Okamoto, Courtesy of the LBJ Library and Museum

9

NGUYEN VAN THIEU:
A MERRY-GO-ROUND IN
A CHAMBER OF HORRORS

The 1968 campaign spun itself out through the late summer and early autumn with the bloodshed in Vietnam often in the headlines, but usually occupying only the background of increasingly hot political debates in the United States. The front-runner, Richard Nixon, refused to discuss the war in any detail. He was ahead and, as he well knew, taking a direct stand on the conflict could splinter his supporters. On the other hand, coming down hard on the need for law and order could only add votes from frightened undecided voters and even rank-and-file Democrats. George Wallace did not want to discuss the war because he cared little about it, compared with his campaign cries blasting crime, antiwar protesters, and civil rights marchers. If he mentioned the bloodshed, moreover, it might only remind voters of the extreme, sometimes loony, statements made by his vice presidential running mate, General Curtis LeMay. Hubert Humphrey could not discuss the war except within the narrow confines set by the Johnson administration in which he had served as vice president. Lyndon Johnson would see to that.

By late September, therefore, the national debate on the one issue that was ending hundreds of American lives each week was arid. Antiwar protests continued. Humphrey encountered hecklers at his public appearances. Through the first half of the campaign, however, most Americans seemed to feel that they were helpless to change a complex, fourteen-year, U.S. commitment 10,000 miles away. They instead sought the candidate who seemed best prepared to make streets safe for their children. The war's lack of progress reinforced such feelings. Through the summer and fall it seemed to offer only more of the same: more fighting, more false starts for any negotiations in Paris, more excuses and misrepresentations from Washington officials, more dead, more soldiers returning to California hospitals terribly maimed in both body and mind from fighting in dense, booby-trapped Vietnamese villages and jungles.

Americans were on an out-of-control merry-go-round in a chamber of horrors. And no one knew how to push the "off" switch and find the exit. The hopes raised by Johnson's March 31 speech, when he dropped out of the race and offered to stop much of the bombing in order to open peace talks, fell to the ground like a pin-pricked balloon.

The pins in this case were two. The first was Johnson's demand that in return for a halt to the bombing, the North Vietnamese would not try to take advantage of the U.S. pullback, especially in the sensitive demilitarized zone that separated North and South Vietnam, or in the cities that had been hit by the January Tet offensive. The communists showed little interest in weakening themselves by meeting this demand. The second pinprick came from the North Vietnamese. They demanded that their southern arm, the NLF, have a separate place at the peace table and not be included as part of the North's delegation to Paris. This demand presented major problems. The NLF occupied a strong position in the South, notably in the countryside, but it also depended on its communist colleagues in the North for vital support.

Of special importance, if the U.S.-backed South Vietnamese government of Nguyen Van Thieu accepted the NLF as an equal at the peace table, Thieu would at that very moment have compromised his own control over—and legitimacy in—South Vietnam. No regime in Saigon could recognize the NLF as an independent entity unless it wanted to end up committing political suicide—or unless the United States could somehow greatly weaken the NLF while greatly strengthening the South Vietnamese government. For nearly a decade no one in Washington or Saigon had been able to figure out how to do that.

Thus, President Thieu saw NLF representation at Paris as literally a life-or-death issue for his country and probably for himself. It would be Thieu, even more than the North Vietnamese communist leader, Ho Chi Minh, who at critical moments in the 1968 peace discussions threw ice water on the proceedings and—according to some observers—lost the U.S. presidency for Hubert Humphrey. Thieu was no amateur. He had been involved in Vietnamese politics and military affairs for decades, although not usually on the winning side.

Thieu was forty-five years old in 1968, young for a politician in a country whose people venerated age and experience (both of which the 78-year-old Ho Chi Minh had in abundance). Thieu's two brothers had escaped from their small village to enter politics and one, who worked for the French colonial rulers, helped educate Thieu politically. Thieu later claimed that in 1945 he joined Ho Chi Minh and the nationalist resistance against the French (who were trying to reimpose their colonial control), but declared he left when he discovered Ho's group was communist controlled. He instead entered the military, studied under French instructors, and in 1957 attended an officer training course in the U.S. Army school at Fort Leavenworth, Kansas. After the Kansas experience, he spoke English well, a talent that considerably increased his popularity with the monolingual U.S. administrators and journalists in Vietnam. But he had picked the wrong side: Ho and his fellow nationalists drove the French out of Vietnam in 1954. Thieu then joined the Americans who, by the late 1950s, were at war with Ho's forces.[1]

One of Thieu's battlefield experiences was revealing. In 1953, while an officer with the French, he found himself fighting around his home village. The enemy nationalist forces had set up headquarters in his family's house. They believed Thieu would not attack it. He directed mortar and artillery fire on the entire neighborhood until Ho's forces retreated. Observers were struck by Thieu's act, especially since Vietnamese honored their home villages. He seemed, moreover, especially soft-spoken and indirect. One close associate complained, "I like Thieu, but sometimes he talks to me for an hour, and I don't know what he has said." U.S. officials would later utter the same complaint. But they, especially Johnson and Humphrey, learned that—as he had demonstrated in his family's village—he could be ruthlessly decisive if his own position depended on it.[2]

In the early 1960s, Thieu joined the U.S.-supported Ngo Dinh Diem regime by becoming commander of an army division. Of special note, he converted from Buddhism (the religion of 90 percent of Vietnamese) to Roman Catholicism (Diem's religion). The conversion was once again a poor political decision. Thieu soon realized that Diem's regime was losing control of the war and falling out of grace with the United States. Rescuing himself once more, Thieu joined army officers who (with U.S. approval) overthrew Diem in October 1963. Colonel Thieu soon became General Thieu. The new military leaders, however, failed to stabilize South Vietnam in 1964–1965 (a major reason why President Johnson believed he had to escalate the number of U.S. troops so dramatically at that time).

In mid-1965, the revolving door of South Vietnam's military politics finally brought Thieu to power, along with a fellow military officer, Nguyen Cao Ky. A dashing air force officer, Ky was known to admire beautiful women and, more unfortunately, the social order of Hitler's Germany. Under these Young Turks of the military, the political situation seemed to stabilize, especially after Johnson committed a half million troops to support the Thieu-Ky regime. In September 1967, the two men guided South Vietnam from a military government to a constitutional republic, at least in form, to meet repeated demands from the Johnson administration that something be done to make the country's government more acceptable to American critics. In a series of moves that left Ky stunned, the older and more senior Thieu, with the support of key officers in the powerful Armed Forces Council, assumed the presidency while allowing the much weakened Ky to be vice president. Johnson and Secretary of State Dean Rusk happily pointed to the new "republic" and the elections that put Thieu into the presidency, as well as the setting up of a two-house legislature, as triumphs of American democratic ideals.

In reality, the elections were corrupt and manipulated by Thieu's group. The president instituted land reforms to win back villagers who were moving under communist control. He also removed some corrupt officials, which meant little but pleased Americans. Corruption was eating away at all levels of South Vietnam's political and military structures. Army officers bought commands for $10,000, while provincial chiefs paid as much as $100 for power. Thieu's military numbered 700,000 troops, plus 70,000 police, but many existed merely on paper so officials could take the salary owed to these ghost recruits and put it in their own bank accounts. Key divisions were woefully undermanned and suffered from too little modern equipment. The unit most observers had considered the best fighting force, the First Division, was one of the notable victims of the embarrassing Tet offensive. Meanwhile, Thieu cracked down on dissent, stopped local elections he could not control, and began to shift U.S. aid into his personal bank account. Above all, however, as even Prime Minister Tran Van Huong admitted, corruption was "the national cancer."[3]

It was the weakness and corruption of his military forces and his own regime that forced Thieu to an important conclusion: he could never allow the communists of the stronger NLF to have an equal place with him at the peace table. The communists were better organized, more aggressive militarily, and in control of much of the countryside, where they were brutally effective against opposition. Any peace settlement that recognized the NLF's legitimacy in the South, even by giving the communists a separate seat at the table, would force Thieu into a political and military struggle he probably could not win—especially since the United States might well use any settlement as an excuse to pull out of Vietnam immediately.

Thus, Johnson's sudden announcement on March 31 that he was dropping out of the presidential race in order to seek peace hit Thieu and Ky like a bolt of lightning. They wanted no part of talks in Paris, where things might get out of hand as the Americans searched for a way out of the war. Any possible coalition with the NLF, they insisted, in the words of one reporter, "would take place, literally, over their dead bodies." Nor did the two Vietnamese leaders want any part of the Robert Kennedy and Eugene McCarthy candidacies that surged to the forefront after Johnson withdrew. The South Vietnamese believed Kennedy the more dangerous, not only because he had a greater chance of winning, but because he seemed not to want to understand the stakes in Vietnam and instead emphasized the overwhelming needs of American minorities and the poor. Thieu's determination only grew in May 1968 when the communist attempt to launch a variation of the earlier Tet offensive fizzled. Another expected offensive by the North and the NLF in August never occurred. That month, Thieu repeated his assertion that "we will never agree to talk to the front [The NLF]. We are willing to talk to Hanoi," he added, but "I would never accept any Communist to run in an election in Vietnam."[4]

As the pressure for peace built in the spring of 1968, the military situation changed little except for the increased number of those killed. Thieu attempted to whipsaw the Americans. In early April he stunned them by declaring they could begin withdrawing from Vietnam by the end of the year. South Vietnam, he claimed, was effectively mobilizing large numbers of its own men to fight. In other words, he seemed to be saying, if the Americans were going to force an unwelcome peace on his government, they could leave. "We're surprised by this," a top U.S. military officer said, "very surprised." It was not what the Americans expected: if they withdrew, U.S. officials feared, the South could fall in a short time. Thieu then backtracked. Having gotten Washington's full attention, he said such a withdrawal would occur only if the United States requested it—and if the Americans did, he warned, "They are avoiding their responsibility. . . . They are deserting the free world." U.S. officials might play with peace terms and contemplate withdrawal, Thieu said sadly and with effect, but "so far as the Vietnamese people are concerned, we are determined to stay, since we have no place to go." Thieu hit all the chords to try to shame, if he could not convince, Americans to his point of view that South Vietnam could not survive peace negotiations, especially if Washington recognized the NLF as a legitimate participant.[5]

In late June 1968, U.S. and North Vietnamese officials held secret talks (just as the fearful Thieu suspected). The Americans made a move. If the North would simply indicate the steps it would take when the bombing stopped (and, the U.S. side emphasized, this could be merely a signal, nothing put down on paper), Johnson would halt the bombing and pretend it was being done unilaterally. But the North Vietnamese again did little, so Johnson again dug in his cowboy boots in what he saw as a test of will with Ho Chi Minh: a Texan versus a North Vietnamese communist.

By late July, the president was back to telling aides he wanted to "knock the hell" out of North Vietnam. The Americans, nevertheless, were also taking initiatives to find some way to begin the peace talks, even if their search might go too far for Thieu and not far enough for Ho. At a Honolulu summit conference in July, Thieu again surprised the Americans by raising the stakes. He asked LBJ to pledge that the bombing would not stop (in other words, that the peace talks would not start). Secretary of Defense Clark Clifford's fears were now confirmed. He had told Johnson that Thieu did not want the war to end because of the protection provided by U.S. troops and the "golden flow of money" from Washington.[6]

This apparent stalemate, the riots on Chicago streets during the Democratic Party convention, and LBJ's insistence that the vice president walk the narrow line of the president's policies—all helped condemn Humphrey to the distressing possibility that in November he would finish behind not only Nixon but even Wallace. In late September, however, George Ball, the undersecretary of state who had repeatedly questioned Johnson's decisions to escalate in 1965 and was now the U.S. ambassador to the United Nations (UN), had a conversation with the president that led Ball to resign his UN post. LBJ was fed up with the North Vietnamese refusal to negotiate. "I am not," the angry president told Ball, "hell-bent on agreement." Angry and frustrated with Johnson's stubbornness, Ball left the UN to work for Humphrey, whom he had already been quietly helping.[7]

Trailing twenty points in the polls, Humphrey would have to walk a very high, very thin wire: do something drastic to show he wanted peace in Vietnam, but do nothing so dramatic that he would further anger Johnson. The vice president, however, was reaching his limits with LBJ. According to Humphrey's personal physician, who was with him at the time, in late September the president suddenly summoned Humphrey, alone, to the White House. He came out livid. Johnson had accused him of leaking meaningless information (and nothing that involved Vietnam) to a reporter. Johnson, who went berserk whenever he read leaked information in newspapers, now unjustly blamed Humphrey. "Do you know what he had the nerve to say to me, after all the insults I've taken from him the last four years?" he asked his doctor. "He said that if I didn't watch my p's and q's, he'd see to it personally that I lost Texas [on

election day]. . . . He said he'd dry up every Democratic dollar from
Maine to California—as if he hasn't already." The vice president added,
"I had trouble holding back, but I wasn't going to come down to that bas-
tard's level. I didn't answer . . . I just turned around and walked out."[8]

With his poll numbers and relationship with Johnson at rock bottom, Humphrey began to separate himself from LBJ on the war. Taking advantage of Ball's help, and pushed by many friends who warned
he could save his political life only by moving out from Johnson's
shadow, Humphrey struck a new tone in a speech on September 30 at
Salt Lake City: "As president, I would stop the bombing of the North
as an acceptable risk for peace." These words, however, were carefully
covered by another phrase: "Now if the government of North Vietnam
were to show bad faith, I would reserve the right to resume the bombing." This condition was lost in the front-page stories of Humphrey's
supposed new policy. He carefully said nothing about including the
NLF in the talks. Nor did he provide a list of specifics he would demand from the North. As Secretary of Defense Clifford recalled, the
speech differed little from the official U.S. negotiating position. But
the tone sent a signal that Humphrey was separating himself from
LBJ. Before the speech was given, Ball read the crucial words over the
phone to Johnson. The president replied he assumed Ball would tell
the press the words did not mean Humphrey was departing from
White House policies. "I'm sorry, Mr. President," Ball responded,
"but that's not quite the name of the game."[9]

The Salt Lake City speech, mild as it was, seemed to free
Humphrey from both Johnson's apparent dead-end policy and the
Texan himself. The next day in Nashville, the Minnesotan noticed
signs that said in so many words, "If you mean it, we're with you." He
also endured much less heckling that day. Significant amounts of
money began to flow into Humphrey headquarters for the first time.
Democrats could now begin to plan to attack Nixon with a major television campaign in the last two weeks before the election. (One of
the Democrats' often repeated television spots was only ten seconds
long: "Nixon has not won an election on his own in sixteen years. Let's
keep a good thing going.") Protesters at Humphrey speeches dropped
in number. At a Boston rally one person held a sign reading, "Former
Heckler for Humphrey." Democrats who had looked for an excuse to

return to their political home had finally found one. It was not much, but it was more than Nixon or Wallace offered. A powerful Democratic organization, Americans for Democratic Action (ADA), had earlier favored McCarthy for the nomination, then remained silent after Humphrey became the candidate at Chicago. Now the ADA came out for the vice president.[10]

Even Richard Nixon had to respond. He would not debate Humphrey and Wallace on national television, as Democrats demanded. Nixon's unfortunate experience debating John Kennedy in the 1960 campaign made him determined not to appear again on the medium unless he could control the questions and the surroundings. In any case, as front-runner, he had little to gain and much to lose in a public debate. As the buzz grew over Humphrey's words, however, Nixon had to say something about Vietnam. It was lame: he accused the vice president of "pulling the rug out from under our negotiations" in Paris because the bombing was "the only trump card" the U.S. negotiators held. Humphrey and Ball, however, anticipated such criticism. They had talked with the U.S. negotiators who had no objection to the speech.[11]

Earlier in September, Nixon had taunted Humphrey by declaring the vice president "has not disagreed with one policy" of Lyndon Johnson's. Now Humphrey had slightly separated himself, began to rise in the polls, and collected $300,000 in contributions over the next two weeks. A law-and-order speech brought in another $300,000. The vice president picked up ten points in the polls. "People don't give money to losers," one happy Democratic adviser concluded.[12]

Nixon stuck with promising to "de-Americanize" the war (as the Republican platform had phrased it) through a secret plan he refused to reveal. Humphrey meanwhile grew increasingly specific: "I would stop the bombing," he declared on October 9, "as Hanoi shows good faith," and would then push for a "cease-fire, for de-Americanizing the war and for free elections in South Vietnam with all the factors participating." Later in California he went farther: if there were no peace by the time he became president in January, he would meet with Thieu to plan a "systematic reduction of the American forces." Such words set off alarm bells in Saigon. Thieu later recalled he had concluded that Humphrey's victory "would mean a coalition government in six months" that would effectively put the communists in charge. "With Nixon at least there was a chance," Thieu and Ky believed, for them to survive.[13]

On October 11, 1968, with the presidential election just three weeks away, events began to rush to a climax. North Vietnamese officials had been insisting they would only negotiate with Americans, and never with Thieu's government. But it became apparent that the Soviets, on whom the North Vietnamese depended heavily for aid, were pushing them to negotiate as long as the bombing stopped. Moscow officials, it seemed, wanted Humphrey, not Nixon, to be president. The North Vietnamese secretly asked whether Johnson would halt the bombing if they agreed to negotiate with Thieu as well. The next day, October 12, U.S. ambassador to South Vietnam Ellsworth Bunker secretly told Washington he believed Thieu would agree to stop the bombing on four conditions: if "serious talks" followed, if Thieu's government fully participated, if the demilitarized zone between North and South Vietnam was respected by the communists, and if the North's shelling of the South's cities stopped. Or, at least, Bunker believed he had obtained Thieu's agreement to these terms after he and other U.S. officials exerted enormous pressure—in English—in a 190-minute meeting with the South Vietnamese President. On October 17, Thieu came back with specific objections. He underlined his old horror that the NLF might end up as a separate participant in the talks. Johnson and Rusk nevertheless believed they and Bunker could manage (i.e., silence) Thieu.[14]

On October 25, Humphrey's advisers concluded their candidate's sudden "upswing" was "very dramatic," and that "the smart money is now coming in." On October 27 in the secret Paris talks, the communists and Americans finally agreed that Johnson would announce a bombing halt and then formal negotiations would begin on November 2, just before the election. Several days later after the Paris agreement, Eugene McCarthy finally overcame his own ego as well as his disdain for Humphrey and Johnson to endorse the vice president, albeit with a notable lack of enthusiasm.

On Thursday, October 31, Johnson went on television to announce dramatically that the bombing would stop and talks would begin one day after the election. He demanded no preconditions from the communists. Privately, U.S. officials thought they had reached agreement that North Vietnam would stop attacking the demilitarized zone and the South's cities. The president added that Thieu's government was "free to participate" in the talks—wording that indicated Washington might not be fully certain what Thieu might do. The last weekend before the election, polls showed Nixon and Humphrey neck and neck. One survey even concluded that the Democrat had done the miraculous: he was slightly ahead.[15]

Thieu then played his final card to ensure that Richard Nixon would become president. On October 31, Ambassador Bunker told Thieu about the content of Johnson's speech. The South Vietnamese president concluded he was being pressured to enter talks, probably directly with the NLF. He wanted no part of them. Bunker reported that Thieu responded emotionally and with some confusion. "You are powerful," Thieu lectured the U.S. ambassador. "You can say to small nations what you want . . . but you cannot force us to do anything against our interests. This negotiation is not a life and death matter for the US, but it is for Vietnam."[16]

Johnson began to back down. On the eve of the election word came out of the White House that the Paris talks had to be delayed. Some days before, on October 25, Nixon had issued a statement alleging that Johnson possessed evil motives for announcing at this particular time the opening of peace talks—but then coolly blamed others for actually saying such things and thinking so badly of the president. The Republican candidate declared he had "been advised" that "top officials in the administration" were driving hard for an agreement. "I am also told," he added, that this "spurt of activity is a cynical, last-minute attempt by President Johnson to salvage the candidacy of Mr. Humphrey. This," Nixon then neatly added after making the accusation public, "I do not believe." Johnson went ballistic when he heard this charge, then blasted Nixon for making "ugly and unfair" accusations. Moreover, LBJ recalled, he had carefully told all three major presidential candidates on October 16 that a bombing halt might occur, and that its timing would not be dictated by the election campaign. Nixon then announced he wanted to make it "clear that I did not share the views of those that thought the President would use these negotiations politically."[17]

Obviously Nixon was lying. If he had not been deeply suspicious of
the timing of the administration's announcements, he would not have
been human. On November 1, the South Vietnamese declared they
were not yet willing to go to Paris. The president publicly backed
down. Nixon's charges, indirect as they were, appeared to be true:
Johnson had been caught trying unfairly to put a last-minute charge
into his vice president's campaign. It is not clear why the president
wanted to attempt this late peace initiative, when throughout 1968 he
had indicated greater confidence that Nixon, not Humphrey, would
carry on his Vietnam policies. Perhaps he finally had enough of Nixon,
that "chronic campaigner," as LBJ labeled the Republican in 1966. Or
perhaps he was impressed by Humphrey's surge in the final days and
decided to help a possible winner. Or perhaps, as Johnson later
claimed, the timing of the announcement had little to do with the
election and much to do with the changing North Vietnamese position. Whatever his reasons, he had decided that Humphrey was
preferable to Nixon, and he had further decided "that if we could
make a substantial move toward peace in Vietnam," Humphrey "could
overcome all other obstacles."[18]

What is clear is that Johnson pushed aside his promise in his March
31 speech that he intended to concentrate on obtaining peace and
would not distract himself with political campaigns. Just two days before Americans went to the polls, Johnson stood beside Humphrey at
a large rally in the Houston Astrodome and called for his election. It
was the first time the president had so resoundingly endorsed his vice
president in public. Perhaps an early endorsement by LBJ would not
have helped with the average voter (given his own personal unpopu-
larity), but he could have helped Humphrey immeasurably by pushing Democratic organizations to support the candidate and by tapping
the spigots of money the president could turn on. While terming
Humphrey a "healer and builder" who brought people together, LBJ
told the large throng in the Astrodome that his vice president was not
a candidate who would use "clever campaign tactics of concealment
and evasion."

This last comment was, of course, an attack on Nixon, but only Johnson, Humphrey, Nixon, and relatively few others knew why the furious president used these precise words. During the previous several

weeks, Johnson had learned from illegal wiretaps set by U.S. intelligence officials that Anna Chennault was telling President Thieu to drag his feet on the Paris peace talks. If Nixon won, she told Thieu, he would do much more to protect the South Vietnamese regime than would Johnson or, especially, Humphrey. Thieu, for good reasons of his own, took Madame Chennault's advice. She had been closely working with, and communicating to Thieu through, the South Vietnamese ambassador to the United States, Bui Diem. Thus, she was not the average citizen.

Born in China and wed to a World War II hero, General Claire Chennault, who had helped defend precommunist China with his fabled Flying Tiger air squadron, Madame Chennault became a major political player after moving to the United States. She was active in the famous (or, as many had it, infamous) China Lobby that worked in Washington to help the exiled Nationalist Chinese government on Taiwan, while doing everything possible to keep the United States at odds with communist China. She raised so much money for Nixon and other Republicans that she became vice chair of the Republican National Finance Committee, and chair of the Republican Women for Nixon. Madame Chennault was determined not only to elect Nixon but to isolate and defeat North Vietnam, which received vital aid from communist China. Her attempts to kill the Paris peace talks by convincing Thieu not to attend were known by Johnson, who termed them treasonous.

He indirectly let Nixon know he knew about Madame Chennault ("Little Flower," as the president's advisers began to call her) and her chicanery. The Republican nominee predictably denied that he had any knowledge of her attempts to back-stab the peace talks. Johnson believed Nixon was lying, and later evidence indicated the president was correct. LBJ now regarded Nixon as even less honest and trustworthy than he had in 1966. But he could do little because the evidence had been gathered through FBI and CIA wiretaps, some of which were doubtfully legal, others based on espionage gathered about the innermost secrets of Johnson's supposed ally, South Vietnam. LBJ concluded he could not make the evidence public without damaging the reputation of the presidency. He did, however, turn some of the material over to Humphrey. The vice president decided to do nothing with it, in part because Nixon was fervently denying any personal role in Chennault's operation. Humphrey's refusal probably further convinced Johnson that his vice president lacked the primitive instinct for the jugular vein necessary in a politician who was reaching for the nation's highest office.[19]

Secretary of Defense Clifford later flatly stated that Nixon's assurance to President Thieu that a Republican president would better protect South Vietnam—an assurance secretly conveyed by "Little Flower"—was "probably decisive" in leading Thieu to undermine Johnson's attempts to start the peace talks. Certainly Ambassador Averell Harriman, who had painstakingly set up the Paris negotiations—and who, unlike the president, enthusiastically supported Humphrey—was furious at the Republican and the South Vietnamese double-dealing. Damning Thieu's "ridiculous performance," the crusty, experienced Harriman urged LBJ to go ahead without South Vietnam. Clifford privately and angrily pointed out that Americans were dying while it seemed a few South Vietnamese were making the real decisions. But Thieu and Madame Chennault were only part of the undercover conspiracy against Humphrey. Harvard Professor Henry Kissinger, enjoying close ties to U.S. officials in both Washington and Paris, passed privileged information on to the Nixon camp about American policy. One motive for this double-dealing was Kissinger's lusting after a top job in a future Nixon administration. Historian George Herring correctly calls the Harvard professor's operation "one of the more sordid episodes in recent political history."[20]

Ironically, the Paris talks probably would not have made much progress even (perhaps especially) if Thieu had joined them. The North Vietnamese, encouraged by Communist China, which wanted the United States to be dragged down in a long, costly war (with little cost to the Chinese), had no interest in any compromise acceptable to the United States. It would take five years, not mere months, before such a deal could be worked out by Nixon and his national security adviser, Henry Kissinger. The immediate effect of the various Chennault-Nixon-Kissinger-Thieu operations, however, was felt on election day.

Embarrassingly, apparently hopelessly, behind just weeks before, Humphrey finally lost by less than a million votes out of 72 million cast. The Republican candidate received 30.7 million votes, or 43.4

percent of the ballots; the Democrat 30.5 million or 42.7 percent; and Wallace 9.5 million or 13.5 percent. Humphrey lost more decisively in the Electoral College, 301 to 191, while Wallace's 10 million votes garnered 46 electoral votes, all from states in the Deep South. To measure how far the Democrats had fallen during four years of war and riots, observers noted that Johnson won in 1964 with 45 million votes, or 61 percent, while taking 44 states and 486 electoral votes.[21]

The Vietnam War, including the abortive last-minute peace talks attempt, was part of the reason for Nixon's win. Johnson himself realized, however, there was another major cause for Humphrey's defeat: "The average voter thought we had pushed too far and too fast in social reform," while "the blue collar worker felt that the Democratic party had traded his welfare for the welfare of the black man"—who in turn "began demanding his rightful share of the American promise faster than most of the nation was willing to let him have it."[22] This mixture of political, social, and economic dynamite finally exploded on American streets, in the assassination of revered (and hated) leaders, and during a Democratic political campaign whose candidate and his advisers could not figure out how to deal with the explosions without attacking the administration in which that candidate served as vice president.

The war, then, did not form the single influence shaping the 1968 election—an election that, as can be seen in retrospect, transformed the American political landscape for more than a generation. But the conflict 10,000 miles away did come home to play a major part in all the forces that shaped both the election results and the America that emerged, amid blood and riots, from the crucible of 1968.

CONCLUSION

In early 2003, as the George W. Bush administration prepared the United States to go to war against Iraq, Adam Hochschild, an author of important work on colonialism in Africa, warned that Americans should be most careful about questioning Bush's public reasons for entering battle. "Unlike the earlier generations stampeded into war by *The Maine* [in 1898] and the Gulf of Tonkin [in 1964] incidents, we'd be better off detecting such lies when they are made instead of years later."[1]

The Gulf of Tonkin resolution, which Congress overwhelmingly passed to give President Lyndon Johnson too much authority to wage war against North Vietnam, was indeed based on misleading information that tragically short-circuited congressional debate. It was, however, only part of the fundamental problem in the 1960s and later: the Johnson administration's (and the American people's) belief that a supposedly deadly communist threat in Vietnam could only be dealt with through an escalation of U.S. military force.

It turned out by 1968 that these beliefs were wrong. Vietnam posed no deadly threat to the United States. The North Vietnamese and many in the South fought the U.S. military presence not because they planned to make the world (or even Southeast Asia) communist, but because they were nationalists who had fought foreign invaders for more than a thousand years. Military force could not ultimately accomplish the goals U.S. presidents from Truman to Johnson had sought to reach—especially since those goals often turned out to be confused and contradictory. (For example, if, as they said, Vietnam posed such a serious danger, why did not these presidents mobilize American society, including a full-scale military draft as in World War II, instead of trying to wage war on the cheap?)

By 1968, it was clear that Americans had been lied to and misled by their government in 1964, even while their sons and daughters died in a war U.S. officials could not convincingly explain. In 1964, however, most people in the United States had believed Johnson. Many of them paid for that faith with their lives or the lives of loved ones. By 1968, the nation was sharply divided among those who continued to support the president, those who searched for a face-saving way out of Vietnam, and those who—having given up working within the system—resorted to rioting and/or a countercultural lifestyle often fueled with drugs. These divisions over the war were sharpened, indeed taken to new, unanticipated, and often violent levels, by the civil rights movement and the reaction to it. Martin Luther King and Robert Kennedy represented the growing belief that justice, equality, and equal opportunity for all could not be achieved at home until the war in Vietnam—with its $30 billion of expenditures, its corruption of the U.S. faith in government, and its bloodshed that too easily transferred to American streets—was ended.

The United States has never made its society more equal and just while fighting a war. Nearly 140 years before, Alexis de Tocqueville, in his *Democracy in America*, had arrived from France, closely examined U.S. democracy, and, as noted at the beginning of this book, warned that Americans could lose their much-loved personal freedoms not to a Caesar (i.e., to a military officer who would seize power), but gradually, inevitably to their quest for security. They might, Tocqueville feared, so easily—and patriotically—turn to their government for protection that the government would gladly promise protection in return for the people entrusting their legal rights and personal freedoms to the government. An American founder, Alexander Hamilton, in 1788 had anticipated Tocqueville when he issued a similar warning in the eighth paper of that American political bible, *The Federalist*:

> Safety from external danger is the most powerful director of national conduct. Even the ardent love of liberty will, after a time, give way to its dictates. The violent destruction of life and property incident to war . . . will compel nations the most attached to liberty to resort . . . to institutions, which have a tendency to destroy their civil and political rights. To be more safe they, at length, become willing to run the risk of being less free.

It did not happen in the 1960s, however, exactly as Tocqueville and Hamilton had prophesied. Instead of quietly accepting the U.S. government's explanation for waging war and then trusting Washington with their security, Americans—led by journalists and, above all, those voluntary associations (such as teach-ins, church groups, and antiwar societies that had informed themselves about the conflict)—demanded fuller and more accurate explanations from U.S. officials.

Having noticed these types of voluntary associations in the 1830s, Tocqueville had praised them as peculiar (he had never seen such groups on this scale in Europe), but quickly understood they amounted to an all-important strength in American society. Here he was again prophetic. For in the mid-1960s these voluntary groups worked in both the antiwar and the civil rights movements to question, fundamentally, governmental explanations and policies Americans had long taken for granted. Then, when they believed their government was unresponsive, if not wrong, they took to the streets in Washington, New York, San Francisco, Detroit and, notably, in August 1968, Chicago, among many other places.

As in all such historic movements since 1776, these activists formed only a small percentage of the total population. But they continually challenged and disoriented the rest of the country. In one of the most influential analyses of the 1968 election, Richard Scammon and Ben Wattenberg concluded that the central actor in the unfolding campaign was not the antiwar or civil rights protesters, but the mythical housewife in Dayton, Ohio. She did not angrily march into the streets but was nevertheless angry and frustrated because she could no longer take her family out on streets that were safe.[2] She blamed the protesters when her family had to walk in violent streets, but she also blamed the Johnson administration—both for getting her family into this mess and then not doing enough to guarantee its safety. In his classic formulation, therefore, Tocqueville had been half-correct: tens of millions of Americans resembled the Dayton housewife in demanding security from their government, but at the same time their society had created groups that ensured the government would not be able to provide that security at the cost of individual liberties.

This liberalism of a relative few was a fortunate gift to the rest of the American people. It was, in the longer view, a gift from the civil rights activists and other reformers of the past century who had used government not to restrict individual liberty or to favor moneyed elites over the mass of Americans, but to protect social and individual rights and to provide opportunities—as, most notably, in Franklin D. Roosevelt's New Deal and Lyndon Johnson's Great Society spending programs that built infrastructure such as highways and rural electrical complexes, or created needed cultural improvements such as the Public Broadcasting System.

More precisely, American liberalism turned out to be half blessing and half damnation. The same liberalism that at home had created the most extended length of economic prosperity and social stability in American history between 1941 and the mid-1960s had overseas been plagued by a parochialism that proved to be deadly. This parochialism led to a misunderstanding of Southeast Asian cultures. It thus resulted in an anticommunism that blinded rather than enlightened. And it concluded with the belief that the use of force could somehow finally resolve problems produced by the parochialism and narrow anticommunism that actually guided the use of force.

One part of the parochialism turned out to be especially lethal. It was enforced by Americans' belief in their exceptionalism (the belief that God had given them both unique blessings and a unique opportunity to spread those blessings around the world, whether others—such as Vietnamese—wanted them or not). If they believed they were exceptional, then it followed that Americans had God-given rights to act unilaterally, whatever the objections of others. Such close allies as France and Great Britain had warned since the mid-1950s that U.S.

policies in Vietnam were tragically wrong, but Americans who had been triumphant in populating a continent, winning a world war, and creating apparently eternal economic prosperity now trusted their own supposed God-given exceptionalism rather than considering advice from the Old World.

By 1968, then, not only was this split-personality liberalism being questioned, but the centuries-old belief of Americans that they were God's unique gift to progress and civilization was being ripped down in both Europe and on U.S. city streets. As Martin Luther King phrased it, "Somewhere along the way we have allowed the means by which we live to outrun the ends for which we live."[3]

Resembling millions of other Americans, the Dayton housewife trusted neither the protesters nor the government to show her the way to realize "the ends for which we live." Meanwhile, the assassinations of King and the two Kennedys, along with the hundreds of dead in civil rights riots, the hundreds of thousands dead in a never-ending Vietnam conflict, and the televised breakdown of law and order at the Democratic National Convention—all signaled a crisis in American society more severe than any since 107 years before when the nation dissolved into civil war. The frustration took many forms, including that of the taxi cab driver who declared he wanted to obliterate Vietnam. North Vietnam? he was asked. "No," he replied, "Vietnam."[4]

Senator Edmund Muskie of Maine, the Democratic vice presidential nominee, was, in the words of widely read *Life* magazine, "the only congenial new face to come out of the national campaign." Muskie summarized the crisis by observing, "It is the uneasy fate of our generation to be caught in the crossfire of discontent."[5] Anyone who seemed capable of taking Americans out of that "crossfire" would receive most of their votes. In 1968, the revealing statistic was not Nixon's narrow victory over Hubert Humphrey, but that Nixon-Agnew and Wallace-LeMay altogether received 56 percent of the vote. That the four most conservative candidates could garner such a percentage after one of the great liberal political landslides in American history just four years before—and after the previous thirty-five years of mostly liberal rule—was remarkable.

Nixon tapped into the raging discontent by acting as a restrained major party candidate who supposedly had a secret plan to end the war and was determined to restore order in American cities. His support came especially from suburbs, small towns, and farming areas. Wallace and LeMay were unrestrained third-party candidates who loudly promised to run over any protesters who lay down in front of their motorcade. The Alabama governor's 10 million popular votes resulted from the most significant third-party campaign in forty-four years. (The frustrations and divisions were further illustrated by election results that for the first time since 1848 produced a president of one party and both houses of Congress controlled by the opposing party.)

On one level, Nixon was a shrewd, calculating politician who understood something few others seemed to notice: the South, solidly Democratic since the post–Civil War years, was ripe for Republicanism. Nixon understood that prosperous suburbs around such rapidly growing cities as Atlanta, Nashville, and Houston; a long-standing pride in being the most patriotic region in the country (and, thus, the least tolerant of antiwar protests); and, above all, an area whose longtime white political and social structure faced fundamental challenges from Johnson's civil rights acts and civil rights marchers—all these, allowed him to capture the longtime Democratic border states as Kentucky, Missouri (by a hair), and even formerly Solid South states as South Carolina.

Under the unrelenting pressure of the mid-1960s crises, the tectonic plates of American politics were shifting. Nixon could now play to southern worries without losing significant votes in the North, where dislike of street riots and antiwar protests was also widespread. Hoping to pick up strong southern support, he shrewdly refrained from going too far in his attacks on Wallace. Humphrey, on the other hand, blasted the Alabama governor and Muskie did not hide his dislike. When a large Wallace banner was unfurled during a speech in New Jersey, Muskie responded, in the words of one observer, as if someone was "waving a red flag in front of a bull." "That's the man we've got to defeat," Muskie exclaimed, "and we've got to defeat him so badly that his kind and his message is never heard from again in America." Although Wallace ruthlessly played to some of the worst in American nature with his calls for a strong arm to end civil rights and antiwar protests, and while Nixon more politely called for the same strong arm, Humphrey and Muskie could not, in the words of *Life* magazine, "out-extreme

Nixon or Wallace" on the critical issue of law and order. Instead, as Muskie's outburst in New Jersey exemplified, they tended to condemn such extremes and ask instead that "people . . . be more trusting of one another." But this response, *Life* accurately observed, "was saying too little about everybody's worries and fears."[6]

Nixon was more polite and calm than Wallace for two reasons: because he had a different personality and, more importantly, because he intended to entice the Alabama governor's southern followers over to the Republican Party. This seduction could not be accomplished by calling Wallace bad names. All in all, Nixon waged a smart campaign in which he, and especially Agnew, used code words to indicate they wanted to slow the march of equal rights for minorities. With a so-called southern strategy, Nixon picked off Wallace's votes, especially in the last weeks of the campaign when his supporters realized the Alabama governor had no chance of winning. The Nixon–Agnew emphasis on law and order thus cut a number of ways. It served as an attack on civil rights marchers and antiwar protesters who took to the streets, as campaign rhetoric that pleased the Dayton housewife, and as a successful tactic to raid Wallace's camp.

Meanwhile, Nixon's refusal to take a specific position on the Vietnam War turned out to be a short-term stroke of political genius. If he had bluntly attacked Johnson's policies in detail, he would have been accused of being unpatriotic and would have aroused the president's vehement opposition. If he had urged either major escalation or deescalation of the war, he would have lost the votes of "doves" and "hawks" respectively—and the "hawks," who thought they could end the war by using massive force, were in larger numbers than "doves." Nixon instead let Humphrey take the political heat for the Johnson administration's refusal to either win or get out. The Republican remained quiet, and no doubt was amused as the Wallace ticket was condemned for General LeMay's outrageous remarks about ending the war. Of particular importance, Nixon entered the White House in 1969 with the freedom to follow whatever path he thought best in Vietnam. Little he had uttered during the campaign narrowed his freedom to maneuver as president.

Nixon might have been a smart political operator in 1968, but he was so secretive, paranoid, prone to lying, and otherwise unethical that in

1974 he became the first U.S. president forced to resign from office. Leonard Garment, a prominent lawyer and close adviser to several presidents, later noted that the men in the White House do not have normal personalities: "The presidential gene is filled with sociopathic qualities—brilliant, erratic, lying, cheating, expert at mendacity, generous, loony, driven by a sense of mission, a very unusual person. Nixon was one of the strangest of this strange group."[7] In the 1968 campaign, however, Nixon's strangeness was hardly noticeable in a society grown so strange that it spawned political assassinations, the murder of civil rights advocates, a war whose strategy became destroying villages in order to save them, and political conventions in cities where the most prominent smell was of tear gas. In such a society, during such a war, Nixon's strangeness blended into the chaotic background.

The war meanwhile trapped Hubert Humphrey. He could not attack U.S. policy in Vietnam, or even remain silent, without losing the all-important support of the president or without attacking his own role in the escalation of the conflict since he had become vice president in early 1965. But neither could he enthusiastically agree with the policy, as Johnson demanded, without losing large numbers of Democrats who were critical of the U.S. involvement. Perhaps above all, as *Life* magazine noted, Humphrey was trapped by the growing demand, especially by the many who agreed with that Dayton housewife, that he come out strongly for law and order—and be specific about how he would achieve it if he became president. An old friend warned him in mid-1968 that if he ran a law-and-order campaign, as increasing numbers of people wanted him to do, Humphrey would be rejecting the past twenty years of his own liberalism. For many Americans, the friend emphasized, law and order now meant keeping minorities and the poor in their place and treating protesters harshly.[8]

A Humphrey emphasis on law and order, in other words, would endear him to millions of blue-collar workers who had long voted Democratic and wanted peace in their neighborhoods, but would also drive away millions of African Americans and other minority voters, as well as many antiwar protesters, who were essential to any chance for a Humphrey victory. It was a terrible dilemma.

His Salt Lake City speech, which for the first time separated him, at least a little, from Johnson's Vietnam policy, gave Humphrey some maneuvering room. He could now call for law and order without appearing as much to condemn those who opposed the president on the war. But even then, the vice president had to be careful. In the campaign's final weeks he told his staff, "It is absolutely imperative that we rerun our Law-and-Order speech in selective market areas." He quickly defined those areas, however, as the border states and Texas, not states further north where African American and antiwar protest voters could determine the outcome.[9] As earlier noted, voters in many of the border states finally believed, for good reasons, that Nixon, not Humphrey, was the more committed law-and-order candidate.

African Americans turned out in large numbers to vote overwhelmingly for Humphrey. Their numbers, however, were below the 6 million who voted in 1964, and while their help was a key to Democratic wins in Michigan and Pennsylvania, their support fell from 1964 levels in such pivotal states as Ohio. Similarly, many blue-collar workers, who had long been the backbone of Democratic strength in large cities, finally turned away from their infatuation with Wallace when it was apparent he could not win. But they then evenly split their votes between Humphrey and Nixon.[10]

There were many reasons for Humphrey's problems with minority, blue-collar, and poorer Americans. Two need to be noted. First, Democratic tax cuts in 1962 and 1964 had helped corporations more than lower wage earners. The income gap between rich and poor grew, while the largest corporations used their new capital to buy up competition, dominate key sectors of the economy, and invest overseas—especially Europe. Highly respected business analyst Peter Drucker termed the business consolidation that had occurred since the 1950s "the biggest increase in economic concentration ever recorded in this or any other country."[11] Labor's power endured a severe post-1950s decline, even under Democratic presidents. Second, both African American and white blue-collar communities knew their sons and daughters were dying in Vietnam in disproportionate numbers to the whole population. As historian David Steigerwald has noted, the average soldier in Vietnam was a little over nineteen years old. (World War II troops averaged twenty-six years of age.) Up to 80 percent of them came from working-class backgrounds. African Americans were drafted roughly according to their percentage in the

overall population (11 percent), but in the first years of the ground
war had been killed at twice that rate—meaning they were doing
much of the toughest fighting.[12] Given these realities in the U.S.
economy and on Vietnam battlefields, minorities and blue-collar
workers not surprisingly lost some of their enthusiasm for voting
Democratic—or for even turning out to vote at all.

The 1968 election marked the breakup of the thirty-year-old New
Deal coalition of workers, African Americans, ethnic groups, and new
entrepreneurs that Franklin D. Roosevelt had pieced together to reshape America. Many economic and social changes were already
weakening this coalition, including the growing alienation of voters
from their usual party home. As Democrats and Republicans appeared (unlike the 1930s) to have few differences on foreign policy
and the economy, voters became less anchored in a particular political party and more likely to vote for special, personal reasons, or not
vote at all. Poorer and minority voters especially began to drop out of
the political arena. They ironically, and unfortunately, did so just as
they suffered the most from Washington's economic and military policies. Many Americans simply gave up politically.[13]

A major problem was that for more than a century voters had been
educated about issues by their political parties. This education could
be good or bad, but by the 1960s, as party organization weakened, potential voters were conspicuously ignorant about issues. In the early
1960s only half of adult Americans polled knew how many senators
their state sent to Washington and 77 percent knew nothing about the
Bill of Rights that guaranteed their freedoms. By the mid-1960s,
nearly half of Americans polled believed that "most people don't have
enough sense to pick their leaders wisely."[14]

The life-or-death bet on the Vietnam War thus occurred in a rapidly changing political arena. Antiwar and prowar protesters tried to
capture that arena by marching in the streets or disrupting conventions of political parties that had lost some of their old legitimacy.
Richer Americans spent large sums of money to buy off the political
parties and then use the new media to convince the country to accept
their message. A respected political theorist, Sheldon Wolin, has argued that beginning in 1968, election campaigns were used to define
the people, instead of the people defining the politics. Great amounts

of money are collected, Wolin wrote, "to create an 'electorate' that is worked over intensively" through television and the candidate's organization. Once the election is over, "the electorate disappears, leaving behind a 'mandate' that stands as the legitimating principle for a new 'administration.'"[15]

In 1968, this approach worked so well for Nixon that in terms of the Vietnam War he could claim that his "mandate" was whatever he personally might decide it was. Collecting tens of millions of dollars, he outspent Humphrey for television time by nearly 2 to 1. The Democrat tried to catch up by blitzing the TV channels in the last days of the campaign, but it was not enough to overtake Nixon's early lead. And, to use Wolin's words, Nixon and his handlers used those vast sums of money to package the candidate for television so that the old Nixon—who had been mistrusted in the 1950s and defeated in the 1960 presidential campaign—turned into a new Nixon, or at least a new image. This new image was fashioned not by radically new beliefs or a new personality, but by professional public relations people who knew how to manipulate what the voter saw.[16]

Precisely because the debate over the war during the 1968 campaign proved to be so meaningless, Nixon could continue to commit U.S. troops to the conflict for five more years and nearly 30,000 more American battlefield deaths. The Paris peace talks went nowhere for three years. But the Nixon camp's involvement with Madame Chennault and the South Vietnam government's attempts to kill the Paris talks just before the election rose up out of the past like a ghost to haunt Nixon. In January 1973, when Congress began investigating the White House–inspired criminal break-in of Democratic Party offices in Washington's Watergate Hotel, Nixon in desperation tried to blackmail Johnson so the former president would stop the investigation. Nixon threatened to reveal that Johnson had illegally wiretapped the Nixon–Agnew campaign in 1968. Johnson countered by threatening to make public how the Nixon camp maneuvered, with the help of Madame Chennault and Henry Kissinger, to sabotage the Paris peace talks for selfish political gain. Nixon backed down and Johnson died shortly after.[17]

There were also other, more important ghosts (as the great playwright Henrik Ibsen would call them) from the 1968 election and the

tragic war that shaped the results. A most important ghost, indeed, a giant specter that haunted U.S. foreign policy for the next generation, was
the American people's determination never again to become trapped in
a Vietnam-like quagmire. Expert observers in 1968 could see this ghost
forming simply by watching the political campaign. Americans were finally losing their naïveté about their power and capabilities, British Ambassador Sir Patrick Dean reported back to London. "Until recently it
has been an accepted part of American myth that, given the will and the
resources, and a good cause, there is nothing the United States cannot
achieve," Dean observed. "It has finally been borne in on the average
American that whatever the truth of this dictum may be in domestic
terms, it simply does not apply in foreign affairs."[18]

Secretary of State Dean Rusk gave his own, blunter version of what
Ambassador Dean called a new isolationism. In "the present state of
public opposition to the United States overseas commitments," Rusk
was quoted as saying, "there would not even be 20 votes in the [U.S.]
Senate in favor of an alliance with God."[19] Prestigious private foreign
policy groups, such as the New York Council on Foreign Relations,
surveyed the leading business, academic, and political figures in their
memberships and then concluded that Americans, as powerful as they
were, could not fight everywhere in the world, even for such fine objectives as democracy, while at the same time dealing effectively with
the racism, environmental pollution, and poverty that threatened
their society. Not even Americans had the power, and necessary attention span, to do all of this successfully.[20]

Over the next several generations, certain U.S. leaders, who again
wanted to take the country into foreign wars, did everything in their
power to make Americans believe that the Vietnam tragedy was actually a noble cause. Or they argued that greatly increased U.S. power
would have been able to act more effectively in Vietnam, and at less
cost (at least at less cost to Americans). Or, especially, that the chaos
and frustration of the 1960s, especially the 1968 election, were caused
not by an apparently endless war that was wrecking the economy and
society, but by the protesters who took to the streets to show they opposed the war and/or supported civil rights.

These officials and their followers hoped that somehow the protests
of the 1960s could be blamed for centuries of civil rights abuses and

years of failed U.S. policies in Southeast Asia. The ghosts of Vietnam nevertheless refused to go away—at least for those who carefully studied the 1960s and its last presidential election that exemplified, and helped climax, the most domestically dangerous, chaotic American era since the Civil War. U.S. presidents had made the life-and-death bet that they could somehow commit the American people to a long war against a foe they never understood, and, at the same time, maintain order, peace, and constitutional stability at home. The presidents lost and disappeared in disgrace. The ghosts survived.

NOTES

INTRODUCTION

1. Hendrik Hertzberg, "Scaling Mt. Kennedy," *New Yorker,* November 20, 2000, p. 92.

2. *New York Times Magazine,* September 17, 1967, pp. 30–31.

3. *Department of State Bulletin,* February 19, 1968, p. 228.

4. *New York Times,* August 1, 1967, p. 4.

5. "NSC-68, copy no. 3, A Report to the National Security Council," April 14, 1950, Department of State Lot File 63D.357, Box 4108. National Archives, Washington, D.C. I am indebted to David Langbart for the copy of this document that was finally (and accidentally) declassified in 1975.

6. Alexis deTocqueville, *Democracy in America* (New York: Alfred A. Knopf, 1945), 2:268–69.

7. Charles DeBenedetti, *An American Ordeal: The Antiwar Movement of the Vietnam Era* (Syracuse, N.Y.: Syracuse University Press, 1990), p. 187.

8. Lewis L. Gould, "Never a Deep Partisan: Lyndon Johnson and the Democratic Party, 1963–1969," in Robert A. Divine, ed., *The Johnson Years* (Lawrence: University Press of Kansas, 1987–), 3:30.

9. Tom Wicker, "Remembering the Johnson Treatment," *New York Times,* May 9, 2002, p. A39.

10. Terry Dietz, *Republicans and Vietnam, 1961–1968* (New York: Greenwood, 1986), pp. 104–10, 123–24.

11. Dietz, *Republicans and Vietnam*, pp. 108–10.

12. George Herring, "The War in Vietnam," in Robert A. Divine, ed., *The Johnson Years*, vol. 1, *Foreign Policy, the Great Society, and the White House* (Lawrence: University Press of Kansas, 1987), pp. 38–39.

13. Philip E. Converse, Warren E. Miller, Jerrold G. Rusk, and Arthur C. Wolfe, "Continuity and Change in American Politics: Parties and Issues in the 1968 Election," *American Political Science Review*, December 1969, p. 1105.

14. Samuel Zaffiri, *Westmoreland: A Biography of General William C. Westmoreland* (New York: William Morrow, 1994), p. 178.

15. Gould, "Never a Deep Partisan," p. 33.

16. Dietz, *Republicans and Vietnam*, p. 111.

17. Arthur S. Link, *Wilson: Campaigns for Progressivism and Peace, 1916–1917* (Princeton, N.J.: Princeton University Press, 1965), p. 399.

18. Louis Heren, *No Hail, No Farewell* (New York: Harper & Row, 1970), pp. 178–79, for both the McNamara and Westmoreland quotes.

19. San Antonio speech of September 29, 1967, in *Vital Speeches of the Day*, October 15, 1967, p. 2.

20. Assistant Secretary of Defense John McNaughton, quoted in William H. Chafe, *The Unfinished Journey: America since World War II* (New York: Oxford University Press, 1980), p. 297.

21. Joseph A. Califano Jr., "When There's No Draft," *Washington Post*, April 6, 1999, p. A23.

22. Carol Fink, Philipp Gassert, and Detlef Junker, *1968: The World Transformed* (New York: Cambridge University Press, 1998), p. 17.

23. J. William Fulbright, "The Great Society Is a Sick Society," *New York Times Magazine*, August 20, 1967, p. 96.

CHAPTER I

1. Analysis of the survey is in *U.S. News & World Report*, August 21, 1967, p. 46; LBJ's quote is in *Vital Speeches of the Day*, October 15, 1967, p. 3.

2. General William P. Westmoreland, *A Soldier Reports* (Garden City, N.Y.: Doubleday, 1976), esp. pp. 10–11, 18–21, 25–27, 68–70; David L. Anderson, *The Columbia Guide to the Vietnam War* (New York: Columbia University Press, 2002), p. 175.

3. David Steigerwald, *The Sixties and the End of Modern America* (New York: St. Martin's, 1995), p. 84.

4. Westmoreland, *A Soldier Reports*, pp. 225–26.

5. Westmoreland, *A Soldier Reports*, p. 233.

6. Lloyd C. Gardner, "Lyndon Johnson and Vietnam: The Final Months," in Robert A. Divine, ed., *The Johnson Years* (Lawrence: University Press of Kansas, 1987–), 3:200; Robert Buzzanco, *Masters of War* (New York: Cambridge University Press, 1996), chap. 9; Marilyn Blatt Young, *The Vietnam Wars, 1945–1990* (New York: Harper Collins, 1991), p. 210; Westmoreland, *A Soldier Reports*, p. 234.

7. *Department of State Bulletin*, January 15, 1968, p. 75.

8. Ambassador Sir Patrick Dean to Sir Paul Gore-Booth, February 2, 1968, FCO/7/741, Public Record Office, Kew, UK.

9. George C. Herring, *America's Longest War: The United States and Vietnam, 1950–1975*, 4th ed. (New York: McGraw-Hill, 2002), p. 228; Steigerwald, *Sixties*, p. 85.

10. *New York Times*, February 2, 1968, p. 15.

11. McNamara's statement is in his annual report to Congress, *New York Times*, February 2, 1968, p. 16; Buchwald is quoted in William H. Chafe, *The Unfinished Journey: America since World War II* (New York: Oxford University Press, 1980), pp. 345–50, in context of analysis of Tet offensive.

12. *New York Times*, February 2, 1968, p. 16.

13. Herring, *Longest War*, p. 235, for Wheeler's evaluation; *New York Times*, February 2, 1968, p. 15, for LBJ's lament.

14. For LBJ and the demand for more troops, see *Department of State Bulletin*, February 19, 1968, has president's text; Young, *Vietnam Wars*, p. 225, for Rusk's quote and context; for an important interpretation of Westmoreland's reaction, note Buzzanco, *Masters of War*, pp. 312–17.

15. A good discussion of this credibility problem is in Allen J. Matusow, *The Unravelling of America: A History of Liberalism in the 1960s* (New York: Harper & Row, 1984).

16. Young, *Vietnam Wars*, pp. 227–28.

17. A succinct discussion of these themes for the mid-1960s is Daniel C. Hallin, *The "Uncensored War": The Media and Vietnam* (New York: Oxford University Press, 1986), esp. pp. 122–34.

18. George H. Gallup, *The Gallup Poll: Public Opinion, 1935–1971* (New York: Random House, 1972), 3:2103.

19. Gallup, *Gallup Poll*, 3:2099, 2106–7.

20. Gallup, *Gallup Poll*, 3:2107.

21. Young, *Vietnam Wars*, p. 226.

22. Herring, *Longest War*, pp. 243–44.

23. Dean to Sir Paul Gore-Booth, March 2, 1968, FCO/7/741, Public Record Office, Kew, UK.

24. Bunker to George S. Franklin Jr., Council on Foreign Relations, Records of Meetings, July 1968–June 1969.

CHAPTER 2

1. U.S. Government, *Public Papers of the President . . . 1964* (Washington, D.C.: U.S. Government Printing Office, 1965), p. 1204.

2. George Rising, *Clean for Gene: Eugene McCarthy's 1968 Presidential Campaign* (Westport, Conn.: Greenwood, 1997), pp. 52–53.

3. Carole Fink, Philipp Gassert, and Detlef Junker, eds., *1968: The World Transformed* (New York: Cambridge University Press, 1998), pp. 16–17.

4. Rising, *Clean for Gene,* pp. 53–54; Charles DeBenedetti, *An American Ordeal: The Antiwar Movement of the Vietnam Era* (Syracuse, N.Y.: Syracuse University Press, 1990), pp. 200–1.

5. David Steigerwald, *The Sixties and the End of Modern America* (New York: St. Martin's, 1995), p. 27; Rising, *Clean for Gene,* p. 3.

6. Rising, *Clean for Gene,* p. 17.

7. Rising, *Clean for Gene,* pp. 56–57.

8. Rising, *Clean for Gene,* pp. 57–58.

9. Eugene J. McCarthy, *Eugene McCarthy on the Record* (New York: Coalition for a Democratic Alternative, 1968), p. 2.

10. Eugene J. McCarthy, *America Revisited: 150 Years after Tocqueville* (Garden City, N.Y.: Doubleday, 1978).

11. DeBenedetti, *American Ordeal,* pp. 201–2.

12. Kathleen J. Turner, *Lyndon Johnson's Dual War: Vietnam and the Press* (Chicago: Chicago University Press, 1986), pp. 206–8.

13. George H. Gallup, *The Gallup Poll; Public Opinion, 1935–1971* (New York: Random House, 1972), 3:2093; DeBenedetti, *American Ordeal,* p. 209.

14. DeBeneditti, *American Ordeal,* p. 211.

15. Richard T. Stout, *People* (New York: Harper & Row, 1970), pp. 164–65; Irwin Unger and Debi Unger, eds., *The Times Were a Changin'* (New York: Three Rivers, 1998), p. 322; *Time,* March 22, 1968, p. 15.

16. Melvin Small, *Johnson, Nixon, and the Doves* (New Brunswick, N.J.: Rutgers University Press, 1988), pp. 140–41, 153.

17. McCarthy, *McCarthy on the Record,* pp. 20–21, 28–29.

18. McCarthy, *McCarthy on the Record,* p. 29.

19. Senator Eugene J. McCarthy, *First Things First: New Priorities for America* (New York: New American Library, 1968), pp. 18–19.

20. McCarthy, *First Things First*, p. 24.

21. McCarthy, *First Things First*, pp. 21, 24.

22. Ambassador Sir Patrick Dean to Sir Paul Gore-Booth, March 1, 1968, FCO/7/741, Public Record Office, Kew, UK.

23. *Business Week*, March 16, 1968, p. 33.

24. David Broder, "Election of 1968," in Arthur M. Schlesinger Jr. and Fred L. Israel, eds., *History of American Presidential Elections, 1789–1968* (New York: Chelsea House, 1971), 4:3718.

25. Philip E. Converse et al., "Continuity and Change in American Politics: Parties and Issues in the 1968 Election," *American Political Science Review*, December 1969, 1092; Rising, *Clean for Gene*, p. 68; *U.S. News & World Report*, March 25, 1968, pp. 40–41.

26. Converse et al., "Continuity and Change," p. 1093.

27. Broder, "1968," p. 3719; Gallup, *Gallup Polls*, 3:2112.

28. Quoted and analyzed in Daniel C. Hallin, *The "Uncensored War": The Media and Vietnam* (New York: Oxford University Press, 1986), p. 197.

29. *U.S. News & World Report*, March 25, 1968, p. 41.

CHAPTER 3

1. *New York Times*, September 30, 2001, p. 3.

2. *Public Papers of the Presidents of the United States: Lyndon Johnson, 1964* (Washington, D.C.: U.S. Government Printing Office, 1965), p. 320; Ibid., *1965*, p. 600; *Department of State Bulletin*, February 19, 1968, p. 230. *Public Papers of the Presidents* can be found online at www.access.gpo/nara/pubpaps/srchpaps.html.

3. Clark Clifford with Richard Holbrooke, *Counsel to the President; A Memoir* (New York: Random House, 1991), p. 476; George Reedy, *Lyndon Johnson, A Memoir* (New York: Andrews & McMeel, 1982), p. 150.

4. The authoritative account, written in the U.S. Army Center of Military History, is William M. Hammond, *Public Affairs: The Military and the Media, 1962–1968* (Washington, D.C.: Center of Military History, U.S. Army, 1988); Clifford, *Counsel to the President*, p. 474.

5. "Notes of the President's Tuesday Luncheon Meeting," February 6, 1968, Lyndon Johnson Papers, Lyndon Baines Johnson Presidential Library, Austin, Texas.

6. *New York Times,* February 17, 1968, p. 4; Benjamin Read Oral History, Johnson Papers, Johnson Library, esp. pp. 29–30.

7. U.S. Congress, Senate, Foreign Relations Committee, 90th Cong. 2d sess., *The Gulf of Tonkin: The 1964 Incidents* (Washington, D.C.: U.S. Government Printing Office, 1968). Lloyd C. Gardner, "Lyndon Johnson and Vietnam: The Final Months," in Robert A. Divine, ed., *The Johnson Years* (Lawrence: University Press of Kansas, 1987–), 3:201–2.

8. Charles DeBenedetti, *An American Ordeal: The Antiwar Movement of the Vietnam Era* (Syracuse, N.Y.: Syracuse University Press, 1990), pp. 232–33.

9. Ambassador Sir Patrick Dean to Sir Paul Gore-Booth, March 1, 1968, FCO/7/741, Public Record Office, Kew, UK.

10. *New York Times,* April 26, 1966, p. 42.

11. The aide was Bill Moyers, his press secretary, who recorded the incident in "The Final Word," *Among Friends of LBJ,* July 15, 1985, 9; David Broder, "Election of 1968," in Arthur M. Schlesinger Jr. and Fred L. Israel, eds., *History of American Presidential Elections, 1789–1968* (New York: Chelsea House, 1971), 4:3708.

12. Irwin Unger and Debi Unger, eds., *The Times Were a Changin'* (New York: Three Rivers, 1998), pp. 13–15.

13. *New York Times,* January 15, 1968, p. C51 for the background and the Belgian's quote; J. J. Servan Schreiber, *The American Challenge,* trans. Ronald Steel (New York: Atheneum, 1968), esp. pp. 3–6.

14. Robert M. Collins, "The Economic Crisis of 1968 and the Waning of the American Century," *American Historical Review,* April 1996, pp. 396–422, esp. p. 411; *Department of State Bulletin,* February 26, 1968, p. 280.

15. Burton I. Kaufman, "Foreign Aid and the Balance-of-Payments Problem: Vietnam and Johnson's Foreign Economic Policy," in Robert A. Divine, ed., *The Johnson Years,* vol. 2 (Lawrence: University Press of Kansas, 1987), esp. pp. 90–95; *New York Times,* May 6, 1968, p. 72, for the gold figures.

16. *American Foreign Policy Discussion Meeting Report,* January 17, 1968, *Records of Groups,* 122 (1967–1968), Council on Foreign Relations, New York City.

17. Gardner, "Lyndon Johnson and Vietnam," pp. 207–11.

18. Lewis L. Gould, "Never a Deep Partisan: Lyndon Johnson and the Democratic Party, 1964–1969," in Robert A. Divine, ed., *The Johnson Years* (Lawrence: University Press of Kansas, 1987–), 3:39; U.S. Congress, Senate, Foreign Relations Committee, *Executive Sessions of the Senate Foreign Relations Committee,* Historical Series, vol. 18, 89th Cong., 2d sess., 1966 (Washington, 1993), p. 593.

19. Doris Kearns, *Lyndon Johnson and the American Dream* (New York: New American Library, 1976), p. x.

20. The previous two paragraphs are based especially on Elmo Roper, "The Mood of America," *Saturday Review,* June 8, 1968, pp. 30–31; Collins, "Economic Crisis of 1968," p. 419.

21. Collins, "Economic Crisis of 1968," has the Symington quote and the background for Clifford's reevaluation.

22. Clifford, *Counsel to the President,* pp. 493–94; Gardner, "Lyndon Johnson and Vietnam," p. 204; David Steigerwald, *The Sixties and the End of Modern America* (New York: St. Martin's, 1995), p. 89.

23. David L. Anderson, *The Columbia Guide to the Vietnam War* (New York: Columbia University Press, 2002), p. 176; Marilyn Blatt Young, *The Vietnam Wars, 1945–1990* (New York: HarperCollins, 1991), pp. 228–29.

24. Harry McPherson Oral History, Johnson Papers, Johnson Library, tape no. 5, pp. 16–17; George C. Herring, *America's Longest War,* 4th ed. (Boston: McGraw-Hill, 2002), p. 250.

25. Rostow to the President, March 15, 1968, National Security File, Subject File, Press contacts—Memos to the President, Johnson Papers, Johnson Library; McPherson Oral History, tape no. 5, p. 7.

26. Neil Sheehan et al., eds., *The Pentagon Papers* (New York: Bantam, 1971), p. 612; Herring, *America's Longest War,* p. 240.

27. Melvin Small, *Johnson, Nixon, and the Doves* (New Brunswick, N.J.: Rutgers University Press, 1988), pp. 135–36; George E. Reedy, *The Twilight of the Presidency* (New York: World, 1970), pp. 70–72.

28. James R. Jones, "Behind LBJ's Decision Not to Run in '68," *New York Times,* April 16, 1988, p. 31; *Newsweek,* August 15, 1968, p. 26.

29. Jones, "Behind LBJ's Decision," p. 31; Small, *Johnson, Nixon, and the Doves,* p. 158; *Newsweek,* April 15, 1968, p. 26.

30. Ambassador Sir Patrick Dean to Sir Paul Gore-Booth, April 2, 1968, FCO/7/741, Public Record Office, Kew, UK; William H. Chafe, *The Unfinished Journey: America since World War II* (New York: Oxford University Press, 1980), p. 360.

31. Louis Heren, *No Hail, No Farewell* (New York: Harper & Row, 1970), pp. 225–26; Gareth Porter, ed., *Vietnam: A History in Documents* (New York: New American Library, 1981), pp. 364–65, for the Wheeler instruction; Young, *Vietnam Wars,* p. 235; Herring, *America's Longest War,* p. 257.

32. Johnson to Nguyen van Thieu, April 7, 1968, White House, Confidential Files, Box 113, "Vietnam, 1968." Johnson Library.

CHAPTER 4

1. Ambassador Sir Patrick Dean to Sir Paul Gore-Booth, April 2, 1968, FCO/7/741, Public Record Office, Kew, UK.

2. *New York Times*, April 5, 1960, p. 26.

3. David J. Garrow, "The FBI and Martin Luther King," *Atlantic Monthly*, July–August 2002, p. 80; *Biography* (New York: Oxford University Press, 1999), 12:703–7; Michael Eric Dyson, *I May Not Get There with You: The True Martin Luther King, Jr.,* (New York: Free Press, 2001); *Washington Post*, April 5, 1968, p. A6; *New York Times*, April 5, 1968, p. 26.

4. *Washington Post*, April 5, 1968, p. A6.

5. Theodore H. White, *The Making of the President, 1968* (New York: Atheneum, 1970), p. 276.

6. The previous three paragraphs on King's evolving views on Vietnam are based especially on Dyson, *I May Not Get There with You,* pp. 54–55, 59–61; David Levering Lewis, *King: A Biography* (Urbana: University of Illinois Press, 1978), pp. 358–61; *Washington Post*, April 5, 1968, p. A6.

7. *New York Times*, April 5, 1968, p. 26; David Steigerwald, *The Sixties and the End of Modern America* (New York: St. Martin's, 1995), p. 67; William W. Boyer, ed., *Issues, 1968* (Lawrence: University Press of Kansas, 1968), p. 64.

8. Charles DeBenedetti with Charles Chatfield, *An American Ordeal: The Antiwar Movement of the Vietnam Era* (Syracuse, N.Y.: Syracuse University Press, 1990), pp. 176–78; Lewis, *King,* p. 358; Dyson, *I May Not Get There with You,* p. 62.

9. DeBenedetti, *American Ordeal,* p. 217.

10. U.S. Government, *Report of the National Advisory Commission on Civil Disorders* (New York: Dutton, 1968), pp. 1–2; *Time*, March 8, 1968, p. 27.

11. These two paragraphs are based on U.S. Government, *Report of the National Advisory Commission on Civil Disorders,* esp. chaps. 6–8; good summaries and analyses of the report are in *Newsweek*, March 11, 1968, pp. 39–40; *U.S. News and World Report*, March 11, 1968, pp. 33–34; and especially *Time*, March 8, 1968, pp. 26–27, from which parts of these paragraphs are drawn.

12. *Newsweek*, March 11, 1968, p. 42; *Newsweek*, March 18, 1968, p. 16.

13. *Time*, March 15, 1968, p. 16.

14. This theme and these episodes are well discussed in *Newsweek*, March 11, 1968, esp. p. 40.

15. Carson, "King, Martin Luther, Jr.," p. 706.

16. DeBenedetti, *American Ordeal,* p. 218; author's personal experience, April 4–5, 1968.

17. Ambassador Sir Patrick Dean to Foreign office, April 11, 1968, FCO/7/860; and Dean to Sir Paul Gore-Booth, May 1, 1968, FCO/7/741, both documents in Public Record Office, Kew, UK.

18. Ambassador Sir Patrick Dean to Sir Paul Gore-Booth, May 1, 1968, FCO/7/74l, Public Record Office, Kew, UK.

19. Carson, "King, Martin Luther, Jr.," p. 706.

20. Ambassador Sir Patrick Dean to Sir Paul Gore Booth, May 1, 1968, FCO/7/741, Public Record Office, Kew, UK.

CHAPTER 5

1. Daniel Bell, *The End of Ideology: On the Exhaustion of Political Ideas of the Fifties* (Glencoe, Ill.: Free Press, 1960).

2. Arthur M. Schlesinger Jr., *Robert Kennedy and His Times* (Boston: Houghton Mifflin, 1978), p. 372.

3. Ronald Steel, *In Love with the Night: The American Romance with Robert Kennedy* (New York: Simon & Schuster, 2000), p. 59; Thomas Powers, "The Interesting One," *New York Review of Books*, November 11, 2000, p. 22.

4. James W. Hilty, *Robert Kennedy: Brother Protector* (Philadelphia: Temple University Press, 1997), pp. 144–64, 409.

5. *New Yorker*, November 20, 2000, pp. 94–98.

6. Joseph A. Palermo, *In His Own Right: The Political Odyssey of Senator Robert F. Kennedy* (New York: Columbia University Press, 2001), pp. 14–15; Kahin's views can best be studied in his *Southeast Asia: A Testament* (New York: Routledge Curzon, 2002), especially chaps 9–12.

7. Palermo, *In His Own Right*, pp. 20–21, 64–65; Allen J. Matusow, *The Unraveling of America* (New York: Harper & Row, 1984), p. 384.

8. Palermo, *In His Own Right*, especially chap. 8, pp. 161–87.

9. Palermo, *In His Own Right*, pp. 104–6.

10. The last two paragraphs are drawn especially from *Time*, March 22, 1968, p. 16; *New York Times*, March 17, 1968, p. 1; Richard Stout, *People* (New York: Harper & Row, 1973), p. 186.

11. *Economist*, September 16, 2000, p. 92; Clark Clifford with Richard Holbrooke, *Counsel to the President; A Memoir* (New York: Random House, 1991), p. 505.

12. Robert F. Kennedy, "Conflict in Vietnam and at Home," in William W. Boyer, ed., *Issues, 1968* (Lawrence: University Press of Kansas, 1968), esp. pp. 30–31, 40–44.

13. Kennedy, "Conflict in Vietnam," pp. 29–31.

14. Schlesinger, *Robert Kennedy,* pp. 874–77.

15. Hendrik Hertzberg, "Scaling Mt. Kennedy," *New Yorker,* November 20, 2000, p. 92.

16. Charles DeBenedetti, *An American Ordeal: The Antiwar Movement of the Vietnam Era* (Syracuse, N.Y.: University of Syracuse Press, 1990), pp. 216–24; George C. Herring, *America's Longest War,* 4th ed. (Boston: McGraw-Hill, 2002), pp. 260–61.

17. Powers, "Interesting One," p. 25.

18. Lloyd C. Gardner, "Lyndon Johnson and Vietnam, the Final Months," in Robert A. Divine, ed., *The Johnson Years* (Lawrence: University Press of Kansas, 1987–), 3:215; Charles W. Yost, "The Problems of Vietnam in 1968," April 29, 1968, Council on Foreign Relations Ad Hoc Discussion Group on Vietnam, *Records of Groups* 123 (1968).

19. David Broder, "Election of 1968," in Arthur M. Schlesinger Jr. and Fred L. Israel, eds., *History of American Presidential Elections, 1789–1968* (New York, 1971), 4:3723.

20. Steel, *In Love with the Night,* pp. 172–76; Powers, "Interesting One," p. 25.

21. David Steigerwald, *The Sixties and the End of Modern America* (New York: St. Martin's, 1995), p. 31.

22. Palermo, *In His Own Right,* pp. 226–28.

23. Broder, "1968," p. 3724; Steel, *In Love with the Night,* pp. 184–85.

24. Ambassador Sir Patrick Dean to Stewart, July 16, 1968, FCO/7/778, Foreign Affairs, Public Record Office, Kew, UK.

CHAPTER 6

1. *Atlantic Monthly,* January 2002, p. 27.

2. *Webster's* defines "terror" as "intense, sharp, overmastering fear," and "any period of frightful violence or bloodshed," while "terrorism" is "the use of terrorizing methods" and "the state of fear and submission so produced."

3. David English, *Divided They Stand* (Englewood Cliffs, N.J.: Prentice-Hall, 1969), p. 9

4. These paragraphs on Nixon's background are drawn from a number of sources; some of the most useful and succinct are Joan Hoff, "Nixon, Richard Milhous," in Bruce W. Jentleson and Thomas G. Paterson, eds., *Encyclopedia of U.S. Foreign Relations* (New York: Oxford University Press, 1997): 3:246–47; David Steigerwald, *The Sixties and the End of Modern America*

(New York: St. Martin's, 1995), esp. pp. 278–80; David Broder, "Election of 1968," in Arthur M. Schlesinger Jr. and Fred L. Israel, eds., *History of American Presidential Elections, 1789–1968* (New York: Chelsea House, 1971), esp. 4:3711.

5. *Public Papers of the Presidents . . . Lyndon Baines Johnson . . . 1966* (Washington, D.C.: U.S. Government Printing Office, 1967), p. 1323.

6. Richard Nixon, "Asia after Vietnam," *Foreign Affairs*, October 1967, pp. 111–25.

7. Broder, "1968," p. 3713.

8. W. M. Dower to D. J. Swan, December 20, 1967, FCO/7/739, Public Record Office, Kew, UK.

9. Charles Debenedetti, *An American Ordeal: The Antiwar Movement of the Vietnam Era* (Syracuse, N.Y.: Syracuse University Press, 1990), p. 216.

10. Broder, "1968," p. 3712.

11. Norman Mailer, *Miami and the Siege of Chicago* (New York: World, 1968), p. 138.

12. Broder, "1968," p. 3710, gives a brief, general background on Reagan.

13. Broder,"1968," p. 3706; *Time*, August 16, 1968, pp. 12–15.

14. Robert Coate to Hubert Humphrey, June 3, 1968, Personal Political Correspondence, Individuals, Hubert Humphrey Papers, Minnesota Historical Society, St. Paul, Minnesota.

15. Joe McGinniss, *The Selling of the President, 1968* (New York: Trident, 1969), p. 103.

16. Michael Kelly, "The Game," *New York Times Magazine*, October 31, 1993, p. 67. The "likeability gap" and "Would you buy" are in *Time*, April 14, 1967, p. 30; Godfrey Hodgson, *America in Our Time* (Garden City, N.Y.: Doubleday, 1976), pp. 73–74.

17. Steigerwald, *Sixties*, p. 282; Broder, "1968," pp. 3726–27.

18. John Ehrlichman, *Witness to Power: The Nixon Years* (New York: Simon & Schuster, 1982), p. 46.

19. *U.S. News & World Report*, August 19, 1968, pp. 28–29.

20. Jeffrey Kimball, *Nixon's Vietnam War* (Lawrence: University Press of Kansas, 1998), pp. 72–73.

21. Kimball, *Nixon's Vietnam War*, p. 76.

22. Broder, "1968," p. 3728; Terry Dietz, *Republicans and Vietnam, 1961–1968* (New York: Greenwood, 1986), pp. 138–40.

23. *Time*, August 16, 1968, pp. 10–11.

24. The previous three paragraphs on Agnew are drawn especially from *Time*, August 16, 1968, pp. 18–19; Broder, "1968," pp. 3729–30; and an interesting British view, including the comment on looters, in British Embassy,

Washington, to Foreign Office, August 16, 1968, FCO/740, Public Record Office, Kew, UK.

25. DeBenedetti, *An American Ordeal,* p. 222; Larry Berman, *No Peace, No War: Nixon, Kissinger, and Betrayal in Vietnam* (New York: Free Press, 2001), p. 27; and see chap. 9.

26. Broder, "1968," p. 3731.

27. Theodore H. White, *The Making of the President, 1968* (New York: Atheneum, 1970), pp. 161–69.

28. Ambassador Sir Patrick Dean to Sir Paul Gore-Booth, October 1, 1968, FCO/7/742, Public Record Office, Kew, UK.

CHAPTER 7

1. Norman Mailer, *Miami and the Siege of Chicago* (New York: World, 1968), p. 122; Walter W. Heller to Hubert Humphrey, October 2, 1968, Personal Political Correspondence, Individuals, Hubert H. Humphrey Papers, Minnesota State Historical Society, St. Paul, Minnesota.

2. Harry McPherson Oral History, tape no. 1, pp. 30–31, Johnson Library, Austin, Texas.

3. A good discussion of the Wilson speech and its ramifications is in Lloyd C. Gardner, *Safe for Democracy: Anglo-American Response to Revolution, 1913–1923* (New York: Oxford University Press, 1984), esp. p. 260.

4. Theodore H. White, *The Making of the President, 1968* (New York: Atheneum, 1968), p. 338; *Dun's Review,* June 1968, p. 11.

5. Robert A. Caro, "The Orator of the Dawn," *New Yorker,* March 4, 2002, esp. p. 46; White, *Making of the President,* p. 8; Donald A. Ritchie, "Humphrey, Hubert Horatio," in Bruce W. Jentleson and Thomas G. Paterson, *Encyclopedia of American Foreign Relations* (New York: Oxford University Press, 1997), 2:334.

6. *New York Times,* December 9, 1967; April 26, 1966, p. 42.

7. Lewis L. Gould, "'Never a Deep Partisan,'" in Robert A. Divine, *The Johnson Years,* vol. 2 (Lawrence: University Press of Kansas, 1987–), esp. pp. 40–41.

8. Steigerwald, *Sixties, p. 32.*

9. Freeman to Humphrey, June 10, 1968, Personal Political Correspondence, Individuals, Humphrey Papers.

10. Win Griffith to Humphrey, June 19, 1968, Personal Political Correspondence, Individuals, Humphrey Papers.

11. Melvin Small, *Johnson, Nixon, and the Doves* (New Brunswick, N.J.: Rutgers University Press, 1988), p. 159; *Business Week,* March 16, 1968, p. 33.

12. Ambassador Sir Patrick Dean to Sir Paul Gore-Booth, May 1, 1968, FCO/7/741, Public Record Office, Kew, UK.

13. Hubert Humphrey to Warren Robbins, June 18, 1968, Personal Political Correspondence-Harris, Humphrey Papers.

14. *Time,* April 14, 1967, p. 28, for the state organizations; Clark Clifford with Richard Holbrooke, *Counsel to the President: A Memoir* (New York: Random House, 1991), p. 528.

15. William Drower to D. J. Swan, February 15, 1968, FCO/7/760, Public Record Office, Kew, UK.

16. Charles DeBenedetti, *An American Ordeal: The Antiwar Movement of the Vietnam Era* (Syracuse, N.Y.: Syracuse University Press, 1990), pp. 224–25; Small, *Johnson, Nixon, and the Doves,* pp. 1158–59; Irwin Unger and Debi Unger, eds., *The Times Were a Changin'* (New York: Three Rivers, 1998), esp. pp. 328–29, a useful overview and collection of documents.

17. David English, *Divided They Stand* (Englewood Cliffs, N.J.: Prentice-Hall, 1969), p. 307.

18. Broder, "1968," p. 3736; White, *Making of the President, 1968,* p. 343; Gould, "'Never a Deep Partisan,'" pp. 41–42.

19. Quoted, with a fascinating analysis of the context, in Mailer, *Miami and the Siege of Chicago,* p. 163.

20. Broder, "1968," pp. 3732, 3737.

21. DeBenedetti, *American Ordeal,* pp. 226–28; Broder, "1968," p. 3738.

22. Mailer, *Miami and the Siege of Chicago,* pp. 180, 210.

23. Unger and Unger, *The Times Were a Changin',* pp. 334–39, a valuable source for the report; DeBenedetti, *American Ordeal,* p. 229; Sir Patrick Dean to Sir Paul Gore-Booth, September 2, 1968, FCO/7/742, Public Record Office, Kew, UK, analyzes poll data; George Rising, *Clean for Gene; Eugene McCarthy's 1968 Presidential Campaign* (Westport, Conn.: Greenwood, 1997), p. 85.

24. Tad Szulc, "The Legacy of Prague," *Washington Post,* August 20, 1978, p. C5; *New York Times,* October 6, 1968, p. 52; especially useful for placing the Chicago convention in the context of the Czech invasion is Robert V. Daniels, *Year of the Heroic Guerrilla* (Cambridge, Mass.: Harvard University Press, 1989), particularly chapter 9.

25. Broder, "1968," p. 3744; *New York Times,* September 26, 1968, pp. 1, 13.

26. EMK to Orville Freeman and enclosure, October 4, 1968, Personal Political Correspondence, Individuals, Humphrey Papers.

27. Campaign Policy Committee, October 5, 1968, Personal Political Correspondence, Humphrey Papers; Democratic National Committee, "Political News Summary," October 4, 1968, Personal Political Correspondence, Press Releases, Humphrey Papers; Campaign Policy Committee Minutes, September 18, 1968, Personal Political Correspondence, Humphrey Papers.

28. Campaign Policy Committee Minutes, October 7, 1968, Personal Political Correspondence, Humphrey Papers; Humphrey to Bob McCandless, October 8, 1968, Personal Political Correspondence, Humphrey Papers.

29. Bill Moyers to Hubert Humphrey, June 6, 1968, Personal Political Correspondence: Moyers, Bill, Humphrey Papers.

CHAPTER 8

1. Ambassador Sir Patrick Dean to Sir Paul Gore-Booth, October 1, 1968, FCO/7/742, Public Record Office, Kew, UK.

2. Jody Carlson, *George C. Wallace and the Politics of Powerlessness: Wallace Campaigns for the Presidency, 1964–1976* (New Brunswick, N.J.: Transaction, 1981), pp. 1–3. Carlson's is a useful book for understanding Wallace and the southern background.

3. Carlson, *George C. Wallace*, p. 72; David Steigerwald, *The Sixties and the End of Modern America* (New York: St. Martin's, 1995), p. 238; David Broder, "Election of 1968," in Arthur M. Schlesinger Jr. and Fred L. Israel, eds., *History of American Presidential Elections, 1789–1968* (New York: Chelsea House, 1971), 4:3716.

4. Irwin Unger and Debi Unger, eds., *The Times Were a Changin': The Sixties Reader* (New York: Three Rivers, 1998), p. 342; Broder, "Election of 1968," p. 3743; Steigerwald, *Sixties*, pp. 237–39.

5. Chandler's passive role in the Jackie Robinson drama is analyzed in Jules Tygiel, *Baseball's Great Experiment: Jackie Robinson and His Legacy* (New York: Oxford University Press, 1982), esp. pp. 80–82.

6. The press conference is in *New York Times*, October 4, 1968, p. 50.

7. Carlson, *Wallace*, pp. 82–83; *New York Times*, October 4, 1968, p. 50.

8. Stephen C. Shadegg, *Winning's a Lot More Fun* (London: Macmillan, 1969), pp. 256–57.

9. *New York Times*, October 13, 1968, p. 79; ibid., p. 39; Democratic National Committee, "Political News Summary," October 9, 1968, Personal Political Correspondence, Press Releases, Hubert H. Humphrey Papers, Minnesota Historical Society, St. Paul, Minnesota.

10. The platform is excerpted in *New York Times,* October 14, 1968, p. 41.

11. *New York Times,* September 26, 1968, pp. 1, 53.

12. *New York Times,* October 14, 1968, p. 41.

13. Carlson, *Wallace,* p. 129.

14. Carlson, *Wallace,* p. 130.

15. Carlson, *Wallace,* pp. 91–92.

16. *New York Times,* September 26, 1968, pp. 1, 53.

17. Broder, "1968," pp. 3745–46; Carlson, *Wallace,* p. 94; *New York Times,* September 15, 1968, p. E2.

18. *New York Times,* October 22, 1968, p. 29.

19. Humphrey to Orville Freeman, September 19, 1968, Personal Political Correspondence, Individuals, Humphrey Papers; Ambassador Sir Patrick Dean to Sir Paul Gore-Booth, October 1, 1968, FCO/7/742, Public Record Office, Kew, UK.

20. Carlson, *Wallace,* p. 83; Broder, "1968," p. 3746.

21. Broder, "1968," pp. 3740–41.

22. Carlson, *Wallace,* p. 82; Broder, "1968," pp. 3740–42; Democratic National Committee, "Political News Summary," October 9, 1968, Personal Political Correspondence, Press Releases, Humphrey Papers.

23. Broder, "1968," p. 3748, refers to the polls.

CHAPTER 9

1. This and the following two paragraphs rely heavily on A. J. Langguth, "Thieu and Ky Think about the Unthinkable," *New York Times Magazine,* April 14, 1968, pp. 21, 72–78, one of the most revealing contemporary analyses found on Thieu; and David L. Anderson, *The Columbia Guide to the Vietnam War* (New York: Columbia University Press, 2002), p. 148.

2. Langguth, "Thieu and Ky," esp. p. 76; Clark Clifford with Richard Holbrooke, *Counsel to the President: A Memoir* (New York: Random House, 1991), p. 552.

3. Langguth, "Thieu and Ky," esp. p. 76.

4. *New York Times,* August 28, 1968, p. 40; ibid., April 3, 1968, p. 40.

5. *New York Times,* March 3, 1968, p. 40.

6. Clifford, *Counsel to the President,* pp. 351–352; George C. Herring, *America's Longest War: The United States and Vietnam, 1950–1975,* 4th ed. (Boston: McGraw-Hill, 2002), pp. 256–57.

7. Lloyd C. Gardner, "Lyndon Johnson and Vietnam: The Final Months," in Robert A. Divine, ed., *The Johnson Years* (Lawrence: University Press of Kansas, 1987–), 3:222.

8. Edgar Berman, *Hubert: The Triumph and Tragedy of the Humphrey I Knew* (New York: Putnam's, 1979), pp. 210–11.

9. Hubert H. Humphrey, *The Education of a Public Man* (Garden City, N.Y.: Doubleday, 1976), p. 403; David Broder, "Election of 1968," in Arthur M. Schlesinger Jr. and Fred L. Israel, eds., *History of American Presidential Elections, 1789–1968* (New York: Chelsea House, 1971), 4:3747.

10. Campaign Policy Committee Minutes, October 25, 1968, Personal Political Correspondence, Hubert H. Humphrey Papers, Minnesota Historical Society, St. Paul, Minn.; Democratic National Committee, "Political News Summary," October 10, 1968, Personal Political Correspondence, Press Releases, Humphrey Papers.

11. Broder, "1968," p. 3747.

12. Broder, "1968," p. 3746; Democratic National Committee, "Political News Summary," October 22, 1968, Personal Political Correspondence, Press Releases, Humphrey Papers, October 27, 1968.

13. Democratic National Committee, "Political News Summary," October 10, 1968, Personal Political Correspondence, Press Releases, Humphrey Papers; ibid., October 25, 1968; Larry Berman, *No Peace, No Honor: Nixon, Kissinger, and Betrayal in Vietnam* (New York: Free Press, 2001), p. 32.

14. Berman, *No Peace, No Honor*, pp. 27–28; Clifford, *Counsel to the President*, pp. 575–78.

15. Broder, "1968," p. 3750; Campaign Policy Committee Minutes, October 25, 1968, Personal Political Correspondence, Humphrey Papers.

16. Herring, *America's Longest War*, p. 264.

17. Lyndon Baines Johnson, *The Vantage Point: Perspectives of the Presidency, 1963–1969* (New York: Holt, Rhinehart & Winston, 1971), p. 550.

18. Johnson, *Vantage Point*, p. 550.

19. A good, concise account is Irwin Unger and Debi Unger, *LBJ: A Life* (New York: Wiley, 1999), pp. 490–91; details and new documentation can be found in Berman, *No Peace, No Honor*; the best insider's detailed analysis is Clifford, *Counsel to the President*, pp. 582–96; see also Broder, "1968," pp. 3759–60.

20. Clifford, *Counsel to the President*, pp. 582–86; Herring, *America's Longest War*, pp. 263–66.

21. *U.S. News & World Report*, November 18, 1968, p. 41.

22. Johnson, *Vantage Point*, p. 549.

CONCLUSION

1. Adam Hochschild, "War or Peace? . . . " *San Francisco Chronicle,* January 19, 2003; reprinted online at Tomeditor@aol.com, January 21, 2003.

2. Richard M. Scammon and Ben J. Wattenberg, *The Real Majority: An Extraordinary Examination of the American Electorate* (New York: Coward-McCann, 1970).

3. *Washington Post,* April 5, 1968, p. A6.

4. A contemporary overview of this problem is Thomas Griffith, "What the Election Wasn't About," *Life,* November 15, 1968, pp. 36–40; the taxicab driver's view is related in J. A. Thomson of Cabinet Office, Memorandum, December 9, 1969, FCO/7/1418, Foreign Affairs, Public Record Office, Kew, UK.

5. Griffith, "What the Election Wasn't About," p. 39.

6. Democratic National Committee, Political News Summary, October 25, 1968, Personal Political Correspondence, Press Releases, Hubert H. Humphrey Papers, Minnesota Historical Society, St. Paul, Minn.; Griffith, "What the Election Wasn't About," p. 39.

7. *Wall Street Journal,* April 25, 1997, p. A14.

8. Win Griffeth to Humphrey, June 19, 1968, Personal Political Correspondence, Individuals, Humphrey Papers.

9. Humphrey to O'Brien, October 21, 1968, Personal Political Correspondence, Humphrey Papers.

10. *Time,* November 15, 1968, p. 21.

11. Daniel Bell and Irving Kristol, eds., *Capitalism Today* (New York: Basic, 1971), p. 75.

12. David Steigerwald, *The Sixties and the End of Modern America* (New York: St. Martin's, 1995), p. 86.

13. Lee Benson and Joel Silbey, "The American Voter" (paper given at the 1978 Organization of American Historians Annual Meeting), pp. 7–8; paper in possession of authors. There is a succinct analysis of the breakdown of the party system, indeed of electoral democracy, in William Chafe, *Unfinished Journey: America since World War II* (New York: Oxford University Press, 1986), pp. 457–60.

14. *Washington Post,* May 18, 1980, p. D2. A work that puts such findings in a larger context and emphasizes the 1960s is Eric R. A. N. Smith, *The Unchanging American Voter* (Berkeley: University of California Press, 1990).

15. Sheldon Wolin, "Reagan Country," *New York Review of Books,* December 18, 1980, p. 10.

16. Michael Kelly, "The Game," *New York Times Magazine,* October 31, 1993, p. 67.

17. Larry Berman, *No Peace, No Honor: Nixon, Kissinger, and Betrayal in Vietnam* (New York: Free Press, 2001), pp. 35–36.

18. Ambassador Sir Patrick Dean to Stewart, July 16, 1968, FCO/7/778, PRO.

19. Memorandum of Rusk–Michael Stewart Conversation, October 11, 1968, FCO/7/803, PRO.

20. Summary Report of the Discussion Group on New Forces in World Politics, September 1970, Record of Groups, 131 (1969–1970), p. 5, Council on Foreign Relations, New York.

BIBLIOGRAPHY

Studies of the Vietnam War are among the most voluminous on any subject in four centuries of U.S. history. Places to start are George C. Herring, *America's Longest War: The United States and Vietnam, 1950–1975*, 4th ed. (Boston: McGraw-Hill, 2002), an excellent one-volume study that is updated in each new edition with recently released governmental records; Robert Schulzinger, *A Time for War: The United States and Vietnam, 1941–1975* (New York: Oxford University Press, 1997), well written by a leading historian; Marilyn Blatt Young, *The Vietnam Wars, 1945–1990* (New York: HarperCollins, 1991), outspokenly and interestingly carries the story beyond the war's formal ending; Mitchell Hall, *The Vietnam War* (New York: Pearson, 1998), a good, succinct account; David L. Anderson, *The Columbia Guide to the Vietnam War* (New York, Columbia University Press, 2002), the best reference work; Neil Sheehan et al., *The Pentagon Papers as Published by the New York Times* (New York: Bantam, 1971), a helpfully edited abridgement of the sensational multivolume official record collection leaked in 1971; Gareth Porter, ed., *Vietnam: A History in Documents* (New York: New American Library, 1979), a useful collection edited by a noted expert on Southeast Asia; Andrew J. Rotter, ed., *Light at the End of the Tunnel: A Vietnam War Anthology*

(Wilmington, Del.: Scholarly Resources, 1999), a superb collection of important essays on the war (note especially chapters 3 and 10 on the war at home); David L. Anderson, ed., *Shadow on the White House: Presidents and the Vietnam War 1945–1975* (Lawrence: University Press of Kansas, 1993), excellent essays on the White House perspective and its critics; David L. Anderson, ed., *The Human Tradition in the Vietnam Era* (Wilmington, Del.: Scholarly Resources, 2000), highly revealing on some of the human and social cost, even among policymakers; Don Oberdorfer, *Tet: The Turning Point in the Vietnam War* (Baltimore: Johns Hopkins University Press, 2001), a new edition of a classic account by a leading journalist; Ronald H. Spector, *After Tet: The Bloodiest Year in Vietnam* (New York: Free Press, 1993), on the aftermath by a respected military historian; Christian G. Appy, *Working-Class War: American Combat Soldiers and Vietnam* (Chapel Hill: University of North Carolina Press, 1993), exploring the socio-economic-racial divisions that helped fuel the explosions at home in 1968; William M. Hammond, *Public Affair: The Military and the Media, 1962–1968* (Washington, D.C.: Center of Military History, U.S. Army, 1968), a classic account demonstrating why the U.S. casualty rate—not the media—turned Americans against the war; Donald C. Hallin, *The "Uncensored War": The Media and Vietnam* (New York: Oxford University Press, 1986), still an important, dependable study; William J. Duiker, *Sacred War: Nationalism and Revolution in a Divided Vietnam* (New York: McGraw-Hill, 1995), an important starting point for understanding the Vietnamese views, as is Duiker's splendid *Ho Chi Minh* (New York: Hyperion, 2000). Two books that offer excellent comprehensive overviews of the antiwar movement are Charles DeBenedetti and Charles Chatfield, *An American Ordeal: The Antiwar Movement of the Vietnam Era* (Syracuse, N.Y.: Syracuse University Press, 1990); and Melvin Small, *Anti-Warriors: The Vietnam War and the Battle for America's Hearts and Minds* (Wilmington, Del.: Scholarly Resources, 2002).

On the 1968 election and its immediate background, note especially Lewis L. Gould, *1968: The Election That Changed America* (Chicago: Ivan R. Dee, 1993), a well-researched account; Theodore White, *The Making of the President, 1968* (New York: Atheneum, 1969), a classic by a leading journalist who was there; Richard M.

Scammon and Ben J. Wattenberg, *The Real Majority* (New York: Coward-McCann, 1970), a highly influential analysis of public opinion in the campaign that goes well beyond the war; David Broder, "Election of 1968," in Arthur M. Schlesinger Jr. and Fred L. Israel, eds., *History of American Presidential Elections, 1789–1968*, vol. 4 (New York: Chelsea House, 1971), an important, detailed view by another journalist who was there; Lewis Chester et al., *An American Melodrama: The Presidential Campaign of 1968* (New York: Viking, 1969), a fascinating, you-cannot-believe-it's-happening view of the election by three prominent British journalists; for a similar British perspective, note David English's readable *Divided They Stand* (Englewood Cliffs, N.J.: Prentice-Hall, 1969); Edward W. Knappman, ed., *Presidential Election, 1968* (New York: Facts on File, 1970), highly useful for its chronology and documents, including speeches and party platforms; Philip E. Converse et al., "Continuity and Change in American Politics: Parties and Issues in the 1968 Election," *American Political Science Review*, December, 1968, still a valuable, highly revealing analysis of the campaign; Melvin Small, *Democracy and Diplomacy: The Impact of Domestic Politics on U.S. Foreign Policy, 1789–1994* (Baltimore: Johns Hopkins Press, 1996), an excellent source for an understanding of the larger political context and questions; Kurt Taylor Gaubatz, *Elections and War: The Electoral Incentive in Democratic Politics* (Stanford, Calif.: Stanford University Press, 1999), a pioneering attempt to examine the interrelationship between war and domestic politics.

For the broad socioeconomic and political backgrounds that framed the 1968 election, start with Maurice Isserman and Michael Kazin, *America Divided: The Civil War of the 1960s* (New York: Oxford University Press, 2000), a well-written, well-researched, and wide-ranging overview of the sociopolitical background; Irwin Unger and Debi Unger, eds., *The Times Were a Changin': The Sixties Reader* (New York: Three Rivers, 1998), an excellent collection of contemporary materials; David Steigerwald, *The Sixties and the End of Modern America* (New York: St. Martin's, 1994), highly readable and important for its many insights; Charles Kaiser, *1968 in America: Music, Politics, Chaos, Counterculture, and the Shaping of a Generation* (New York: Weidenfeld & Nicolson, 1988), the subtitle tells it all in this in-depth look;

Robert V. Daniels, *Year of the Heroic Guerrilla* (Cambridge, Mass.: Harvard University Press, 1989) and Jeremi Suri, *Power and Protest: Global Revolution and the Rise of Détente* (Cambridge, Mass.: Harvard University Press, 2003), important for understanding the broader international context; Carole Fink et al., eds., *1968: The World Transformed* (New York: Cambridge University Press, 1998), all the chapters (and especially Chester Pach's) for a discussion of how the war was reflected globally, notably in European societies; Todd Gitlin, *The Sixties: Years of Hope and Days of Rage* (New York: Bantam, 1987), by a leading activist and respected sociologist; Paul Berman, *A Tale of Two Utopias: The Political Journey of the Generation of 1968* (New York: Norton, 1996), a personal, bittersweet account of the time and the aftermath.

General William C. Westmoreland, *A Soldier Reports* (Garden City, N.Y.: Doubleday, 1976), is the general's important autobiographical perspective; Samuel Zaffari, *Westmoreland: A Biography of General William C. Westmoreland* (New York: William Morrow, 1994), is the standard biography; and U.S. Congress, Senate, Committee on Armed Services, 90th Cong., 2d sess., *Nominations of William C. Westmoreland . . . July 4 and July 18, 1968* (Washington, D.C.: U.S. Government Printing Office, 1968), has useful background information. But see especially the sweeping, original interpretation in Robert Buzzanco, *Masters of War* (New York: Cambridge University Press).

Material on Lyndon Johnson is plentiful, but start with his autobiography, *Vantage Point: Perspectives of the Presidency, 1963–1969* (New York: Holt, Rinehart & Winston, 1971); Lloyd C. Gardner, *Pay Any Price: Lyndon Johnson and the Wars for Vietnam* (Chicago: Ivan R. Dee, 1995), which superbly links the man, his domestic policies, and his foreign policies; Robert Dallek, *Flawed Giant: Lyndon Johnson and His Times, 1961–1973* (New York: Oxford University Press, 1968), a leading biography of the vice presidential and presidential years; Irwin Unger and Debi Unger, *LBJ: A Life* (New York: John Wiley, 1999), a useful one-volume account of his entire career; Michael Hunt, *Lyndon Johnson's War: America's Cold War Crusade in Vietnam, 1945–1968* (New York: Hill & Wang, 1996), by a leading scholar of U.S.-Asian relations; Doris Kearns, *Lyndon Johnson and the American Dream* (New York: New American Library, 1977), a fascinating personal account of Johnson and his White House;

George C. Herring, *LBJ and Vietnam: A Different Kind of War* (Austin: University of Texas Press, 1994), by a leading scholar of the war; Jeffrey W. Helsing, *Johnson's War, Johnson's Great Society: The Guns and Butter Gap* (Westport, Conn.: Greenwood, 2000), helpful on the crucial economic strain; Dean Rusk, as told to Richard Rusk, *As I Saw It* (New York: Norton, 1990), a revealing account by the secretary of state, who professed few second thoughts but agonized even as he helped lead the intervention; Clark Clifford with Richard Holbrooke, *Counsel to the President: A Memoir* (New York: Random House, 1991), a most valuable inside account of 1968 policies and governmental perspectives; Henry F. Graff, *The Tuesday Cabinet* (Englewood Cliffs, N.J.: Prentice-Hall, 1970), useful insights into Johnson's inner-circle decision making; Kathleen J. Turner, *Lyndon Johnson's Dual War: Vietnam and the Press* (Chicago: University of Chicago Press, 1985), important on the adversarial relationship; Robert D. Schulzinger, "Walt Rostow: Cheerful Hawk," in David L. Anderson, ed., *The Human Tradition in the Vietnam Era* (Wilmington, Del.: Scholarly Resources, 2000), one of the best insights into LBJ's adviser who spearheaded the war effort in 1968; Warren I. Cohen and Nancy Bernkopf Tucker, eds., *Lyndon Johnson Confronts the World: American Foreign Policy, 1963–1968* (New York: Cambridge University Press, 1994), especially helpful on both Vietnam and the larger foreign policy context, as is H. W. Brands, ed., *The Foreign Policies of Lyndon Johnson: Beyond Vietnam* (College Station: Texas A&M Press, 1999). David M. Barrett, ed., *Lyndon Johnson's Vietnam Papers: A Documentary Collection* (College Station: Texas A&M Press, 1997) is a useful 800-page, wide-ranging selection of primary documents.

For material on Eugene J. McCarthy, five of the Minnesota senator's own books provide insight: *First Things First: New Priorities for America* (New York: New American Library, 1968); *Eugene McCarthy on the Record: Excerpts from His Speeches Compiled by Dorothy Dunbar Bromley and Ruth Gage-Colby* (New York: Coalition for a Democratic Alternative, 1968); *The Year of the People* (New York: Doubleday, 1969); *The Limits of Power: America's Role in the World* (New York: Holt, Rinehart & Winston, 1967); and his autobiography, *Up 'til Now: A Memoir* (San Diego: Harcourt, Brace, Javonovich, 1987). Richard T.

Stout, *People* (New York: Harper & Row, 1970), is the best journalistic account that focuses on McCarthy's 1968 campaign; George Rising, *Clean for Gene: Eugene McCarthy's 1968 Presidential Campaign* (Westport, Conn.: Greenwood, 1997), is an outstanding study of the senator's run; and Melvin Small and William D. Hoover, eds., *Give Peace a Chance: Exploring the Vietnam Antiwar Movement* (Syracuse, N.Y.: Syracuse University Press, 1994), provides a useful larger context.

Martin Luther King Jr.'s work in 1968 and before has attracted a large number of important studies, including David Levering Lewis, *King: A Biography* (Urbana: University of Illinois Press, 1978); Stephen B. Oates, *Let the Trumpet Sound: The Life of Martin Luther King, Jr.* (New York: Harper & Row, 1983); Michael Eric Dyson, *I May Not Get There with You: The True Martin Luther King, Jr.* (New York: Free Press, 2000); Michael Friedly with David Gallen, *Martin Luther King Jr.: The FBI File* (New York: Carroll & Graf, 1993), tracing the FBI's misplaced suspicions of King; David J. Garrow, ed., *Martin Luther King, Jr.: Civil Rights Leader, Theologian, Orator,* 3 vols. (Brooklyn, N.Y.: Carlson, 1989), with a valuable preface by Garrow; Michael G. Long, *Against Us, But for Us: Martin Luther King, Jr., and the State* (Macon, Ga.: Mercer University Press, 2002), on a (the?) central theme in King's political career; and Michael L. Krenn, ed., *The African American Voice in U.S. Foreign Policy since World War II* (New York: Garland, 1999), highly important for context, with the Moss, Levy, and Fairclough chapters good contributions on King and 1960s foreign policies.

For Robert Kennedy, note Jeff Shesol, *Mutual Contempt: Lyndon Johnson, Robert Kennedy, and the Feud That Defined a Decade* (New York: Norton, 1997); Ronald Steel, *In Love with the Night: The American Romance with Robert Kennedy* (New York: Simon & Schuster, 2000), a sensitive, critical account; Joseph A. Palermo, *In His Own Right: The Political Odyssey of Senator Robert F. Kennedy* (New York: Columbia University Press, 2001), a first-rate political analysis of events that climaxed with the final campaign; Evan Thomas, *Robert Kennedy: His Life* (New York: Simon & Schuster, 2000); the complete biography; Arthur Schlesinger Jr., *RFK and His Times* (Boston: Houghton-Mifflin, 1978), the most detailed analysis by a Kennedy insider; Jack Newfield, *RFK: A Memoir* (New York: 2003), by a friend and important journalist, with a new introduction added to the 1969 edition; James W. Hilty, *Robert Kennedy: Brother Protector* (Philadelphia: Temple University Press, 1997), a highly revealing account of the tough Kennedy; and Jules Witcover, *85 Days: The Last Campaign of Robert Kennedy* (New York: Quill, 1988), written by an experienced journalist who was there.

The career of Richard Nixon has been extensively chronicled, and his 1968 victory has been analyzed from many perspectives. His own is *RN: The Memoirs of Richard Nixon* (New York: Grosset & Dunlop, 1978, 1990); Herbert S. Parmet, *Richard Nixon and His America* (Boston: Little, Brown, 1990), is an excellent one-volume biography; Jules Witcover, *The Resurrection of Richard Nixon* (New York: Putnam, 1970), provides a highly detailed journalistic account of Nixon's climb during the 1960s; Jeffrey Kimball, *Nixon's Vietnam War* (Lawrence: University of Kansas Press, 1998), is an outstanding account with a first chapter that is unsurpassed in understanding Nixon's view of the war in the year before his presidency; Joe McGinniss, *The Selling of the President, 1968* (New York: Trident, 1969), shows how the Nixon camp exploited the media; Richard J. Whalen, *Catch the Falling Flag* (Boston: Houghton, Mifflin, 1972), is an insider's account of the campaign by a self-described nonpolitician; Stephen C. Shadegg, *Winning's a Lot More Fun* (London: Macmillan, 1968), is also by an insider, but one who believes war was a central issue for Democrats although not for Republicans; Terry Dietz, *Republicans and Vietnam, 1961–1968* (New York: Greenwood, 1986), is an excellent overview of the party's debate.

Hubert H. Humphrey has had surprisingly few books written about his long and important career. His own *The Education of a Public Man: My Life and Politics* (Garden City, N.Y.: Doubleday, 1976) catches the Humphrey personality and concerns; Carl Solberg, *Hubert Humphrey: A Biography* (New York: Norton, 1984), is a comprehensive scholarly account (reprinted in 2003); Robert Mann, *The Walls of Jericho: Lyndon Johnson, Hubert Humphrey, Richard Russell, and the Struggle for Civil Rights* (New York: Harcourt, Brace, 1996), covers one important part of the story; Edgar Berman, *Hubert: The Triumph and Tragedy of the Humphrey I Knew* (New York: Putnam's, 1979), has to be used carefully but includes fascinating material. Arnold

Offner, the highly respected biographer of Harry S. Truman and his foreign policies, is writing a major biography of Humphrey.

George C. Wallace's third-party movement has interested many scholars. A place to begin is Jody Carlson, *George C. Wallace and the Politics of Powerlessness* (New Brunswick, N.J.: Transaction, 1981), a superb study of the 1964–1976 campaign themes; Marshall Frady, *Wallace* (New York: World, 1976), is a succinct biography by an author who knows the South well; Dan T. Carter, *The Politics of Rage: George Wallace, the Origins of the New Conservatism, and the Transformation of American Politics* (Baton Rouge: Louisiana State University Press, 2000), tracks Wallace and his legacy in considerable detail; Stephan Lesher, *George Wallace: American Populist* (Reading, Mass.: Addison-Wesley, 1994), is especially useful on the Alabama background; and Joseph A. Fry, *Dixie Looks Abroad: The South and U.S. Foreign Relations, 1789–1973* (Baton Rouge: Louisiana State University Press, 2002), provides the large context within which Wallace often appears to be a poor fit.

For Thieu and the climax of the campaign, note Peggy Duff, *Truth about Thieu: South Vietnam, the Facts* (London: Indochina Solidarity Conference, 1973); and Larry Berman, *No Peace, No Honor: Nixon, Kissinger, and Betrayal in Vietnam* (New York: Free Press, 2001), now the definitive, highly important account of how and why the peace talks were delayed at the last moment before the election; and also see the footnotes to the last two chapters of the present book, especially Clark Clifford's *Counsel to the President,* cited in the Lyndon Johnson section of this bibliography.

INDEX

ABOUT THE AUTHOR

Walter LaFeber is Andrew H. and James S. Tisch Distinguished University Professor and a Weiss Presidential Teaching Fellow in the Department of History at Cornell University. He is the author of numerous articles, and his most recent books include *Michael Jordan and the New Global Capitalism* and *America, Russia, and the Cold War, 1945–2002*.

VIETNAM
America in the War Years

Series Editor
David L. Anderson
California State University Monterey Bay

The Vietnam War and the tumultuous internal upheavals in America that coincided with it marked a watershed era in U.S. history. These events profoundly challenged America's heroic self-image. During the 1950s the United States defined Southeast Asia as an area of vital strategic importance. In the 1960s this view produced a costly American military campaign that continued into the early 1970s. The Vietnam War was the nation's longest war and ended with an unprecedented U.S. failure to achieve its stated objectives. Simultaneous with this frustrating military intervention and the domestic debate that it produced were other tensions created by student activism on campuses, the black struggle for civil rights, and the women's liberation movement. The books in this series explore the complex and controversial issues of the period from the mid-1950s to the mid-1970s in brief and engaging volumes. To facilitate continued and informed debate on these contested subjects, each book examines a military, political, or diplomatic issue; the role of a key individual; or one of the domestic changes in America during the war.

Volumes Published

Melvin Small. *Antiwarriors: The Vietnam War and the Battle for America's Hearts and Minds*.

Edward K. Spann. *Democracy's Children: The Young Rebels of the 1960s and the Power of Ideals*.

Walter LaFeber. *The Deadly Bet: LBJ, Vietnam, and the 1968 Election*.

E 851 .L33 2005

LaFeber, Walter.

The deadly bet

GAYLORD S